EX LIBRIS

Randy Manning

Hannibal's Oath

HANNIBAL'S OATH

---

*The Life and Wars of
Rome's Greatest Enemy*

John Prevas

DA CAPO PRESS

Designed by Timm Bryson
Set in 11 point Adobe Jenson Pro by Perseus Books

Library of Congress Cataloging-in-Publication Data
Names: Prevas, John, author.
Title: Hannibal's oath: the life and wars of Rome's greatest enemy / John
Prevas.
Description: Boston, MA: Da Capo Press, 2017. | Includes bibliographical
references and index.
Identifiers: LCCN 2017007554 (print) | LCCN 2017012699 (ebook) | ISBN
9780306824258 (e-book) | ISBN 9780306824241 (hardback)
Subjects: LCSH: Hannibal, 247 B.C.–182 B.C. | Punic War, 2nd, 218–201
B.C. | Generals—Tunisia—Carthage (Extinct city)—Biography. |
Rome—History—Republic, 265–30 B.C. | Carthage (Extinct city)—History. |
BISAC: BIOGRAPHY & AUTOBIOGRAPHY / Historical. | HISTORY /
Asia / Central Asia.
Classification: LCC DG249 (ebook) | LCC DG249 .P74 2017 (print) | DDC
937/.04092 [B] —dc23
LC record available at https://lccn.loc.gov/2017007554
ISBN: 978-0-306-82424-1 (hardcover)
ISBN: 978-0-306-82425-8 (ebook)

Published by Da Capo Press
An imprint of Perseus Books, LLC, a subsidiary of Hachette Book Group, Inc.

www.dacapopress.com

Da Capo Press books are available at special discounts for bulk purchases
in the U.S. by corporations, institutions, and other organizations. For more
information, please contact the Special Markets Department at Perseus Books,
2300 Chestnut Street, Suite 200, Philadelphia, PA 19103, or call (800) 810-
4145, ext. 5000, or e-mail special.markets@perseusbooks.com.

LSC-C
10 9 8 7 6 5 4 3 2 1

To Mavis Gibson

CONTENTS

PREFACE

MY INTENT IN writing this book has been to produce a readable and engaging biography of Hannibal for the nonhistorian—a book that does not require extensive knowledge of the historical context of the period in order to follow the narrative. Mine is not a book for scholars; it is a book for general readers interested in history and adventure. It is something to be read and enjoyed, not studied. The Punic Wars between Rome and Carthage, for a general reader at least, are a relatively obscure period in ancient history even though those wars transformed Rome from a regional republic on the Italian mainland into an empire that stretched from one end of the ancient world to the other and set the course for the development of Western civilization. Hannibal played a defining role in that transformation.

My interest in Hannibal began over twenty-five years ago while I was teaching Latin in a suburb of Washington, D.C. I was translating the works of the Roman historian Livy with some of my advanced students, and we initially focused on the grammar and vocabulary found in the story of Hannibal's crossing of the Alps. As the words were translated from Latin into English and their grammatical context brought into focus, something entirely unexpected and delightful began to take place in that classroom. History came alive. A story of adventure, hardship, and accomplishment began to unfold on the pages of my students' composition books. The further we delved into Hannibal's story, the more the interest, excitement, and anticipation of the students began to build. The drudgery of grammatical constructions and the tedium of endless vocabulary drills were soon replaced by a fascinating story from the ancient world.

Students were intrigued by this African hero, this leader who did what everyone in the ancient world thought impossible. At first I thought their interest was intended to get me off track, something students are inclined to do. But Hannibal's story opened the mysterious and hedonistic world of Carthaginian North Africa and then carried us into Spain, over the Pyrenees, and into southern France. We crossed the Rhone River with Hannibal and followed him into the Alps, fighting nature and the primitive mountain tribes who lined the route. Livy's words brought to life, often in fascinating detail, how Hannibal, with his mercenaries and elephants, marched over a thousand miles, fighting hostile Iberian and Gallic tribes, crossing rivers and then struggling over the highest, most remote and treacherous passes of the Alps to reach Italy and begin a major war. Students wanted to learn more, so we even began looking at the sources in ancient Greek.

My students learned how Napoleon duplicated Hannibal's feat in the spring of 1800 when he led his army over the Alps to surprise his Austrian enemies. Napoleon bested everyone, not simply by crossing the Alps but by building a road over them that is still used today. Later, in exile, Napoleon wrote, "Hannibal was the most daring of all men, perhaps the most astonishing; so bold, so assured, so broad of vision in all things. At the age of 26 he conceived what was scarcely conceivable and carried out what was deemed impossible. He scaled the Pyrenees and the Alps, then came down into Italy paying with half his army the price just to attain a battlefield and the right to fight."[1] Hannibal became for my students, young men and women of the evolving digital age, a larger-than-life action hero from the past. Here was an ancient leader who overcame the elements of nature, beat the odds against survival, won every battle he fought in Italy against the Romans just to lose the war in the end. Why, my students asked, are we so fascinated by this tragic figure?

To prepare for this book I walked in Hannibal's footsteps. Everywhere Hannibal went in the ancient world, I went. I covered every battlefield where he fought, crossed every river and mountain pass he crossed, and visited the site of every ancient city he laid siege to. I began in Tunisia, at Carthage where Hannibal was born, and ended on the Asian side of Turkey in a small port town where he died. In the course of my travels, I went to Spain where Hannibal learned to be a soldier and a leader. I visited the ruins of Saguntum, where the war with Rome began, and then followed his path through France, over the Alps, and all through Italy, from the north to the south. I went to Ephesus in Asia Minor and then to Crete and the ruins of Gortyna where Hannibal hid in exile. What that experience taught me, and I hope is reflected in my writing, is how important it is for an author to follow in the footsteps of those whose stories he or she is trying to tell, whether it be a Carthaginian Hannibal, a Persian Cyrus, an Athenian Xenophon, a Macedonian Alexander, or a Roman Caesar or Augustus. Seeing where these leaders went and developing even a partial feel for what they must have experienced matters when it comes to trying to bring them to life and recounting for my readers their accomplishments and failures.

When it comes to the source materials for the study of Hannibal, nothing new has come to light over the last few decades. Those of us who write about Hannibal all rely on the same Greek and Latin literary sources, and then we try to give them a slightly different spin. The current trend is to question, with some reserve, the accuracy and even usefulness of the ancient sources. A form of political correctness seems to have permeated ancient studies. The ancient Greeks and Romans are viewed with skepticism, either because they are regarded as so biased against Carthage and Hannibal due to their hatred of the Semitic civilization that they purposely distorted their accounts and vilified their enemies or because they moved in the opposite direction and exaggerated the strength of their enemies to inflate Rome's greatness. So, the sources are either hypercritical of Hannibal or excessively complimentary, making it difficult for any author to sort out which is which and develop a balanced perspective. But Roman attitudes, like most things, changed over time. Hannibal was undoubtedly a terrifying figure in the third century B.C.—a threat to Rome's very existence. During the war and shortly thereafter, the Romans portrayed him as untrustworthy, perfidious, avaricious, and cruel in nature, a man of inherently violent disposition who lived for one thing—to destroy. But later, that attitude moderated, and by the time of the empire, Roman writers adopted a positive view of him. Hannibal came to embody the noble adversary, with the virtues and characteristics that had heretofore been reserved for their heroes from antiquity. That image has carried forward over the centuries and into our own time. But as this work will show, Hannibal was a complicated mix of the best and worst in human nature—a man of incredible self-confidence, intelligence, tactical genius, generosity, and compassion on the one hand and unfathomable cruelty, callousness, and greed on the other.

CHRONOLOGY

800 B.C.   Legendary date for the founding of Carthage.

753 B.C.   Legendary date for the founding of Rome.

600 B.C.   Carthaginian colonization of western Sicily and Sardinia.

275 B.C.   Rome begins the consolidation of her power in southern Italy. The Greek king Pyrrhus invades southern Italy and wages war with Rome.

264 B.C.   Rome invades Sicily and the First Punic War begins.

249 B.C.   Hamilcar Barca, the father of Hannibal, takes command of the Carthaginian land forces in Sicily and begins a successful guerilla campaign against the Romans.

247 B.C.   Hannibal is born at Carthage, the eldest of the three Barca brothers, who will become known as "the lion's brood."

247–243 B.C.   Hamilcar is successful in Sicily against the Romans, but restrained by the senate in Carthage from carrying the war across the straits into Italy.

241 B.C.   When the Roman navy destroys a Carthaginian supply fleet on its way to Sicily, Carthage, unable to resupply

its forces in Sicily and worn out by the war, sues for peace. The First Punic War ends.

240 B.C. Hamilcar evacuates his army from Sicily to North Africa. The senate refuses to pay the mercenaries their wages and a savage war begins. Hamilcar takes command of a new Carthaginian army and defeats the mercenaries he led in Sicily. Rome annexes the Carthaginian islands of Sardinia and Corsica.

237 B.C. Hamilcar begins to build an empire for Carthage in Spain and a dynasty for his family. The Carthaginians found the coastal city of Cartagena or "new Carthage."

229 B.C. Hamilcar is killed and his son-in-law, Hasdrubal the Handsome, becomes the new commander of the Carthaginian forces and governor of the province. Hasdrubal increases the Carthaginian hold over Spain and tutors young Hannibal in war and diplomacy.

221 B.C. Hasdrubal is assassinated by a Celtic slave, and Hannibal, at age twenty-six, is proclaimed the commander of the army.

220 B.C. The Carthaginians and the Romans come into conflict over Saguntum, a Greek city on the Spanish coast just a few miles north of modern-day Valencia.

219 B.C. Hannibal captures Saguntum and the Second Punic War begins.

218 B.C. Hannibal takes the initiative and reaches northern Italy by way of the Alps, defeating the Romans at the Ticinus and Trebbia Rivers.

217 B.C. Hannibal crosses the Apennine mountain range into central Italy and draws a Roman army into a devastating ambush on the northern shores of Lake Trasimene.

216 B.C.　At Cannae, on the Adriatic coast of southeastern Italy, Hannibal meets and destroys the largest Roman army ever assembled and wins the greatest victory of his career.

215–213 B.C.　Using the momentum of his victory, Hannibal convinces the king of Macedon, Philip V, to join the war against Rome. In response, the Romans dispatch armies to Illyria to keep Philip at bay and send additional reinforcements to Spain.

211 B.C.　The Scipio brothers, two of Rome's best generals, are killed fighting Hannibal's brothers in Spain.

210–208 B.C.　The Roman Senate sends Publius Scipio, son and nephew of the commanders killed in Spain, to take over their armies. Hasdrubal, with a relief force, leaves Spain and crosses the Alps to try and reach his brother.

207 B.C.　The tide of the war turns in Rome's favor. Hannibal is unable to win another victory over the resilient Romans, and the Greek city-states are not defecting to him in the numbers he needs to win the war. At the Metaurus River, just north of the modern-day Italian coastal port of Ancona on the Adriatic Sea, Hasdrubal is killed and his army destroyed. Hannibal is contained in southern Italy as the focus of the war shifts to Spain and North Africa.

206 B.C.　Scipio defeats Hannibal's youngest brother, Mago, in Spain. Hannibal remains confined largely to the southernmost section of Italy and isolated from the war.

205–204 B.C.　Scipio moves to North Africa to enlist Numidian allies and then proceeds to Sicily to train an invasion army. Mago leaves Spain with a fleet in another attempt to reach Hannibal with reinforcements.

203 B.C. Scipio defeats a Carthaginian army in North Africa. Hannibal and Mago are recalled from Italy.

202 B.C. Hannibal tries to negotiate peace with Scipio but is forced into battle southwest of Carthage. Scipio turns Hannibal's own tactics against him and the result is a resounding victory for the Romans. The battle of Zama brings the Second Punic War to an end.

201 B.C. As a result of the treaty ending the war, Carthage is confined to Africa, loses most of its fleet and war elephants, and is forced to pay Rome a heavy war indemnity over a fifty-year period.

200 B.C. Rome wages war against Philip of Macedon in retaliation for his support of Hannibal.

196 B.C. Hannibal is elected chief magistrate at Carthage by the popular assemblies and undertakes to reform the government.

195 B.C. Hannibal flees Carthage to avoid arrest on charges of conspiring to wage war against Rome and finds refuge in the eastern Mediterranean court of the Seleucid king, Antiochus.

193 B.C. Hannibal advises Antiochus to invade Italy. The king invades Greece.

191 B.C. Antiochus is defeated by the Roman army at the battle of Thermopylae and driven from Greece.

190 B.C. The Romans defeat Antiochus at the battle of Magnesia in Asia Minor and Hannibal flees to the island of Crete.

188 B.C. Hannibal leaves Crete to take refuge in the court of King Artaxias of Armenia.

187 B.C. War breaks out in northern Asia Minor between Eumenes II of Pergamum, a Roman ally, and his neighbor,

King Prusias of Bithynia. Hannibal joins Prusias as his military advisor.

184 B.C. Prusias loses the war and agrees to Roman demands that he surrender Hannibal.

183 B.C. Hannibal is cornered by the Romans in Bithynia and commits suicide. Rome undertakes the building of an empire and expands her presence throughout Greece and Asia Minor.

149 B.C. The Third Punic War between Carthage and Rome begins.

146 B.C. Carthage is destroyed by the besieging Roman army and its surviving citizens are sold into slavery.

DRAMATIS PERSONAE

ALIMENTUS, LUCIUS CINCIUS. Roman officer captured by Hannibal in southern Italy. Alimentus spent several years as a prisoner in the Carthaginian camp where Hannibal apparently disclosed to him many details of his crossing of the Alps and his campaign in Italy. Those details subsequently found their way into the chronicles of later Roman historians.

ANTIOCHUS III. King of Syria and descendant of Seleucus I, one of Alexander the Great's generals and successors. Antiochus welcomed Hannibal to his court at Ephesus in 195 B.C.

ARTAXIAS I. King of Armenia, he gave Hannibal refuge after the latter fled Crete.

CATO, MARCUS PORCIUS. Roman senator who fought during the Second Punic War. His hatred and fear of Carthage became a major cause of the Third Punic War and the destruction of the city.

EUMENES II. King of Pergamum in Asia Minor and an ally of Rome. Eumenes helped the Romans defeat Antiochus in 190 B.C. and later fought a naval battle in the Sea of Marmara against Hannibal and Prusias, the king of Bithynia.

FABIUS, MAXIMUS QUINTUS. One of the most respected senators in Rome, Fabius was appointed dictator, the highest office in the republic, on two occasions. After the Roman defeat at Trasimene, he put into place a strategy of shadowing Hannibal but never directly engaging him in battle. The tactic became unpopular with the impatient Romans who came to refer to him pejoratively as "cunctator" or the delayer even though in the end he was proven right.

FLAMININUS, QUINCTIUS TITUS. Consul in command of the Roman armies in the war against Antiochus of Syria, Flamininus pursued Hannibal to Bithynia and forced his suicide.

FLAMINIUS, GAIUS NEPOS. Roman commander killed at the battle of Lake Trasimene.

HAMILCAR. Father of Hannibal and commander of the Carthaginian forces in Sicily during the First Punic War. After the war, Hamilcar established an empire for Carthage in Spain.

HANNO. Nephew of Hannibal and one of his principal commanders, he is often mistakenly referred to by scholars as the fourth son of Hamilcar.

HASDRUBAL. Second of Hamilcar's sons. Hannibal left him in command of Spain and North Africa at the outbreak of the Second Punic War. Late in the war he led an army over the Alps to reach his brother but was killed at the battle of the Metaurus River.

HASDRUBAL. Hannibal's cavalry commander in all the major battles in Italy as well as the campaigns in the south.

HASDRUBAL, GISCO. Carthaginian commander considered one of Hannibal's best generals.

HASDRUBAL THE HANDSOME. Brother-in-law of Hannibal and husband of Hamilcar's second eldest daughter. Following Hamilcar's death, Hasdrubal became his successor in Spain and Hannibal's mentor.

IMILCE. Hannibal's Spanish wife from Castulo, one of the most important cities in upper Andalusia. Her prominent family tie has led historians to speculate that Hannibal's marriage to her might have been a political accommodation.

LIVY. First-century-B.C. Roman who wrote a history of the city that included a detailed account of the war with Hannibal. One of two principal sources when it comes to the study of Hannibal.

MAGO. Youngest son of Hamilcar and one of Hannibal's principal generals. Mago accompanied Hannibal over the Alps and then went on to lead the forces of Carthage against the Romans in Spain. He invaded northern Italy in a second ill-fated attempt to take the Roman pressure off Hannibal in the south. Mago died on a sea voyage back to Carthage.

MAGO, THE SAMNITE. One of Hannibal's principal officers and close friends. Mago commanded an army in Bruttium from 212 to 203 B.C. and was reputed to be as avaricious when it came to money as Hannibal.

MAHARBAL. Numidian cavalry commander who crossed the Alps with Hannibal and fought at the Ticinus, the Trebbia, Lake Trasimene, and Cannae. He is most known for dressing down Hannibal after Cannae for the latter's failure to move immediately against the city of Rome.

MARCELLUS, MARCUS CLAUDIUS. Roman commander in Sicily and then southern Italy, Marcellus took the city of Syracuse and was one of Rome's best generals in the Second Punic War. He was killed fighting Hannibal.

MASSINISSA. Numidian prince and later king of the nomadic tribesmen who inhabited the area of North Africa that today comprises Algeria and eastern Morocco. Massinissa was initially an ally of Hannibal then changed sides and fought alongside Scipio Africanus, helping win the victory at Zama. As a reward, the Romans recognized him as the king of the Numidians.

NERO, GAIUS CLAUDIUS. Roman who commanded in Spain and Italy, then played a major role in defeating Hasdrubal at the battle of the Metaurus River. His foresight, initiative, and boldness at the Metaurus turned the war in Rome's favor.

PAULLUS, LUCIUS AEMILIUS. Co-commander of the Roman forces at Cannae, he was killed in the battle.

PHILIP V OF MACEDON. The king of Macedon. He agreed to aid Hannibal in Italy after the latter's victory at Cannae hoping to extend his kingdom into Greece and parts of Italy. He was defeated by the Romans in 197 B.C. at the battle of Cynoscephalae in Thessaly.

POLYBIUS. A second-century-B.C. Greek historian, he was arrested by the Romans in Greece and placed under a very loose form of house arrest in Rome. During his captivity, Polybius wrote the definitive history of the wars between Carthage and Rome, and to this day, his works, along with those of Livy, remain the principal sources for the study of Hannibal.

PRUSIAS. King of Bithynia in northwestern Asia Minor. He utilized Hannibal's tactical skills in his war with King Eumenes and later betrayed him to the Romans.

SALINATOR, MARCUS LIVIUS. Co-commander with Nero, Salinator helped defeat Hasdrubal at the Metaurus River, ending any chance Hannibal had of winning the Second Punic War.

SCIPIO, GNAEUS CORNELIUS. Uncle of Scipio Africanus and co-commander of the Roman forces in Spain from 218 B.C. until he was killed fighting the Carthaginians in 211 B.C.

SCIPIO, LUCIUS CORNELIUS ASIATICUS. The younger brother of Africanus and co-commander of the Roman forces that defeated Antiochus III in Greece and Asia Minor.

SCIPIO, PUBLIUS CORNELIUS. Roman consul and father of Scipio Africanus. He fought Hannibal at the Ticinus and Trebbia Rivers in 218 B.C. and then was appointed co-commander along with his brother in Spain from 217 until his death fighting the Carthaginians in 211 B.C.

SCIPIO, PUBLIUS CORNELIUS AEMILIANUS. Adopted grandson of Africanus, he became the commander of the Roman forces that destroyed Carthage in the Third Punic War.

SCIPIO, PUBLIUS CORNELIUS AFRICANUS. As a young man, Scipio was given command of the Roman army in Spain following the deaths of his father and uncle. He proved to be the equal of Hannibal as a commander and the savior of Rome.

SEMPRONIUS, TIBERIUS LONGUS. Roman commander defeated at the battle of the Trebbia River when Hannibal drew him out of his camp and into an ambush.

SILENUS. Greek historian from Sicily who served as tutor and biographer to Hannibal. Silenus accompanied Hannibal over the Alps and wrote a history of the expedition that was relied upon by later historians.

SOSYLOS. Greek historian from Sparta, who along with Silenus served as tutor, biographer, and historian to Hannibal.

SYPHAX. King of the Massaesylian Numidians who played both Carthage and Rome against each other. He fought against Scipio in North Africa, was defeated, and was taken as a captive to Rome.

VARRO, GAIUS TERENTIUS. Roman commander defeated by Hannibal at the battle of Cannae. Varro escaped from the battlefield and despite his defeat continued to serve as a general and eventually as ambassador to Carthage.

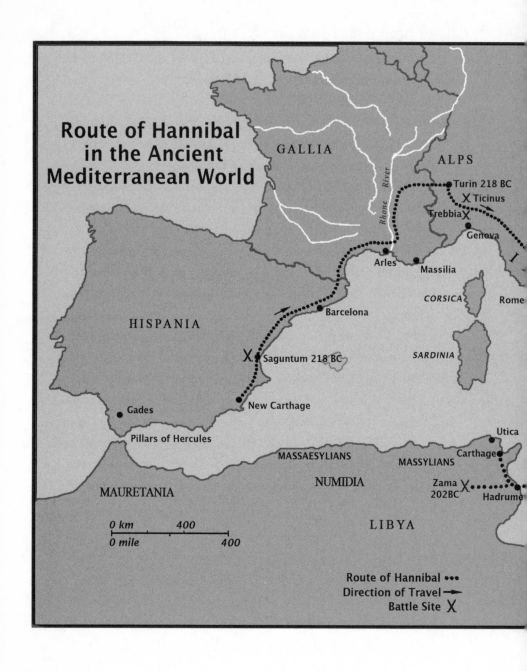

Route of Hannibal
in the Ancient
Mediterranean World

GALLIA

ALPS

Rhone River

Turin 218 BC
X Ticinus
Trebbia X
Genova

Arles
Massilia

CORSICA
Rome

HISPANIA

Barcelona

X Saguntum 218 BC

SARDINIA

Gades

New Carthage

Pillars of Hercules

Utica

MASSAESYLIANS
MASSYLIANS
Carthage

MAURETANIA

NUMIDIA

Zama X
202BC
Hadrume

LIBYA

0 km   400
0 mile   400

Route of Hannibal •••
Direction of Travel ➡
Battle Site X

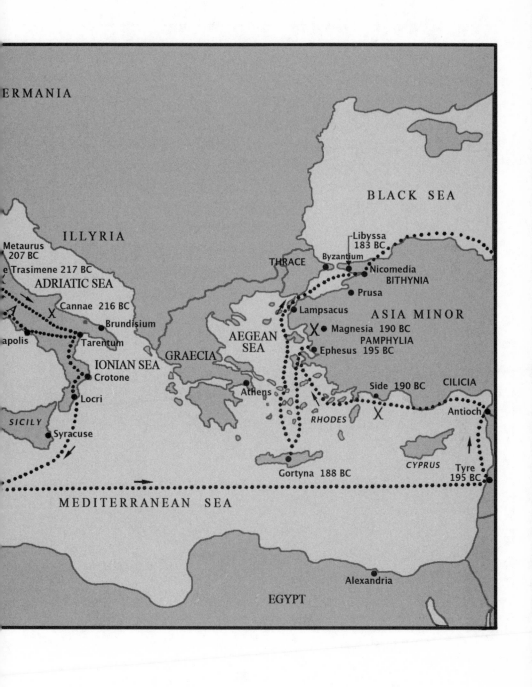

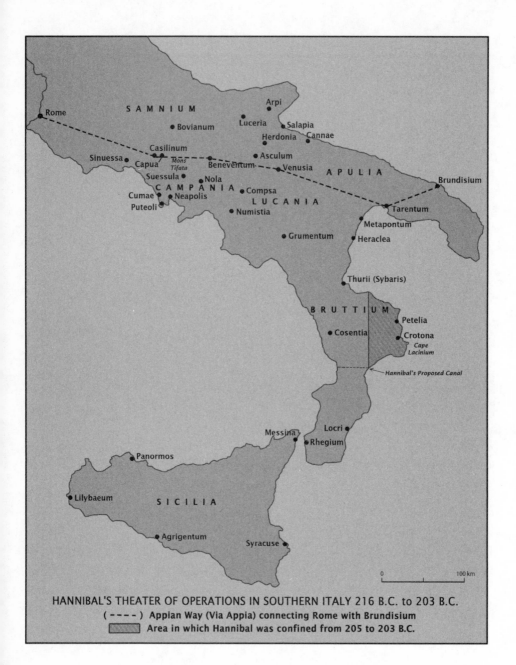

HANNIBAL'S THEATER OF OPERATIONS IN SOUTHERN ITALY 216 B.C. to 203 B.C.
(- - - -) Appian Way (Via Appia) connecting Rome with Brundisium
Area in which Hannibal was confined from 205 to 203 B.C.

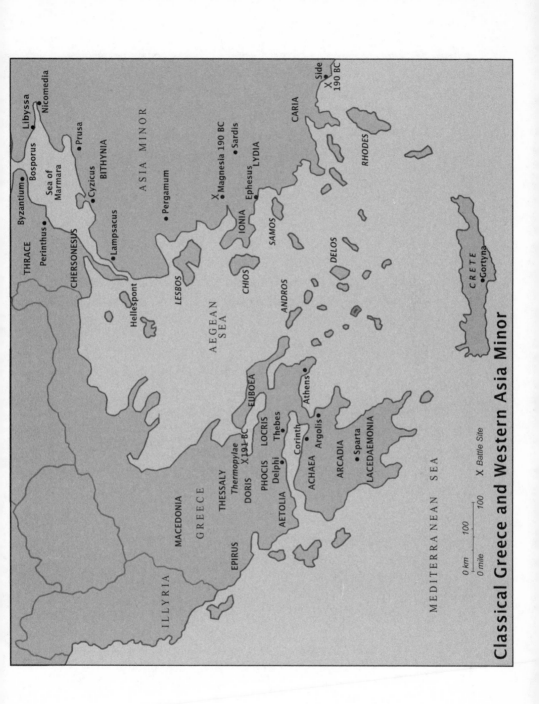

Classical Greece and Western Asia Minor

Libyssa

THRACE   BOSPORUS
Byzantium ●

Nicomedia ●

SEA OF
MARMARA

BITHYNIA

Prusa ●

Cyzicus ●

Lampsacus ●

ASIA MINO
(TURKEY)

HELLESPONT

MYSIA

Pergamum ●

Magnesia 190 BC
X Sardis
● LYDIA

LYCAONIA

CAF

Ephesus ●

PISIDIA

CARIA

PAMPHYLIA

LYCIA Side ● CILICIA

X
190 BC

RHODES

CYPRUS

CRETE ●

Gortyna

MEDITERRANEAN SEA

0 km   200
0 mile   200

X Battle Site

Asia Minor

● T

● Gaza

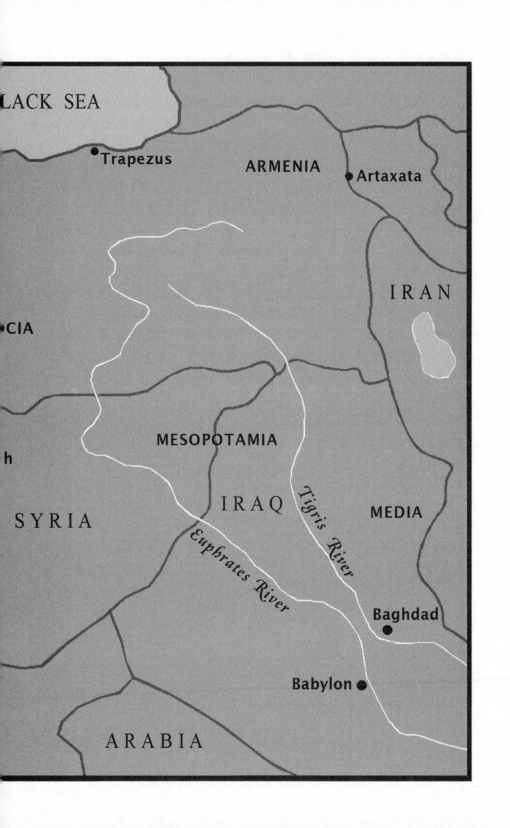

Weigh the ashes of Hannibal on the scales; how much does this great commander come to?

This is the man for whom Africa was too small a land. Even when Spain is added to his dominions he leaps over the Pyrenees; Nature throws in his way Alps and snow: he splits the rocks asunder, and breaks up the mountain-sides with vinegar! And now Italy is in his grasp, but still on he presses: "Nothing is accomplished," he cries, "until my Punic soldiers break down the gates of Rome, and I plant my standard in her midst!"

O what a sight! What a picture, the one-eyed general riding on the Gaetulian monster! What then was his end? A conquered man, he flees headlong into exile, and there he sits, a mighty and marvellous suppliant, in the King's antechamber, until it please his Bithynian Majesty to awake! No sword, stone, or javelin shall end the life which once wrought havoc throughout the world: only a little ring shall avenge Cannae and all those seas of blood. On! on madman, race over those wintry Alps, so that you might become the delight of schoolboys!

—Juvenal, "Satire X,"
from Satires, pps. 147–148

The Ultimate Sacrifice
to Fulfill an Oath

J UST AS THE first rays of dawn swept the eastern wall of the small
castle, a detachment of soldiers quietly landed on the beach below.
They were members of the Bithynian king's royal guard under the command of Romans. They had sailed through the night, west along the
Gulf of Izmit, a tributary of the Sea of Marmara, until they reached
what is today the small Turkish port of Eskihisar on the Asian side
of the Bosporus. It was toward the end of the summer of 183 B.C.,
and Prusias, the king of Bithynia, under pressure from a delegation of
Roman dignitaries, had reluctantly dispatched the soldiers from his
capital, Nicomedia, to the castle with instructions to either capture or
kill Hannibal. Hannibal had fled Carthage twelve years before, seeking
refuge and employment among the Hellenistic kingdoms of the eastern
Mediterranean world. He had been Rome's most formidable enemy for
nearly four decades, fighting in Spain, Italy, and North Africa. Now he
was in the service of these kings as a military advisor and expert on conducting war against the Romans. For the Romans, as long as Hannibal

was alive, anywhere in the ancient world, he was a threat and they could not rest until he was captured or killed.

For years, Hannibal had wandered the eastern Mediterranean, from the court of one king to another, always looking over his shoulder and keeping one step ahead of the Romans. Finally, he thought he had found refuge in Bithynia, a small kingdom in northern Asia Minor ruled by a petty tyrant who had need of him. But the Romans were relentless in their search and when they learned where Hannibal was, they sent a delegation to pressure Prusias to turn him over. The king hesitated at first, pleading not to be forced to violate the laws of hospitality by betraying a guest. But the Roman delegation was led by Flamininus, an ex-consul who was intent on securing his place in history as the man who had rid Rome of her greatest enemy. The Romans were establishing a military presence in Asia Minor and Prusias saw the proverbial handwriting on the wall. He needed and feared them, so laws of hospitality gave way to the tangible rewards of accommodation and cooperation. Prusias gave up Hannibal's location and the Romans went after him.

Once the soldiers landed, it was only a short hike up the hill to the small castle where Hannibal lived in near seclusion. Nicomedia was the capital of Prusias's kingdom and the center of its economic and cultural life, but Hannibal preferred to keep a low profile and so sequestered himself in this remote seaside village. Here, for a while at least, the aging commander, now sixty-four, had found some modicum of peace. But he knew a day like this would come and prepared accordingly. He had never trusted Prusias, finding him to be cowardly and weak, and it came as no surprise that the king had betrayed him. But Hannibal was not one to leave things to chance, waiting for circumstances to dictate his fate. Months before, he supervised the digging of seven secret tunnels, exits that radiated out from the castle. Prusias knew of the existence of the tunnels and revealed them to the Romans. Small contingents of soldiers quickly found and blocked the exits, while the main body of troops prepared to force an entry into the castle.

Flamininus was one of the great personages of Rome at the time. While too young to have played an important role in the war against Hannibal in southern Italy and North Africa, he made his mark in the years after as commander of the Roman armies in their "liberation" of Greece from the oppression of Philip of Macedon. In 189 B.C., Flamininus had returned to Rome in triumph and was elected censor, the culmination of any Roman's successful political career. But as the years passed, his opportunities to gain additional glory diminished, yet he was intent on ending his career by having his name associated with the capture and death of Rome's most feared enemy—Hannibal. Flamininus learned that Hannibal had taken refuge in Bithynia when ambassadors from Prusias came to Rome to explain the king's position in his dispute with Eumenes the king of Pergamum and a Roman ally. At a dinner party hosted by Flamininus, one of the Bithynians inadvertently let slip that Prusias was hiding Hannibal at his court. The next morning, Flamininus went to the senate and demanded authorization to leave for Bithynia and capture Hannibal. The matter engendered considerable debate. There were senators who were skeptical and questioned if it was worth the effort to track down an enemy whom circumstances and time had rendered old and powerless. Hannibal, one senator contended, was like an old bird that had lost its tail feathers and could no longer fly. He should be allowed to live out his remaining years in the east, far from Rome; isolated and harmless.

Flamininus knew which chains to pull in response to calls to leave Hannibal alone. He warned the senators that so long as Hannibal lived, he remained a threat. He reminded them of Hannibal's presence by the side of Antiochus and his role in the victory of Prusias over Eumenes. Funded by another eastern king with aspirations of conquest, Flamininus warned that Hannibal could unexpectedly appear on the shores of

Italy with an army and once more threaten the republic. While Flamininus was willing to concede that Hannibal was old, at least by ancient standards, and that perhaps he had passed his prime in terms of his bodily strength, he had years of accumulated experience as a tactician and strategist and was potentially more of a threat to Rome now than he had been in his youth. There were those in the senate who agreed with Flamininus and wanted Hannibal brought back to Rome in chains to be paraded through the streets and then executed. Flamininus played to them and they carried the day. He was granted his authorization, but the senate sent with him, as co-ambassador to Prusias, Lucius Scipio, the younger brother of Africanus. Lucius had served with Flamininus in the wars against Philip, and then against Antiochus in Greece. In honor of his success, the senate had bestowed upon him the cognomen "Asiaticus." The mission of the two Romans seems to have been to reach an accommodation with Prusias, and then either capture Hannibal and bring him to Rome for execution or kill him on the spot.

A slave on one of the ramparts spotted the soldiers moving into position and awakened his master. Hannibal ordered him to check the other ramparts and the slave returned to report that the castle was surrounded. Resistance was not an option as Hannibal had only a small number of slaves who were no match for the more heavily armed soldiers outside the walls. Hannibal made several attempts to escape through his secret passages, and each time he reached the end of a tunnel, he found it blocked by soldiers and was forced to turn back. He never believed his end would come in Bithynia because he had taken comfort in the words of an oracle that prophesied his time to die would come in North Africa when "Libyssan earth shall cover the body of Hannibal." Hannibal believed this referred to Libya—as North Africa was known in ancient times. But unknown to him, not far from his castle, a small river named Libyssa flowed to the sea and sealed his fate.

As the soldiers forced their entry, Hannibal barricaded himself along with a trusted slave in one of the chambers. Turning to the slave, he said, "Let us now put an end to the great anxiety of these Romans, who think it too long and tedious a task to await the natural death of this hated old man." Then he wound a cloak around his neck and ordered the slave to plant his knee in his back and twisting the cloak choke the life from him. Thus, on a cold stone floor ingloriously and ignominiously came to an end the life of the most known, respected, and feared commander in the ancient world.[1]

CHAPTER I

The Road to Power

H ANNIBAL WAS BORN to an aristocratic Carthaginian family known as the Barcas in 247 B.C. just as the First Punic War between Carthage and Rome was entering its concluding years. His father, Hamilcar Barca, was a figure larger than life, a man of action and unquestionably the most influential force in his son's life. Hamilcar would set the direction for Hannibal's life and determine its end. The father commanded the Carthaginian forces in Sicily and for nearly three years (244–241 B.C.) conducted a successful campaign of guerilla warfare against the Romans on the northwestern part of the island. From a base on Mt. Eryx (now called Monte San Giuliano), Hamilcar Barca harassed the Romans and inflicted the maximum number of casualties wherever he could. Sailing across the Straits of Massena, he raided towns along the southeastern Italian coast, and when the fighting in Sicily became too intense or he risked losing an encounter, he withdrew to the safety of his mountain stronghold to await the next opportunity. This strategy of attacking and retreating while always avoiding a major battle disrupted Roman lines of supply and became a continual drain on their manpower and finances. No Roman commander in Sicily seemed able to counter, much less match, Hamilcar's tactical skills as the war dragged on indecisively.

But Hamilcar was dependent on the Carthaginian navy for his supplies, and that proved to be his Achilles' heel. The navy, in turn, was under the command of an admiral named Hanno, and its mission was to keep Hamilcar supplied with reinforcements, weapons, and most importantly, money to pay his mercenaries. In 241 B.C. a fleet of nearly one thousand ships under Hanno's command sailed from Carthage in an attempt to reach Hamilcar at the port of Trapani on the western tip of Sicily. Before the ships could reach Sicily, they were intercepted by the Roman navy. Those that were not sunk or captured returned to Carthage where Hanno was tried for the defeat and crucified. Support in the senate to continue an expensive war that had gone on for nearly a quarter century was waning, and Hamilcar was ordered to reach an accommodation with the Roman consul in Sicily to stop the fighting.

Hamilcar hated the Romans. He considered his army to be a viable force able to continue the war and so at first he resisted the order. The landowning aristocracy that now controlled the Carthaginian senate had a different agenda. They wanted to end what they saw as a futile, costly, and indecisive conflict and focus the resources of their city on the development of a land-based, largely agricultural empire in North Africa. But Hamilcar was a commander more inclined to do what he thought was right rather than what the senate ordered. Many of the senators at Carthage anticipated that he might refuse to follow their directive and they were prepared to cut off his supplies, negotiate their own peace with Rome, and leave him isolated in Sicily to continue his war on his own. Faced with that prospect, Hamilcar gave in and approached the Romans to negotiate a truce.

The Romans were also tired of a war that had gone on for so long, draining their treasury and depleting their manpower reserves. The consul in charge of the Roman forces in Sicily reached a settlement with Hamilcar that stopped the fighting. Hamilcar agreed to leave Sicily, return all Roman prisoners without ransom, and pay a reparation settlement to Rome of two hundred talents[1] of silver over a twenty-year period. The agreement between the two commanders was contingent upon ratification by their respective senates, and when the Roman senate reviewed the terms, it determined they were too lenient. The amount of the indemnity was substantially increased, the repayment period shortened, and Carthage required to keep its merchant ships out of all waters close to the Italian mainland. While the First Punic War only slightly altered the balance of power in the western Mediterranean, it set the stage for what was to be a shorter but much more destructive conflict, to come within the next twenty years.

Hamilcar returned to his family at Carthage an angry and embittered man. He believed he had been betrayed by aristocrats who were motivated to end the war more out of concern for their own fortunes than the good of the city. The historian Livy described him as *"ingentis spiritus virum,"* a man of great pride who believed that he had come close to defeating the Romans in Sicily, and, if not winning the war, at least bringing it to an honorable draw.[2] Hamilcar Barca traced his lineage to the very founding of Carthage. His was an aristocratic line, wealthy and influential, and he could have enjoyed a life of leisure on his estates south of Carthage or devoted himself to commercial pursuits in the empire with high returns of profit as did so many of his contemporaries. But instead, Hamilcar chose a career of military service, which often took him away from his family for long periods. To Hamilcar's thinking, it was not the Romans who had defeated him in Sicily, but his own people who had withheld the support he needed to win in the final months of the conflict.

Over the next few weeks, nearly twenty thousand mercenaries from Sicily arrived at Carthage. Initially they landed on the shores in small groups to minimize any disruptive impact they might have on the city.

The plan was to pay each group off quickly as it arrived, at a reduced rate, and then send the soldiers back to their countries of origin or on to another assignment before the next group arrived. Many in the senate were unhappy over the enormous indemnity due to Rome and the money already wasted on a war that had been lost. They complained at the prospect of having to raise taxes to pay the mercenaries their full wages, and suggestions came from the senate floor that crucifixion might be a cheaper and more desirable alternative. As the senate stalled the payments by engaging in endless discussion and debate, the agitated mercenaries continued to congregate outside the city, their numbers growing larger by the day as each arriving ship disgorged its load. A volatile mix of Iberians, Gauls, Ligurians, Balearic islanders, Greeks, and Africans began to mass outside the walls, all clamoring for their money. The Carthaginians responded by jeering and throwing stale bread down on them from the safety of their high city walls. The mood grew increasingly uglier and more contentious as each day passed.

Finally, the mercenaries rebelled: rampaging into the countryside, they attacked the villas and plantations, pillaging, raping, and murdering rich and poor alike. The aristocrats at Carthage watched from the ramparts in horror as the smoke from their burning villas and fields filled the sky. A war began which, paraphrased in the words of the Greek historian Polybius, exceeded "human wickedness" and the "ferocity of even the wildest animals." As the mercenaries rampaged, they were joined by local tribesmen, and the atrocities took on "the vindictiveness of insanity." The solidarity of the mercenaries and the Africans can only be accounted for within the context of their mutual hatred for Carthage and its duplicitous leaders.

Carthage had no mercenaries to hire this time. The Carthaginians were faced with the prospect of having to leave the safety of their high-walled city to do their own fighting. Command of a hastily raised citizen army went to the leader of the senate, Hanno "the Great," a politician of long standing and an opponent of the Barca family. While he had led the faction in the senate that negotiated the end of the war with Rome, Hanno was no general and in the field failed to accomplish anything against the mercenaries. The situation became increasingly more alarming, especially to the large landowners who watched as their investments in the countryside continued to be looted and burned.

In desperation, the senate turned to Hamilcar and prevailed upon him to take command. Always resourceful, he was able to recruit a few mercenaries from Italy, employ some renegades from his old army in Sicily, and buy supplies from the Romans. Combining these mercenaries with citizen soldiers, Hamilcar ventured out into the deserts of North Africa to confront the men he had commanded for years in Sicily. The struggle lasted three years (241–238 B.C.), until Hamilcar brought it to an end when he lured the greater part of the mercenary force into a gorge in the desert outside Carthage known as the "saw." There, trapped and exhausted by thirst, hunger, and fatigue, the mercenaries were trampled by Hamilcar's elephants. The few who survived were taken back to Carthage and crucified outside the walls of the city.

The Romans remained relatively neutral throughout the conflict, probably so they would continue to receive their indemnity payments from Carthage. They allowed Hamilcar to recruit mercenaries in Italy, and Roman merchants made handsome profits selling to the Carthaginians, just as the Carthaginians had done for years before in so many other regional conflicts. Then, without warning and in blatant violation of the terms of the peace treaty ending the First Punic War, Rome seized the island of Sardinia from the Carthaginians and shortly thereafter took Corsica. Carthage, worn down by years of fighting and with only a few ships left, was in no position to call Rome to account for her actions, even though voices in the Carthaginian senate clamored for another war. With no practical alternative, the Carthaginians accepted the humiliating reality as Sicily, Sardinia, and Corsica now became the first provinces of what would become the greatest empire the ancient world had ever seen. Hamilcar was furious at what he saw as Roman bad faith, but, powerless to intervene at that moment, he chose to bide his time and find another way to even the score.

When it came to advice about parenting, the ancient Greeks had a saying "as is bent the twig, so grows the tree." Hamilcar was a father who bent his three sons—Hannibal, Hasdrubal, and Mago—with a hatred of Rome and mistrust of those who ruled at Carthage. Hannibal was the oldest, and not only did he resemble Hamilcar physically, he also had his father's temperament, character, and innate sense of leadership. Just as Alexander the Great was the product of his father, Philip II of Macedon, so Hannibal was the product of Hamilcar Barca. As Philip had raised Alexander to make war on Persia, so Hamilcar raised his sons to wage relentless war against Rome. Hamilcar wanted to restore what he considered his lost honor and exact revenge for the Roman taking of Sicily, Sardinia, and Corsica.

Hamilcar had married at Carthage, although we know nothing about his wife beyond the fact that she bore him six children; first, three girls, and then three boys. We do not even know her name. Those girls, when they came of age, were married to secure political and military alliances beneficial to the Barca family—a common practice in the ancient world, especially among the Greeks, Romans, and Carthaginians. The eldest daughter married an aristocrat, who would later command the Carthaginian fleet during the Second Punic War. Their marriage produced a male child, Hanno, who became one of Hannibal's commanders and played a key role in the defeat of the Romans at the battle of Cannae in 216 B.C. This Hanno has often understandably, if not mistakenly, been referred to by scholars as the fourth son of Hamilcar.

The second daughter was also married for political purposes, sometime between 241 and 237 B.C. She was wed to an influential supporter of her father's in the senate, known as Hasdrubal the Handsome.

Hasdrubal and his family had considerable political influence at Carthage, and ancient Roman commentators, who admittedly had their own axes to grind when it came to Carthage, describe him as *adulescens illustris et formosus* (a young man remarkably distinguished and handsome).[3] So handsome was Hasdrubal that apparently Hamilcar developed "a love less honorable than was proper" for him. Cornelius Nepos, a Roman, wrote that Hamilcar, being a great man, was often subject to slander by his opponents, but went on to imply that there may have been something more there than just slander. Because of these allegations, an officer of the state, known as the censor of morals, issued an order that forbade Hamilcar to be in the presence of Hasdrubal. Hamilcar circumvented the order by marrying his daughter to Hasdrubal and then invoking a Carthaginian common law that prevented the state from denying a father the company of his son-in-law.

Stories of bisexual relationships between great leaders are not unusual in the literature of the ancient world. We find them in references to Alexander the Great and Julius Caesar. Caesar's political opponents, and even his soldiers, often disparaged him with allegations that he was "husband to many a woman and wife to many a man." The Hamilcar-Hasdrubal story takes another twist when Roman sources maintain that following the death of Hamilcar, Hannibal was in turn seduced by Hasdrubal. However, some contemporary scholars have tended to either ignore these allegations or dismiss them as little more than "far-fetched tales."[4]

The third daughter of Hamilcar was married to a Numidian chief named Naravas. Of the three marriages this one must have been done to provide a military alliance that secured for Hamilcar the Bedouin cavalry that would prove so effective against the Romans in the Second Punic War. That daughter became the inspiration for the seductive Salammbo in Gustave Flaubert's nineteenth century novel by the same name.

Hamilcar, with the help of Hasdrubal's family, manipulated the senate into assigning him as military governor to Spain. With the recent loss of three of its most valuable overseas possessions, Sicily, Sardinia, and Corsica, and the destruction of large parts of the countryside around Carthage as a result of the mercenary war, the city needed new areas of development if it was to continue to prosper and pay the Romans their war indemnity. Hamilcar argued against the diverting of Carthaginian resources toward the development of a land-based African empire and promoted a continued and even expanded naval and commercial presence in the western Mediterranean to keep the Romans at bay. Hamilcar's assignment to Spain may have been an integral component of a plan to renew a war with Rome. Spain, with its plentiful reserves of manpower and untapped natural resources, was the ideal place to build a base from which the next campaign against the Romans could be launched.

In 238 B.C., the senate authorized Hamilcar to lead a large expeditionary force to Spain, and in keeping with Carthaginian religious practices he sacrificed to the god Baal for a successful mission. As the rituals neared completion, Hamilcar called for Hannibal, then only nine years of age, to join him at the altar. There, the young boy begged his father to take him to Spain, and Hamilcar consented on the condition that Hannibal pledge to the god he would always be an enemy to Rome and to anyone who stood with Rome.

The Carthaginians sacrificed infants and the occasional adult to appease their gods in a systematic, institutionalized practice that appears to have been a part of their culture since the founding of the city and that can be traced back even further, to their Semitic origins in the biblical land of Canaan. The actual rite was termed *molk*, and there is debate among contemporary scholars if living children were sacrificed or only those who died in infancy. None of the Greek or Roman sources that describe the practice ever clearly make the distinction, although Plutarch wrote that children were bought from the poor or from slave markets specifically for that purpose. The largest molk was recorded by the Roman writer Diodorus, who noted it occurred in 310 B.C while the city was under attack by Agathocles, the Greek tyrant of Syracuse.

The Carthaginian aristocracy was called upon by their priests to sacrifice five hundred of their infants to appease Baal, who was allegedly angry because on an earlier occasion, the aristocracy had attempted to "cheat" him by substituting infants and young children bought from the slave markets in place of their own.[5] In no other society in the ancient world was human sacrifice found on such a scale and frequency as at Carthage, and nowhere does the issue raise more interest and engender more passionate debate among contemporary scholars. A succession of Greek and Roman historians have provided details of child sacrifice at Carthage, and although they are unanimous in their condemnation of the practice, on occasion, both their cultures resorted to the sacrifice of adults in times of crisis.[6]

There is no indication in the manuscripts that on this occasion infants or adults were being sacrificed to the god. Still, the very setting itself must have been one that would have terrified anyone, especially a nine-year-old child, since inside the temple the fearsome god Baal was represented by a huge iron furnace, cast in his image, into which victims were burned alive.

Spain at the time was known as Iberia, and over the next decade Hamilcar conquered most of the southern portion along the Mediterranean coast. He established his power over a land of tribal societies that were, by Carthaginian and Greek standards, primitive. There were two primary groups, the Celts and the Iberians, and in many parts of Spain, they had gradually blended into a single warlike people known as the Celtiberians. While they were a strong, brave, and impulsive people, they were undisciplined and took direction poorly. While they were capable of fierce resistance in defending their homes, they were incapable of joining forces with their fellow countrymen in a coordinated effort to defeat an organized and more sophisticated invading army like that of the Carthaginians. Their warriors were aided by finely tempered swords, unsurpassed in the ancient world and to this day Spanish blades continue to set a standard for quality that is second to none.

Hamilcar used these tribes for everything—from slave labor to supplementing his African troops and his mercenaries. In those areas under
direct Carthaginian control, the tribesmen were conscripted directly
into Hamilcar's army, while recruits from outlying areas were enticed
to join by his agents who made them promises of great personal wealth
and glory in battle. Under Carthaginian commanders, many of them
were transformed into disciplined cavalry and infantry.

Once Hamilcar had subdued most of the tribes of southern and eastern Spain, he set about to exploit the natural wealth of the land. Only
the northern areas of the country remained beyond his control and for
the next twenty years, 238 B.C. to 218 B.C., first Hamilcar, then his
successors, Hasdrubal and Hannibal, established a larger and richer
empire in Spain than Carthage had ever possessed in Sicily, Sardinia,
and Corsica. Spain became the private domain of the Barca family as
they founded new cities along the eastern seaboard: Cartagena or "new
Carthage"; Barcelona, "the camp of the Barcas"; and Gades (Cadiz) in
the south. The new empire was developing, just as Hamilcar had intended, into an economic and military base for the launch of the next
war against Rome.

The gold and silver mines of Spain yielded their wealth to the efficiency of their new African masters. Hamilcar's power and wealth increased his influence in Carthage to the point where few in the senate
would dare to criticize him openly or oppose his will. A significant portion of the wealth from Spain flowed into Carthage, which only served
to reinforce Hamilcar's popularity among the people and stifle those
who opposed him in the senate. Hamilcar Barca was not just wealthy;
he was powerful beyond what any Carthaginian had ever achieved. He
had become a de facto king.

Due in large part to Hamilcar's efforts in exploiting the wealth of
Spain, the financial condition of Carthage improved and within a generation the city had regained much of its former wealth and prestige in

the ancient world—a development that came to interest the Romans, who were new at empire building and were quickly realizing its benefits. Their acquisition of Sicily, Sardinia, and Corsica at Carthaginian expense had only whetted their appetite for more. The Romans allied themselves with the prosperous Greek city of Massilia, modern-day Marseilles, which controlled a number of smaller colonies or trading stations along the Mediterranean coasts of France and northern Spain. Among these colonies was the fortress city of Saguntum, modern-day Sagunto, whose walled remains can be found on a high hilltop overlooking the sea just a few kilometers north of present-day Valencia.

Among the inhabitants of Saguntum was a small group who favored closer contacts with Hamilcar and the Carthaginians to their south. This concerned those who controlled the city to such a point that they asked the Romans to send a delegation to Hamilcar to inquire about his intentions toward Saguntum. Hamilcar received the delegation and quickly put them at ease with his assurances that he was content with the southern half of Spain and had no intention of moving north. The delegation returned to Rome and reported to the senate that, for the moment at least, they were content to accept Hamilcar's assurances that he would leave Saguntum alone. The senate was now able to address more pressing concerns for Rome, such as the administration of their new provinces (Sicily, Sardinia, and Corsica) and a threat that was developing among the Gauls in northern Italy.

The Gauls who inhabited the Po Valley in northern Italy had been a concern to the Romans since 390 B.C. when they moved south and sacked the city. The Romans were anxious to keep them contained in northern Italy and to that effort they established two sizable colonies at Cremona and Placentia (modern-day Piacenza) as buffers. A short but fierce and indecisive conflict broke out between the Roman colonists and the Gauls lasting from 225 B.C. until 222 B.C. The Romans managed to put a temporary but uneasy truce in place that lasted until just before Hannibal crossed the Alps and invaded northern Italy. Another Roman concern at the time was piracy stemming from Illyria (Albania) on the Adriatic coast. The Roman navy engaged in an ongoing action to suppress the pirates, while the army kept a watchful eye on Macedonia, which was becoming increasingly restless under a youthful and aggressive new king, Philip V. Both the Gauls and Philip would later come to play parts in Hannibal's war against Rome.

Hamilcar's second-in-command in Spain was his son-in-law, Hasdrubal the Handsome. Years of close collaboration had enabled them to develop a consistency of policy and administration from 238 B.C. until 221 B.C. They seem to have operated independently of Carthage and focused on bringing the tribes under their control and exploiting the natural resources. They depended heavily on their army, which had been built around their personal leadership and charisma, to maintain their power. The soldiers in Hamilcar's army came to owe their allegiance to the Barca family, which paid their wages and provided for them— not to the senate at Carthage. This consistency and stability paid off. When Hamilcar was killed in 229 B.C., there was a smooth transition of power. Hasdrubal became the new regent without opposition, and then with his death in 221 B.C., Hannibal in turn became the new leader of the army and governor of Spain—again without opposition or any major changes in policy and administration.

Hamilcar and then Hasdrubal pacified many of the tribes, utilizing terror when necessary—blinding, maiming, and crucifying those who resisted, while generously including and rewarding those who cooperated. It was a policy of alternating force with diplomacy and the generous benefits of inclusion. The Barca influence extended even off shore to the Balearic Islands, whose soldiers became a part of Hannibal's expeditionary force to Italy. Hamilcar's and then Hasdrubal's policies resulted in the establishment of a native base of support and a system of alliances, which Hannibal later used in his war against Rome. As long as the Barcas kept the money flowing into Carthage, the senate and people there seemed willing to turn a blind eye to the fact that the family had established a dynasty in Spain.

Hamilcar was killed in the winter of 229/228 B.C., and there are three generally similar versions of his death. In the most accepted story, he was killed while conducting operations against a fortified town in the Spanish interior. The besieged town was saved by the arrival of a relief force under the command of the king of the Oretani, a tribe from the La Mancha plateau, and this forced Hamilcar to break off the siege. In the ensuing confusion of his retreat, Hamilcar and his two young sons, Hannibal and Hasdrubal, were separated from their soldiers and pursued by elements of the enemy cavalry. Faced with only one safe avenue for escape, Hamilcar ordered his two sons to take that route while he drew off the pursuing Oretani into a river with a dangerous current. Hamilcar was swept away and drowned. At least that is the story related by one ancient historian.[7] In a second version, Hamilcar died fighting in an unnamed battlefield in Spain, while a third version has him dying in an engagement against a tribe from the area west of modern-day Toledo.[8]

In this last version of the story, Hamilcar's death occurred during an attack in which enemy tribesmen drove oxen pulling carts loaded with hay directly into the Carthaginian soldiers. The hay was set on fire just as the carts engaged Hamilcar's soldiers. The tactic took the Carthaginians by surprise, and Hamilcar was killed in the chaos of the fighting. While the exact circumstances of Hamilcar's death remain unclear, what is certain is that when he died his sons were too young to succeed him. His son-in-law, Hasdrubal the Handsome assumed command of the army, and his position was ratified by the senate at Carthage. Wasting no time, Hasdrubal's first action was to avenge his father-in-law and mentor. The Carthaginian army showed no mercy toward those it held responsible for Hamilcar's death, including their women and children.

It was retaliation pure and simple—with a callous indifference to innocence or human suffering. Many were crucified as an example to other
tribes that might be considering resistance to the Barca dynasty, and in
the process of retaliation, Hasdrubal added considerable territory to the
existing Carthaginian holdings in Spain.

The next three years under Hasdrubal were devoted to the consolidation of Barcid power in Spain. While Hamilcar was a conqueror,
Hasdrubal was a consolidator and administrator. He continued to exploit Spain's manpower and resources, as his role evolved into more that
of a governor than a conqueror. The city of Carthago Nova or New
Carthage (Cartagena) prospered and Hasdrubal built a splendid palace
there. The port city offered easy access by ship to Carthage, and its location made it an ideal administrative center for the new Spanish empire.
Hasdrubal became a king in every sense of the word. He lived in regal
luxury, married an Iberian princess to cement his alliances, and ordered
the minting of gold and silver coins that bore his image.

Carthaginian holdings in Spain grew under Hasdrubal. Large numbers of natives as well as slaves from Africa were forced to work in the
gold and silver mines, often under brutal conditions, ensuring the un-
interrupted flow of precious metals into New Carthage and guarantee-
ing the stability and prosperity of the dynasty. While discontent might
have been widespread among many of the proud Iberians and Celts,
the discipline and organization imposed on the country by Hasdrubal,
enforced by his army and tempered by his diplomacy, kept it suppressed.
The tribal chiefs paid tribute to Hasdrubal as they had to Hamilcar and
were often required to surrender their children as hostages to insure
their fidelity, a practice the Romans quickly saw the value of and utilized
effectively throughout their empire in later years.

Once the Gauls in northern Italy had been quieted and the pirates
suppressed, the Romans took an active interest in Spain. Philip V of
Macedon still remained a potential problem because of his desire to

expand his kingdom into Greece, but the primary attention of the Romans was now focused on Hasdrubal. Emissaries were dispatched to New Carthage in 226 B.C. to negotiate an arrangement that would limit Carthaginian expansion north of New Carthage. Hasdrubal received the Roman delegation in a cordial fashion and conceded that all territory north of what some modern scholars believe might have been the river Ebro, was a Roman sphere of influence. There is some debate about whether the Ebro was that demarcation line since it would have increased considerably the amount of new territory in Spain left free for Hasdrubal's taking and left the city of Saguntum, with its ties to Rome, isolated deep within Carthaginian territory.

A more plausible choice for the boundary is the river Jucar, which flows into the sea just south of Valencia. If the Jucar is taken as the northern limit of Carthaginian territory, the Romans would have succeeded in limiting the area of Spain controlled by Hasdrubal and protecting Saguntum. The debate among modern scholars about exactly which river in northern Spain was the boundary is not just an academic exercise. It is relevant because the location of that river impacts discussions of where the blame for starting the Second Punic War can be placed.[9] Hasdrubal might have accepted the Jucar as the boundary to placate the Romans, since he was probably more concerned with consolidating power over his Spanish territories to the south and west than risking war with Rome. Both Hamilcar and Hasdrubal may have been cautious in dealing with the Romans during this period and careful not to give them any cause to intervene in Spain; Hannibal, however, would change all that in short order.

Exactly when Hannibal arrived in Spain is not clear. We know he accompanied his father initially and that he was with Hamilcar when he was killed. After Hamilcar's death he returned to Carthage, and not long thereafter, Hasdrubal sent for him, probably to begin training for a command position. Hannibal's return to Spain became a matter of

considerable debate in the Carthaginian senate. The pro-Barcid faction
supported him as the logical successor to Hasdrubal and urged that he
be sent to Spain to become "inured to war and succeed to the resources
of his father." The anti-Barcid faction, led by Hanno, strongly opposed
Hannibal's return. Hanno opened his remarks to the senate on a sa-
lacious note—Hannibal should not be sent to Spain to satisfy Hasdrubal's lust—just as Hasdrubal had satisfied Hamilcar's years before.
Hanno thought it "most unseemly" that the young men of Carthage be
sent to satisfy the libidos of her generals.[10] Hannibal should remain at
Carthage, he argued, to be "schooled in the proper submission to the law
and its officers" and remain on an "equal footing with other young men."
He should not be allowed to join Hasdrubal and be corrupted by the
"inordinate powers and regal pomp" his father and Hasdrubal indulged
in. Hanno knew the hatred of the Barcas for Rome, and he feared that
if Hannibal were allowed to return to Spain, that "small spark," as he
called him, might one day kindle a massive conflagration. Even though
Hanno's arguments found favor with many in the senate, the pro-Barcid
faction had the votes to carry the motion, and Hannibal was allowed to
leave for Spain.

When Hannibal arrived, the soldiers celebrated his return. Veterans saw in him the reincarnation of Hamilcar, while younger soldiers
quickly fell under the charismatic spell of the next generation of Barca
leadership. Hasdrubal appointed Hannibal commander of the cavalry,
and the young man began to learn tactics on the plains of Spain, while
in the royal palace at Carthago Nova, Hasdrubal taught him politics and
diplomacy. The sources are clear that Hasdrubal favored Hannibal over
all his other officers, not so much because of their family ties, but because of Hannibal's ability. Hannibal learned quickly at Hasdrubal's side,
watching him as he utilized diplomacy rather than force to settle dis-
putes among the Celtiberians and advance his interests. When force was
necessary to suppress unrest, Hannibal became Hasdrubal's enforcer.

As a commander, Hannibal learned to inspire those he led by example. While on the march, he showed that he could endure the worst nature could throw at him and he asked no more from those he led than he was willing to give—much in the style of Alexander the Great and later Julius Caesar. Hannibal ate and drank in moderation, taking only as much as he needed to sustain his strength. He would sleep lying on the earth in the company of those he led and only when his work was completed—never in the luxury of a commander's tent attended by servants. He took his meals from the same cooking pots as his soldiers and stood his turn on sentry duty throughout the night. His clothes and armor were modest for a man of his royal lineage and rank. Officers and especially the common soldiers loved him because he lived among them in the camps and won their confidence in field operations where he proved time and again his competence and leadership abilities.

Hasdrubal's life came to a violent end in 221 B.C. when a Celtic slave murdered him in the palace. The motive appears to have been retaliation. Hasdrubal had ordered one of the Celt's kinsmen crucified for plotting against him and the Celt took his revenge. Hannibal was twenty-six years old when Hasdrubal was killed, and he took immediate command of the army and political control of the country. The army acclaimed him their leader, and word of their decision was sent to the senate at Carthage to be affirmed. The senate was not about to object.

When Hannibal took command his first action was to lead a punitive expedition against some Spanish tribes that had revolted against Hasdrubal's rule. The tribes inhabited the area of Spain known today as La Mancha, and Hannibal quickly subdued them. He imposed a tribute and then withdrew into winter quarters at New Carthage to await the spring and the start of a new campaign. During the summer of 220 B.C. Hannibal defeated a large force of hostile tribes that had converged in the area of what is today Salamanca. In a preview of the tactics he would come to use against the Romans in Italy, Hannibal withdrew in the face of the enemy, who, bewildered by this unorthodox move, and thinking he was retreating, followed him. It was a brilliant tactical maneuver. Hannibal drew the enemy into a cleverly laid trap at a crossing of the Tagus River, where he had concealed a large contingent of his African cavalry along the riverbank.

As the tribesmen crossed the river, most of them on foot, Hannibal's African cavalry attacked from the flank cutting them down in midstream. Caught by surprise, waterlogged and hampered by their weapons, they panicked. Unable to gain a secure footing because of the swiftly moving waters, most were killed and the few who escaped had only a temporary respite before they were trampled by Hannibal's elephants as they struggled up the banks of the far side of the river.

What Hannibal demonstrated at the Tagus that day was that he could utilize the elements of surprise and advantages of location. The salient characteristic of his military career was that he always retained the initiative and would determine when, where, and how he would fight. He would utilize everything to his advantage that nature could provide—cold or heat, wind and rain, ice and snow. Following the victory at the Tagus, few tribes in central and southern Spain would risk engaging him in battle, and for the next two years, he extended the limits of his control north to the Ebro River—leaving only Saguntum outside his pale.

Hannibal's personal life, beyond some scattered references in the ancient sources, is a mystery. He was evidently well educated during his early years at Carthage, and while his native language was Semitic Punic, his second language became Greek—the lingua franca of the ancient world. We know that Hannibal surrounded himself in Spain with Greek scholars, and so that he could better understand the people he had devoted his life to fighting, he undertook to learn Latin. Hannibal married, taking as his bride the daughter of an Iberian chieftain from Castulo, a town on the Guadalquivir River west of Cartagena.[11]

The area had attracted the Carthaginians because of its mineral wealth, and Hannibal may have entered into the marriage as much for political considerations as out of love. Hasdrubal had taken a Spanish wife soon after succeeding Hamilcar, presumably because it was to his political advantage to take a native bride and tighten his bonds with the Celts, even though he was married to Hamilcar's daughter. Historians have never agreed among themselves if the Carthaginians were essentially monogamous like the Greeks and Romans.

In his epic work *Punica*, the Roman poet Silius Italicus tells us that Hannibal's wife was named Imilce and she bore him a son as he was besieging Saguntum. Apparently this was Hannibal's only child, but Silius Italicus is not considered a reliable source because of suspicions that he was inclined to exaggerate and fabricate in the interests of artistic expression. He was a dramatic poet, writing for the emperor Nero in the first century A.D., over two hundred years after Hannibal's death. Italicus and Livy are the only sources to mention Hannibal's wife.

According to the dramatic account of Italicus, before Hannibal left for Italy he took his wife and child to Gades in the south of Spain to put them on a ship for Carthage—probably to protect them from the vicissitudes of war. There, Imilce begged Hannibal to allow her to accompany him over the Alps to Italy, maintaining that her gender would not prevent her from enduring the same deprivations as any man. Hannibal refused. Later in the poem, Italicus relates the story of how Hannibal's political enemies at Carthage colluded to compel Imilce to surrender her son to be sacrificed to the god Baal. Imilce resisted and obtained from the senate permission to postpone the sacrifice until she could inform her husband and secure his consent. When Hannibal received the demand in Italy, he refused and offered instead to sacrifice a thousand Romans to placate the god.

The people of Saguntum were weary of Carthage and fearful of Hannibal. For security and to keep Hannibal at bay, they relied on their

alliances with the Greek city-states of southern France and in turn the
alliances of those city-states with Rome. As Hannibal became increasingly more active in the region around Saguntum, the Greeks sent a
delegation to Rome seeking a strong commitment to come to the city's
aid in the event of an attack. The Romans in turn sent a delegation to
Hannibal with instructions to demand that he honor the treaty Hasdrubal had signed with Rome some years before, limiting Carthaginian
expansion in northern Spain.

Hannibal was twenty-six, and this meeting was probably the first
time he had confronted the Romans face-to-face. There is a slight discrepancy in the sources regarding exactly where the meeting took place.
One source has the Romans arriving by ship at New Carthage, where
they had met with Hamilcar and Hasdrubal, while another, later source
has them arriving farther north along the coast where Hannibal was
preparing to attack Saguntum.

When Hannibal received the Roman delegation, his manner was reserved and rigid—unlike that of the more affable and diplomatic Hasdrubal. The Romans began by insisting that Hannibal guarantee the
continued independence of Saguntum and agree to restrict his activities
to the area south of the Jucar River. In turn, he lectured the Romans
about the persecution of people living in and around Saguntum who
were allies of Carthage. Carthage, Hannibal argued, had a long tradition of taking up the causes of the victims of injustice and persecution.
The people of Saguntum, he warned the Romans, should not be lulled
into a false sense of security because of any treaty they had with Rome.
He would hold them accountable for their actions. Hannibal's concern
for the "mistreatment and persecution" of people with pro-Carthaginian
sentiments would become the pretext for his attack on the city.

What Hannibal really wanted was the wealth of Saguntum to help
finance his coming war with Rome and to reward his troops. From a
strategic perspective, the taking of Saguntum would serve as a warning

to other Iberian tribes of what could be expected if they deserted him. Equally important, he could not afford to leave a heavily fortified city, easily reachable by sea, behind him when he left for Italy. The Romans could use the city as a base of operations for a campaign in Spain. Saguntum had to be taken.

The Romans left New Carthage, convinced that Hannibal was intent on attacking the city. They reported to the Roman senate in dispatches that Hannibal was obsessed with a hatred for Rome and that they found him to be in a state of "unreasoning and violent anger."[12] They maintained that his allegations about the persecution of the pro-Carthaginian population at Saguntum were fabrications used to justify his impending attack. From Spain, the Roman delegation sailed directly to Carthage, where they requested an appearance before the senate there. While the Romans addressed the senate at Carthage, Hannibal battered the walls of Saguntum. As the Romans demanded that the Carthaginian senate force Hannibal to honor the treaty they had signed with Hasdrubal, his battering rams and siege machines worked mercilessly night and day to demolish the walls of the doomed city.

Initially, the Carthaginian senators listened patiently to what the Romans had to say and then they began to debate the matter. The pro-Barcid faction supported Hannibal and praised his actions, savoring the taste of revenge from the first war. They took pride in what Hannibal was doing and argued that the Roman protests were not about Saguntum, but that Carthage was regaining her place as a leader in the world once more thanks to the Barcas in Spain. Some senators argued that a war now might even allow Carthage to recover her former colonies lost to the Romans and warned the Roman envoys that gone were the days when they could dictate terms. The losses of the first war were behind them, Carthage had recovered, and a new era was dawning. Then some of the Carthaginian senators argued a legal point; the treaty with Hasdrubal had never been ratified by the senate at Carthage and was therefore not binding on them or on Hannibal. It was a treaty that died with Hasdrubal. The Romans countered by demanding that the siege of Saguntum be lifted and Hannibal turned over to them for punishment.[13]

Not everyone in the senate that day approved Hannibal's actions or favored war with Rome. There was a "peace party," led by Hanno, the same Hanno who had led the opposition to Hamilcar Barca at the end of the first war and had objected so strongly to allowing Hannibal to join Hasdrubal in Spain. In deference to Hanno's influence and long years of seniority, the senate became quiet when he rose to speak. Even though it was clear that the majority was in favor of Hannibal's attack on Saguntum, they listened. Hanno began by reminding them that he had warned years before that a day like this would come. He had advised against sending young Hannibal to Spain. Now corrupted by power and driven by his ego, he was attacking Saguntum in violation of the treaty, and it would only be a matter of time before Rome would be battering the walls of Carthage in retaliation. He pointed out that the Roman envoys had come to them, willing to resolve the dispute before it escalated, and the senate, those entrusted with the responsibility to guide Carthage, would not recognize the precarious position Hannibal had placed them in. Hanno reminded the senate of the suffering Carthage endured during the First Punic War and the mercenary war that followed. Saguntum's walls, Hanno railed, will fall on our heads!

Hanno had hated Hamilcar, and now he feared his son "who brandishes the torch of war" and is possessed by the ghost of his father.[14] He urged that Hannibal, if not surrendered to the Romans, should be banished to a place where neither his name nor his reputation could ever disturb the peace of the Mediterranean again. At a minimum, Hanno urged the senate to order Hannibal to withdraw his army from Saguntum, make restitution for the damage and loss of life there, and send ambassadors at once to Rome to mitigate the damage to the relations between them. When Hanno concluded, the senate still remained nearly unanimous in its support of Hannibal. The consensus was that Saguntum had started the war, and its people had no one to blame for their misfortune other than themselves. Senators stood to warn the Romans they would be making a serious mistake to support Saguntum and thus abandon their longstanding treaty of friendship and peace with Carthage. A resolution was passed supporting Hannibal, and the Roman delegation left for Rome.

It took eight months for Saguntum to fall. The city's defenders used every means to drive Hannibal's soldiers from their walls. They poured burning oil and a combination of pitch and tow on the Carthaginians below, setting fire to both men and siege machines. Still, Hannibal's army kept up a relentless assault. At one point in the siege, in an effort to motivate his soldiers, Hannibal led a rash and frenzied attack against a heavily defended portion of the wall. As a result he was badly wounded in the leg by a javelin and collapsed. The javelin could well have been the falarica, a long round shaft with a three-foot iron head. The middle of the shaft was often wrapped in tow and smeared with pitch (sulphur), then set on fire and, in a larger version, fired from a device that resembled a large crossbow.

The sight of Hannibal falling in battle sent a shock wave through his army. As word spread, his soldiers "fell into confusion and dismay," which caused the attack to falter. Hannibal had to be carried from the battlefield for treatment and the fighting stopped. For the next several weeks, Saguntum was under more of a blockade than a siege as the army waited for Hannibal to recover. The direction of the effort fell to one of his subcommanders, Maharbal, an officer who would later play a decisive role at the battle of Cannae in Italy and become a critic of Hannibal.

In leading the assault at Saguntum, Hannibal was playing the classic role of the Homeric hero. The term comes from references to the Mycenaean world of the eleventh century B.C. and the war between the

Greeks and the Trojans. It was a time of mythical warrior-kings and acts of legendary bravery by men like Achilles, Odysseus, Ajax, Agamemnon, and Menelaus. These were kings who ruled because of their courage. In war, they engaged in individual combat with their enemies and led by example, inspiring those who followed them. The warrior-kings put courage in battle and honor above all else, showing no fear of death in their belief that immortality for them was to be found in the collective memory of their people. Battles could be won or lost on the actions of these men, who sought glory above all else and embodied characteristics of leadership that Greeks from the classical age to Alexander the Great would come to venerate.

While a warrior-king might make an impressive action hero, he does not make an effective general. Hannibal would evolve from one to the other as his career developed. Rather than commanding and directing his forces, the warrior-king is involved in the heaviest areas of fighting. Hannibal at Saguntum led an impulsive attack against a heavily fortified position, and it nearly cost him his life. Instead of directing operations from the relative safety of a command post, he put himself and the entire operation at jeopardy by leading his soldiers in combat. Had Hannibal been killed during the assault, and he came perilously close, the siege of Saguntum could have changed the course of the war and history.

Once he recovered, Hannibal left Saguntum, leading a small force to suppress a revolt of Spanish tribes in Castilla la Nueva, the area of central Spain that today constitutes La Mancha and Madrid. These tribes had refused to provide soldiers when ordered and had attacked Hannibal's envoys sent to collect them. Hannibal intended to set an example. He quelled the revolt, and according to Silius Italicus, returned to Saguntum carrying a beautiful shield of bronze made by Galician craftsmen, upon which the entire history of Carthage had been carefully embossed; a shield similar in theme and workmanship to ones carried by earlier epic heroes like Achilles and Alexander.[15]

When Hannibal returned to Saguntum, he found that his engineers, under the supervision of Maharbal, had managed to weaken a section of the city wall. A force of nearly five hundred Africans had dug tunnels under a main section of the wall, and through a combination of their mining operations and constant battering by their rams at ground level, they had caused a section of it to collapse. Now under Hannibal's direction, the Carthaginian assault troops flooded into the breach as the defenders within fought to stem the tide. During a lull in the fighting, two envoys were sent to Hannibal to ask for terms. The survivors of Saguntum were in a terrible state after eight months of siege, and many had been reduced to eating their dead.[16] The envoys begged Hannibal to show compassion for their women and children, and he countered with the harshest of terms, leading to comments among ancient historians that in time of war he was capable of "inhuman cruelty." Hannibal demanded that all the gold and silver in the city be turned over to him and in return he would allow the survivors to leave, unarmed, and carrying no more than one article of clothing each. From Saguntum, he would direct them to a place of exile. There was no negotiation. After hearing the terms, one of the envoys was so terrified that he surrendered to Hannibal immediately, while the second carried back the news to the city.

It had become evident over the months that Saguntum would receive no military aid from Rome, and with the breach of the main wall, there was no chance of holding out any longer. When the envoy announced Hannibal's demands, the people were defiant. They constructed an enormous furnace in the central market place and began collecting all their gold and silver. Once the furnace had reached a high enough temperature, the precious metals were thrown in, and as they melted, base metals were added to render them worthless when they eventually fell into Hannibal's hands. Panic at the impending fall of the city began to spread quickly, and when another section of the main wall suddenly collapsed from the incessant battering, leaving a second gaping entry, many threw their children and then themselves into the furnace.

Saguntum fell, and Hannibal's soldiers unleashed their fury on its survivors in an orgy of looting, rape, and murder. Hannibal ordered his soldiers to put every adult male in the city to death, and the surviving women and children were distributed among the victors as the spoils of war. A vast array of valuables such as apparel, fabrics, furniture, and art works were collected, crated, and shipped to Carthage. In spite of their attempts to debase the gold and silver, a significant amount remained pure and was recovered. Hannibal put a portion in reserve to cover the expenses of his forthcoming war with Rome and sent the remainder to Carthage. When the captured wealth of Saguntum arrived at Carthage, it silenced Hannibal's critics and emboldened his supporters. By appealing to a most basic instinct, greed, Hannibal had brought the people and government of Carthage solidly behind him. He had correctly calculated that Rome would not risk war in Spain by coming to Saguntum's aid, and now, with the full support of Carthage, Hannibal was ready to take his war to Italy.

With the fall of the city, Hannibal now effectively controlled all of Spain and had secured the base he needed to launch the war against Rome that his father had planned for so long. That war was now inevitable, and the horrors at Saguntum were only a mild preview of the suffering that would be repeated in cities and towns all over Italy in the coming years.

When news of Saguntum's fall reached Rome, the senate voted to send another delegation to Carthage in an attempt to avert war. As the most senior Roman ambassador addressed the senate of Carthage, he gathered around him the folds of his toga, holding them tightly about his chest, his hands concealed. He asked for peace between Carthage and Rome, but demanded the surrender of Hannibal and his principal officers to be tried for their violation of the treaty. "I hold in my one hand peace and in the other war," he told the senate. "I will let fall whichever one you choose."[17] Derisive shouts and challenges from the senators emanated from all sections and filled the chamber. "Let fall whichever one you choose" was the refrain, and with that, the ambassador relaxed his grip and said "It is war which has fallen." The senate responded with a resounding cheer, and thus in such a casual, festive manner, began the greatest and most destructive war the ancient world had ever seen.

When word reached Hannibal that Carthage and Rome were at war, he moved immediately to secure the sea routes between Spain and North Africa. A second fleet was dispatched to patrol the waters between Sicily and North Africa. Among the older generations at Carthage, those who remembered the first war years before, there was fear of a Roman invasion of North Africa and an attack on the city. Hannibal moved to ease those fears by sending a large force of Spanish tribesmen to protect the city and the surrounding countryside, while cross-posting his African contingents to reinforce the Carthaginian armies in Spain. Cross-posting or sending soldiers to garrison provinces far from their homes minimized the chances of revolt or desertion among them. The Romans would later adopt the same policy and use it successfully in the garrisoning of their empire from Britain to Palestine. The African troops in Spain were placed under the command of Hannibal's younger brother, Hasdrubal, who would govern in his absence and guard against any possible Roman invasion there.[18] Secure in his preparations and having addressed his contingencies, Hannibal prepared to invade Italy. What lay before him now was a thousand-mile trek north; along the Spanish Mediterranean coast, over the Pyrenees, through southern France, and then over the Alps into Italy.

CHAPTER II

On the March

THE PLAN TO carry the war to Italy by way of the Alps was radical. Conventional thinking at both Carthage and Rome was that a war between the two city-states would be fought initially in Spain and then the decisive campaign would take place in North Africa. For Hannibal, a direct invasion of Italy by sea was fraught with too many risks. The distances were substantial and the seas could be unforgiving for ships largely propelled by oarsmen. The Romans had built a formidable fleet since the end of the First Punic War, and now they actively patrolled the waters around Italy and Sicily. Carthage was no longer the naval power it had once been, and if the Romans were to intercept the slow-moving and heavily laden transport ships or if a storm should catch them at sea, the entire fleet could be destroyed and the war lost before the first battle on land was ever fought.

Exactly whose plan it was to invade Italy by way of the Alps—Hamilcar's, Hasdrubal's, or Hannibal's—is not clear. The sources never tell us outright although it may well have been Hamilcar's idea, carried out by Hannibal, just as over a century before Alexander had carried out his father Philip's plan to unite the Greeks and invade Persia. Whoever in the Barca clan came up with the idea, it rested on the belief that the next war with Rome could not be fought the way the last one in Sicily was. This war would have to utilize an innovative, unexpected move, with Carthage taking the initiative instead of Rome.

The plan was predicated on the fact that Italy at the time was not unified under Rome; something that would happen after the last of the three Punic Wars. Italy was a land of semi-autonomous city-states and tribes; Gauls in the north, Italians in the center, and Greeks in the south, all held together in a loose confederation under an evolving and tenuous Roman hegemony. The Gauls in the north were semi-barbaric and had troubled the Romans ever since they attacked the city in 390 B.C. They were an independent people who valued their freedom and viewed any Roman moves into northern Italy as a threat. For the most part, the Romans preferred to leave them alone whenever possible. The Italians, who populated the middle and some of the southern parts of the peninsula, were mostly small farmers, and their communities were tied to Rome by treaties that required them to pay taxes and send their sons to serve in Rome's legions. They were indigenous tribes like the Sabines, the Volsci, and the Samnites, who had been subjugated by the Romans in a series of relatively short but fierce conflicts during the fourth and third centuries B.C.

In the south of Italy and on the island of Sicily, the Greeks had established a strong and prosperous presence as early as the eighth century B.C. Many of their colonies came to rival their mother cities on the Greek mainland, both in their levels of cultural development and in their wealth. The Greeks had come under limited degrees of Roman control as a result of a war waged earlier in the third century B.C. By the time the Second Punic War erupted, the Romans had considerable control over central and southern Italy, and parts of Sicily, Sardinia, and Corsica. Northern Italy, from Cremona north and west, had been left largely to the Gauls.

Hannibal believed the Italian confederation was inherently weak and would dissolve in the face of a strong challenge to Roman authority. He was confident that the Italians and Greeks resented the Romans, to whom they paid, in varying amounts, taxes and tributes of men and material, to such a degree that many would leave the confederation and join him in what he would promote as a war of liberation. As a result, Rome would lose her hold over Italy and her legions would be tied to the mainland, suppressing insurrections from one end of the peninsula to the other. Hannibal's objective does not seem to have been to destroy Rome, but, instead, to break her hold on Italy, diminish her growing power in the Mediterranean, and keep her restricted to the Italian mainland as much as possible. Keeping the Romans out of Spain and North Africa would protect the commercial interests of Carthage.

An overland route from Spain to Italy would enable Hannibal to avoid the logistical problems which he believed had contributed to his father's loss of the war in Sicily. Hamilcar had been isolated on the island and dependent on ships from Carthage to bring him supplies and reinforcements. When the Carthaginian navy failed him time and again because of a combination of natural disasters, strategic mistakes, and the Roman fleet, Hamilcar had no choice but to end the war. Hannibal intended to remain as self-sufficient as possible—maintaining a limited supply and communication line back to Spain and living largely off the land, both on the way to and once in Italy. His strategy was to seize the initiative, putting Rome immediately on the defensive and keeping her there. In the First Punic War, Rome had taken the initiative by invading Sicily, and Carthage had simply reacted. This war, Hannibal pledged, would be different as he would take the fighting to the Romans; by invading from the one place where they would least expect an enemy to come—over the French Alps. From northern Italy, he intended moving south, living off the land and forcing the Romans to fight his type of war, on his terms.

Hannibal planned to offset the Roman reserves of manpower by supplementing his army with Gauls. Then, by winning a few initial battles in a decisive and dramatic fashion, he believed members of the Roman confederation, especially the Greek cities, would join him and the balance of power in Italy would be quickly recalibrated. As the Italian tribes and Greek city-states defected from the confederation, Roman reserves of manpower would be depleted and the playing field leveled. With the confederation fractured, Hannibal expected, the Roman legions would be overextended and tied down from one end of the Italian peninsula to the other as they tried to suppress multiple rebellions. The Romans would be so busy trying to keep their own house in order that they would have no time to interfere with Carthage in North Africa and Spain.

Hannibal's plan to break apart the confederation depended on convincing the Gauls, Italians, and Greeks that this was a war not only in their economic interests, but to free them from Roman cultural domination. The war would be transformed into a crusade for the liberation of Italy from Roman oppression while masking the real reason—the protection and preservation of Carthaginian economic interests and the revenge of the Barcas.

The Romans apparently never imagined that Hannibal would invade Italy from the north. They calculated correctly that he would never risk coming by sea, given the distance and their naval superiority. An attack on Italy by land, they reasoned, would be equally unlikely given a journey of over a thousand miles through hostile territory and the logistical problems of crossing two high mountain ranges, the Pyrenees and the Alps. While the Pyrenees could be crossed relatively easily by an eastern pass near the Mediterranean Sea called the Col du Perthus, the Alps were another matter altogether. An invasion from those formidable heights was unthinkable. Not only are they the highest mountain range in Europe, but at the time they were populated by the warlike Gauls. The Romans knew little about the Alps at the time and tended to regard them as an impassible natural barrier that protected them. It would only be in the first century A.D., nearly two hundred years following the end of the war with Hannibal, that the Romans would bring the Alps under their control by pacifying the tribes who lived there, building roads over the passes, and establishing colonies at the base of the range.

From the Roman perspective, the next war would be fought in Sicily, Spain, and North Africa. They expected that any Carthaginian invasion, if it came, would probably be launched against Sicily to recover the lost possession, and they prepared accordingly. The prevailing thinking was that Hannibal would probably fight a defensive war, waiting for the legions to invade Spain, which the Romans saw as the next acquisition in their expanding empire. Roman transports could ferry their troops from Italy to the Iberian Peninsula, rarely out of sight of land and with a multitude of safe harbors along the coast they could put into in the event of inclement weather. The second war would be a simple replay of the first; the establishment of naval superiority followed by victories on the ground. What the Romans did not anticipate was that Hannibal, against all odds and with amazing speed, would succeed in accomplishing what they thought impossible and bring the war to their doorstep.

In the early spring of 218 B.C., Hannibal assembled his army for the invasion of Italy. Saguntum had fallen in the autumn of the year before, and his soldiers, content and with money in their pockets, had emerged from winter quarters ready for action. Hannibal assembled his officers and justified the coming war by recounting how the Romans had demanded his surrender, along with many of them, to be punished for the taking of Saguntum. He told them how the Carthaginian senate had rejected that demand, and Rome in response had declared war. Then Hannibal revealed his plan to cross the Alps and carry the war

to Italy, describing the wealth of the lands through which they would
be passing and the spoils to be had. While the route from Spain to
Italy would be difficult, Hannibal assured them, it was passable, and the
Gauls, fierce tribes who hated the Romans, waited on the other side of
the Alps to join them in the war. Then in the traditional peroration of
a commander, he praised their fighting spirit and their level of preparation. The departure date was fixed for the very early onset of summer.

Hannibal's strategy for the first phase of his campaign involved two
levels of preparation; intelligence and logistics. The intelligence centered
around establishing contact with the Gauls who inhabited the Po Valley
to determine if their leaders could be induced to join him, while the
logistics of the operation focused on the route the army would follow
and the provisions necessary. Hannibal had earlier dispatched envoys
to cross the Alps with authority to promise Carthaginian friendship
and aid to the Gauls, ply their chiefs with gifts, and exploit to the maximum their hatred of Rome. They also had the task of surveying the
route through France to the Alps, assessing the terrain and measuring
the level of cooperation or resistance they could expect from the tribes
along the way.

The envoys returned to New Carthage and reported that most of the
Gauls they encountered along the route west of the Alps were inclined
to let him pass safely through their territory—with the payment of
bribes. The more primitive tribes who lived in the most remote reaches
of the mountains might prove hostile—not because they had any fond-
ness for the Romans or dislike of Carthage, but because they were naturally warlike and would probably seek to loot the baggage train. They
reported that the Gauls on the Italian side of the Alps, those Hannibal
counted on the most, eagerly awaited his arrival, and that the passage
over the mountains, though arduous and in places difficult, was not impossible. There were multiple passes by which to cross, so long as they
got over them before they were sealed by snow for the winter. Delays

along the route, for any reason, could prove fatal if the army became stranded in the Alps as cold weather set in.

Hannibal was confident that as his army moved toward Rome he could build a momentum that would draw in the Gauls the way pilgrims are drawn to a crusade, swept up in the passion of the cause. The success of the plan depended on crossing the Alps quickly, organizing the Gauls in Italy, and attacking the Romans before they had a chance to recover from their surprise.

A sizable component of Hannibal's army was the mercenary corps—professional soldiers who had been recruited from diverse parts of the ancient world. Many had been with Hamilcar and Hasdrubal when they campaigned in Spain, and with Hannibal when he took Saguntum. There was a composite force of Africans: Libyans who made up the infantry and Numidians, the skilled Berber horsemen, who comprised the cavalry contingents. In addition to the Africans was a small contingent of Greek hoplites, heavily armed infantry, arguably the best trained and most disciplined soldiers in the ancient world. From the Balearic Islands, off the coast of Spain, Hannibal recruited men who fought with a simple weapon made famous in biblical times by David in his renowned encounter with Goliath. This sling,[1] as it was known, propelled a small ball with deadly accuracy, and these soldiers, known as "slingers," demanded their pay not in gold or silver but in captive women. The largest contingent in Hannibal's army were the Spaniards, the Iberian and Celtiberian tribesmen who also served as infantry and cavalry. They would be supplemented later by the Gauls and become the disposable element, the sacrificial anodes in Hannibal's fighting force. Their principal function on the battlefield was to make up the center of the line and absorb the initial Roman attack. They had the task of inflicting as many casualties as possible and wearing out the enemy until, at the crucial point in the battle, Hannibal sent in his more experienced mercenary corps, backed by the cavalry on the flanks, to turn the tide in his favor.

The men who made up Hannibal's army came from different cultures and spoke different languages. They fought for pay as well as what they could accumulate in the way of plunder from towns and cities looted along the route and stripped from the dead and dying on the battle-fields. Murder and rape must have been their stock-in-trade and the prospect of unlimited spoils the tie that bound them together. Hanni-bal's greatest achievement as a leader was his ability to mold them into a disciplined and loyal fighting force. In that regard he is clearly the equal, of Alexander the Great. When his army reached Italy, they were vastly outnumbered by the Romans by as much as twenty to one. Yet the devastation Hannibal's army would inflict on Italy, both physical and psychological, proved to be far greater than could have been imagined from their small numbers.

Along with his soldiers, Hannibal left Spain with thirty-seven el-ephants and their handlers.[2] His use of elephants as instruments of warfare was nothing new in the ancient world. Alexander the Great was given an elephant as a gift when he first entered India in 327 B.C., and he fought against elephants in his famous battle against King Porus on the River Hydaspes the following year. After Alexander returned to Baby-lon from India, the use of elephants in war caught on in the west, and his successors, the Ptolemais, Seleucids, and Antigonids, all obtained them. While elephants were only partially effective as tools of warfare, they became status symbols among monarchs in the ancient world. The Romans first encountered elephants in battle when they clashed with the Greek king Pyrrhus in the struggle for mastery of southern Italy. Pyrrhus used twenty elephants against the Romans in 280 B.C. and while he won the battle, his losses were so great he returned to Greece. The Romans encountered elephants again fighting the Carthaginians in Sicily during the First Punic War (264–247 B.C.), but judging from descriptions of their panicked reaction when they encountered Han-nibal's phalanx of elephants in northern Italy during the Second Punic

War, they had not acquired any of their own or developed any effective tactics to deal with them when utilized by an enemy. It would be nearly a hundred years after the war with Hannibal before the Romans would use elephants in their army and then on a very limited basis.

There were two species of elephants used for warfare in the ancient world: Indian and African. The consensus among contemporary historians seems to be that most of the elephants Hannibal had on his march were the African variety, of which there were two subspecies: the larger and more aggressive sub-Saharan bush elephant and a smaller, more docile but now extinct elephant from the Atlas Mountains of North Africa. That consensus derives largely from examinations of coins minted by the Carthaginians in Spain around the period of the Second Punic War, which bear images of elephants. The elephants from the Atlas Mountains, known as the Carthaginian elephant, stood about eight feet measured from the shoulder and paled in comparison to the larger, more aggressive African and Indian varieties, which can measure as much as fourteen feet at the shoulder. The smaller elephants were largely extinct by the end of the Roman Empire, having been extensively captured for use in everything from transport and battle to entertainment and slaughter in the arenas.[3]

The elephants were often plied with wine before battle to stimulate their aggression, and while the wine might have done that to some degree, it also seems to have contributed to their tendency to panic and then rampage during the mayhem of the fighting. Because panicked elephants would often turn and trample their own soldiers, with devastating results, their handlers, who rode atop them, carried a spike and hammer. If an animal became unmanageable, the handler drove the spike into the base of its neck, killing it instantly. Several years after Hannibal crossed the Alps, his younger brother, Hasdrubal, also crossed with elephants and managed to make his way across northern Italy to the Adriatic coast. There, at the Metaurus River, just north of modern-day Ancona, Hasdrubal was confronted by a Roman army, and during the ensuing battle more of his elephants were apparently killed by their handlers in this manner than by the enemy.

Hannibal may have had both the Indian and the African varieties with him, since there are references in the sources to elephant handlers known as the *indoi*. It is logical to conclude that the *indoi* came from India along with the elephants, since the Indians were considered the experts in the training of elephants. These Indian handlers could have been hired initially by the Hellenistic kings and then made their way west into the service of the Carthaginians. As a caution, however, the word *indoi* could also be interpreted in a broader context as nothing more than a generic term for elephant handlers. Manuscript references indicate the presence of at least one Indian elephant when Hannibal crossed the Alps. The sources refer to this elephant which Hannibal rode as Syrus—a beast significantly larger than the others. Syrus is interpreted by modern scholars to mean Syrian because the Seleucid kings who succeeded Alexander the Great and ruled Syria were known to have imported elephants from India and even bred them. Hannibal could well have obtained Indian elephants and handlers through the Egyptian trade channels with Syria.

The most pronounced difference between the African and Indian elephants, as seen on coins minted in Spain from the time of the Second Punic War, is in their backs. The back of the African variety dips between its shoulders and the hindquarters, leaving two pronounced humps front and back, while the Indian elephant, again as depicted on coins from roughly the same time period and from other areas of the ancient world, shows an unbroken convex dome over its back. A second difference is found in the hindquarters of both varieties. The hindquarters of the African species are nearly flat, whereas those of the Indian project backwards at a relatively sharp angle. A third characteristic concerns their heads. The African elephant carries its head high, as shown on these coins, while its forehead is flat with large fan-shaped ears. The head of the Indian elephant is carried in a lower position while its forehead is concave and its ears smaller. Finally, there are differences in the trunks of the two species. The African elephant's trunk is marked by ridges and the tip has two "fingers," while the Indian elephant's trunk is smooth with a single "finger."

Indian elephants are generally regarded as easier to train, which is why they are favored by zoos and circuses today. The African variety are more aggressive, ill-tempered, and difficult to work with. Both species have voracious appetites and consume an estimated 200 to 400 pounds of vegetation per day, which further supports an argument for Hannibal's use of the smaller elephants from the Atlas Mountains on his long march from Spain to Italy. Given the choice solely from a battlefield perspective, Hannibal would probably have preferred the Indian variety, but the consensus among scholars is that with one exception, his contingent of elephants was clearly African.

One of the only known battles in which African and Indian elephants were matched against each other occurred on the other side of the Mediterranean, in 217 B.C., the same year that Hannibal reached Italy. In one of the largest battles in ancient history, the battle of Gaza on the coast west of Jerusalem, the Egyptian army of Ptolemy IV and the Syrian army of Antiochus the Great clashed. Ptolemy had a contingent of African elephants and pitted them against the Indian variety of Antiochus. During the battle, the African elephants gave way, allegedly unable to bear the smell, sound, and sight of the Indian variety, who proved to be stronger and more aggressive.[4]

Hannibal left New Carthage in the very late spring or early summer of 218 B.C. with a force reported by the ancient sources to have been as large as ninety thousand foot soldiers, twelve thousand cavalry, and his elephants[5]—numbers many modern historians regard with considerable skepticism. The consensus seems to have settled on about half that number, though the rationale for arriving at that figure is seldom given. In any case, Hannibal's army must have been a considerable collection of everything that could walk—soldiers, horses, elephants, and pack animals for the baggage—as well as camp followers: merchants, craftsmen, artisans, cooks, slaves, and women. Hannibal provided for nearly every political and military contingency that could develop in his absence. With Spain and Carthage secure, he was free to focus his attention on crossing the Alps and the coming war in Italy.

Hannibal had to follow the Mediterranean coastline north for nearly a thousand miles before he even reached the Alps. Then, he had to make it over those mountains and onto the plains of northern Italy. Allowing for an average marching day of six hours at a pace of two to three miles per hour, the army would have covered between twelve and fifteen miles per day. During the Roman conquest of Gaul, nearly two hundred years later, detailed entries in Caesar's military log indicate his army of nearly fifty thousand moved that distance on an easy day and could cover up to twenty-five miles on a forced march when there was no enemy resistance to hamper them.

Food along the route must have been a primary concern as the specter of starvation, especially once the army was well into the mountains, must have weighed more heavily on Hannibal than thoughts about the enemy. With the average soldier burning an estimated four thousand calories per day, and even more during any fighting along the route, that would translate into a minimum of two to three pounds of food per day per man to function at peak efficiency. Feeding an estimated ninety thousand men, plus camp followers and animals would have required between one hundred and two hundred tons of food daily. One of Hannibal's commanders, also named Hannibal, but surnamed Monomachus and referred to as "the Gladiator," feared starvation in the Alps more than he feared fighting the Romans. He proposed that, because of the length of the march and the barren nature of the terrain through which they would have to pass, the soldiers should be conditioned to eating human flesh. Monomachus suggested that small amounts be cooked into their daily rations, and then increased as the army moved farther into the Alps and food became scarce. In that manner, the army would get over the mountains by feeding upon itself as it moved. Hannibal could not accept the prospect of cannibalism and many of the atrocities that would occur later in Italy were blamed on the allegedly sadistic nature of this Monomachus.[6] The column must have stretched some five to eight miles in length and could easily have been a quarter of a mile wide. Like locusts, Hannibal's army must have cut a swath through the countryside, consuming everything in its path, a marching ecological disaster. Small rivers and streams must have been drained and acres of cropland stripped. In the wake of the column must have been a wasteland, devoid of life and polluted beyond comprehension by vast quantities of human and animal waste, discarded materials of every description, and the bodies of the dying and dead. Those unfortunate enough to be caught in its path would most certainly have lost everything; crops, livestock, and probably their lives. An army the size and composition of the one led by Hannibal must have had little compassion for anyone or anything in front of it.

At the end of the column, following in the dust of the army, came the camp followers; merchants who sold the soldiers goods at the end of the day, cobblers to mend boots, blacksmiths to repair equipment, prostitutes, and slaves. Among them would have been opportunists, that predatory element of humanity that seeks to profit from the misfortunes of others by buying anything of value that had been stripped from the dead or looted from the weak and wounded. And there would be plenty of opportunities in the fall of so many cities and towns along the route and in Italy.

The first phase of the march, along the Spanish Mediterranean coast and over the Pyrenees, took several months to complete. Not only did the army move slowly, but it encountered unexpected resistance from tribes that blocked the way. Still, the army moved forward, towns and villages along the route fell and tribes yielded. By the time Hannibal crossed the Pyrenees, most probably by the Col du Perthus where the mountains come down to the sea, his army had covered about half the distance to Italy. The Col is less than 2,500 feet in altitude and, even in ancient times, it must have been a relatively easy passage over the mountains. Today, the pass is a heavily trafficked truck and car route between Spain and France. Once over the Pyrenees, the excitement and euphoria of the early stages of the campaign gave way to the reality of what lay ahead. It became evident that there could be nearly constant fighting as the column moved north, and many of the soldiers became disgruntled and fearful—especially concerning the dangers and hardships to be encountered in crossing the Alps. The fear and apprehension spread, resulting in the first challenge to Hannibal's leadership as nearly three thousand Spanish soldiers, from a tribe called the Carpetani, demanded to return home.

Hannibal had a situation that had to be contained quickly before it demoralized his entire army. As a leader, he had two choices—he could revert to a traditional response by a commander faced with rebellious troops and execute the leaders as an example to the rest. Alexander the Great used that tactic in quelling a mutiny among his soldiers in the east. Instead, Hannibal chose a less harsh course of action. He assembled the army and acknowledged the fear many of them had about what lay ahead. Then he explained that he needed to send some of them back to Spain to reinforce the garrisons there and leave others behind to guard the pass. Thus, Hannibal could dismiss, without confrontation, the most contentious and least dependable elements in his army.

Seven thousand were sent back to Spain, among them the Carpetani.[7] Hannibal had avoided inflicting any harsh punishment this early in the campaign on soldiers who had already endured weeks of hard marching and fighting. More importantly, he avoided a potentially violent confrontation with discontented elements of his army that could easily have spread and compromised his entire campaign. As a leader, Hannibal had been willing to find an accommodation which allowed him to recognize the discontent and defuse it before it degenerated into insubordination. Hannibal showed he was an astute judge of human behavior by recognizing its complexities and variations, especially among men under stress. As a leader, he understood that sometimes more than force is required to command and that effective leadership is often a judicious combination of power tempered by appropriate levels of compromise and accommodation.

The next phase of the march was through southern France—the territory of tribes that inhabited the area between the Pyrenees and the Rhone River. Hannibal's envoys had made these tribes aware that his army only wished to pass through their territory on its way to Italy and meant them no harm. But these were a naturally warlike people, and they had no doubt heard how the Carthaginians had subjugated their cousins in Spain. Perhaps they feared Hannibal might make slaves of them, and force them to work in the Carthaginian gold and silver mines. The prospect of losing their freedom might have alarmed many of the tribes, and they came together at Ruscino (modern-day Castel-Roussillon near Perpignan) ostensibly to resist Hannibal's advance.

Hannibal was anxious to avoid a battle and get over the Alps without delay. Even though it was now summer, every day engaged in fighting would be time lost and could mean he would arrive in the Alps when the passes were sealed by snow and ice. Hannibal sent a delegation to assure the tribal leaders once more that he had no desire to fight unless they compelled him to. The chiefs came to Hannibal's camp in peace, and he showed them such hospitality and lavished so many gifts on them, that they agreed to let his army pass without resistance.

By the time Hannibal's army reached the Rhone River it had covered nearly seven hundred miles and been on the march for over two months. Another two hundred miles remained before the column would reach the pass leading into Italy, and while the longest part of the march was over, the most difficult and dangerous portion remained. His army had been reduced by nearly half, first by the group of malcontents that had been sent back to Spain, and then through casualties, disease, death, and desertions. The ancient sources tell us that by the time Hannibal reached the Rhone, his army was down to fifty thousand infantry and nine thousand cavalry.[8] While his force was now significantly smaller, it may have been far more cohesive—by virtue of its loyalty to its commander and its resolve to see the campaign through to a victorious conclusion.

Hannibal probably reduced the size of his army largely for logistical reasons. Food and supplies, always a concern, would become increasingly harder to find as they moved further into the Alps. The chances of reaching Italy intact might be greater if they were a smaller and more mobile force.

When the Romans first learned that Hannibal was on the move with an army, they thought he was securing sections of northern Spain to prepare for a Roman invasion from the sea. They apparently had no idea he had already reached the Rhone and that his objective was northern Italy. In their standard fashion, they elected the two consuls to command their forces. The first, Publius Cornelius Scipio, was assigned some twenty-five thousand men and ordered to Spain to stop any farther Carthaginian advance to the north. The second consul, Tiberius Sempronius Longus, was ordered to Sicily with a much larger army to establish a defensive base against a possible Carthaginian invasion there. This was the Roman strategy for the opening phase of the war, and it was well formulated based on the information available at the time. In northern Italy, the Romans had secured the area against the Gauls by establishing fortified settlements at Cremona and Placentia and then moving Roman settlers in. This caused considerable resentment among the Gauls, especially those who lived between these new colonies and the Alps. Two tribes, the Boii and the Insubres, perhaps anticipating the arrival of Hannibal and his army, jumped the gun and attacked the Roman settlements.

The attack drove the Roman colonists and the legions sent to protect them to the more secure city of Mutina (Modena). The Gauls followed the retreating Romans, devastating everything in their path. A legion sent from Rome to help in suppressing the rebellion was ambushed because its commander had underestimated the tactical skills of his Gallic adversaries. While the legion was badly mauled, it managed to extricate itself from the carnage and retreat to a fortified town nearby. The Romans now had a small war with the Gauls going on in northern Italy and a larger war with Carthage looming in the south. As a result, the senate ordered a general conscription throughout Italy and sent many of the new recruits north to reinforce the garrisons there. The revolt of the Boii and the Insubres was an unwelcome development for Hannibal as well. It was premature and demonstrated the impulsive and unpredictable nature of his new allies. In response, the Romans reinforced the area—something Hannibal did not want to see happen. Still, the Romans in northern Italy apparently had no idea he was moving rapidly in their direction, and they thought their only problem was with the Gauls in the Po Valley. They had no inkling of the storm developing on the other side of the Alps and moving their way.

The consul Scipio in command of a fleet of sixty transports sailed from Italy in August of 218 B.C., bound for northern Spain. The fleet followed the northwestern coast of Italy and then sailed across the Ligurian Sea to the Greek city of Massilia. At Massilia, they put into port for rest since the voyage had been unusually rough and many of the soldiers had been sick for days. The second consul, Sempronius, left

Rome for Sicily with a fleet of a hundred and sixty ships and a much larger army.

Hannibal had made good time through southern France. He followed the coast north with the sea on his right, passing by the sites of the modern French towns of Narbonne and Beziers, then past Montpellier and finally into one of the most desolate areas in all of France— the Camargue. The Rhone flows south through the center of France until it reaches the Camargue, about thirty miles from the Mediterranean. There the river divides into several smaller and slower-flowing tributaries, which make their way through a vast expanse of flat marshland before reaching the sea. Much of the area is home to wild horses and bulls and is as wild today as it was over two thousand years ago. On the eastern edge of the Camargue is modern-day Marseilles, the site of ancient Massilia.

After passing along the western and northern peripheries of the Camargue, Hannibal reached the Rhone and began preparations to cross. Where exactly he crossed has been a point of speculation among scholars for centuries. Polybius maintains that the crossing took place four days' march from the sea, where the river is still wide, shallow, and flowing sluggishly.[9] Contemporary scholars interested in the question have identified three locations along the river between Arles to the south and Orange to the north.[10] Fourques is the first and just a mile or two north of Arles. The second is Beaucaire/Tarascon, some 10 miles farther upriver, and the third is Roquemaure, just south of Orange, near Chateauneuf-du-Pape. The author recently (2015) surveyed all three sites and believes Beaucaire/Tarascon is the most likely.

Four days' march from the sea would be some thirty to fifty miles inland, assuming an army is moving under the best of conditions. The area along the Rhone is relatively flat in that region and would make for easy marching. Archaeological finds at Beaucaire/Tarascon indicate it was a bridgehead as early as the Bronze and Iron Ages. Extensive findings of seventh-century B.C. Greek, Etruscan, and Carthaginian vases and amphorae used to transport wine confirm the early use of the area as a major passage point for goods moving up and down the river as well as along the east-west land route between Italy and Spain. This road, known as the route of Hercules, would later become the Via Domitia, the oldest Roman road in Gallia Narbonensis, today's Languedoc and Provence.

Nearly a hundred mile markers have been found along sections of this road, which stretches from Beaucaire, Nimes, and Beziers to the Col du Perthus in Spain. While admittedly the markers are all Roman and most date from the first century B.C., some hundred years after Hannibal passed through, indications are that the route had been in constant use for centuries before. East from Beaucaire/Tarascon, the road passes through modern-day Apt (the Roman town of Apta Julia) then along the Durance River to Gap (Vapincum), through Briancon (Brigantium) and then over the Alps by the Col du Mt. Genevre into Italy and the land of the Celtic Taurini. This road is one of two possible routes Hannibal might have intended to use to cross the Alps.

Another method of locating the probable crossing point is by comparing the distances Hannibal is reported to have covered from Spain to known geographical reference points in France. Polybius tells us that Hannibal travelled a distance of sixteen hundred Greek *stadia*[11] or approximately two hundred miles from Ampurias (Empuries) on the Spanish side of the Pyrenees to his crossing point on the Rhone. The actual odometer distance from Empuries to Beaucaire, measured by the author, is 190 miles.

At the point Hannibal selected to cross the river, he found the opposite shore under the control of a particularly aggressive tribe known as the Volcae. They had rebuffed his initial offering of gifts in exchange for a safe crossing because they were probably a naturally warlike people, excited by the prospect of a fight and the spoils in his baggage train. Conversely, they might have been fearful he would pillage their villages and fields, then carry off their women and livestock. The Volcae were isolated in their world and neither knew nor cared about the epic struggle then beginning between Carthage and Rome for mastery of the ancient world. They would have had no comprehension of the changes beginning to take place in the Mediterranean that would radically transform their world over the next century as Rome came to dominate Gaul.

Another tribe in the area, the Arecomici, was more accommodating. Accepting Hannibal's offer of peace, they made considerable sums of money selling him supplies as well as anything that would float to use in his crossing. Hannibal, reluctant to cross the river in a direct frontal assault against the Volcae, sent a sizable detachment of his Spanish and African cavalry out of the camp under cover of darkness. They moved north for several miles along the western side of the riverbank, and then crossed the river just before dawn. All that day they remained hidden from view in the woods, and the next night moved quietly south along the eastern bank of the river until they were in position behind the Volcae. At daybreak, they sent a smoke signal to Hannibal to begin his crossing.

As Hannibal's army entered the Rhone, the Volcae came surging to the riverbank, howling and shouting as was their custom when they prepared to engage in battle. They shook their shields above their heads and brandished their spears. The noise from the Volcae was mixed with the shouts from Hannibal's soldiers struggling through the river and urging each other on. Just as the Volcae prepared to engage the first wave of Hannibal's army, the cavalry who had been in hiding charged their camp and began to burn it. When the Volcae turned to see their camp in flames, they were paralyzed by indecision—should they continue to resist the landing or leave their positions to save their families and possessions? The psychological impact of the surprise, and the resulting confusion while they tried to decide what to do, caused them to lose their advantage in holding the riverbank. Hannibal's advanced landing force secured a foothold, and in short order thousands of his troops were reaching the east bank ready for battle. Caught between Hannibal's army and his cavalry, the Volcae abandoned the fight, many running in panic to seek refuge in the forests while others surrendered. With the battle over, the remainder of the day was spent in ferrying the remaining soldiers, animals, and supplies across the river. By nightfall the Carthaginian camp was firmly established on the eastern bank of the Rhone, and the Volcae were gone.

There was nothing brilliant in Hannibal's tactic at the Rhone crossing. It was essentially a replay of what Alexander the Great had used successfully against the Persian army of King Darius at the Granicus River (334 B.C.) in Turkey and then again several years later against the Indian army of King Porus at the Hydaspes River (326 B.C.). In both battles, Alexander was facing a significantly larger army, entrenched on the opposite riverbank. Alexander launched a direct assault through the rivers in both cases, but only after he had dispatched a sizable cavalry contingent to cross the river several miles upstream and circle down behind the enemy. Hannibal's adversaries, the Volcae, were a far less formidable force than either the Persians or the Indians who faced Alexander. This is not to minimize Hannibal's actions as a commander at the Rhone, but to point out that the tactic he used was not unknown in the ancient world. Hannibal may well have studied Alexander's campaigns.

The following day was taken up by moving the thirty-seven elephants across the river. When they were led to the river's edge, those in the lead refused to enter the water. Even as their mahouts prodded them, some of them violently, the beasts still refused. The engineers constructed a series of rafts lashed together to a width of some forty to fifty feet and extended them out into the river to create a pier nearly two hundred feet

long. When this pier was stabilized, additional rafts were placed at its
far end and held in place by ropes and pulleys attached to trees on the
opposite shore. The idea was to lead the elephants in pairs onto the pier,
then onto the rafts. The rafts would be untied and pulled to the opposite
shore using the ropes, which served as towing and guide lines.

The elephants would have none of it. They would move only to the
water's edge and no farther. The engineers spread dirt and grass on the
pier to make it look like a continuation of the path to the water's edge,
but still the elephants refused to move onto it. In exasperation, one of
the mahouts taunted a bull to such a degree that the enraged animal
turned on him. The mahout leaped into the river to escape and the
bull plunged in after him, followed by several other elephants that had
been goaded to their limits by their handlers. Once the elephants found
themselves in deep water, they eventually calmed and let the current
carry them to the opposite bank.

Most the elephants, however, remained on the riverbank, refusing to
move. Finally, a particularly docile pair of females was brought to the
front of the line and their handlers gently enticed them onto the rafts.
Once the females were on the rafts, the males dutifully followed. However, when the rafts were cut loose from their moorings and began to
drift into the middle of the river, the elephants panicked, capsizing some
of the rafts. Several the mahouts were crushed or drowned, but some
of the elephants seemed to have found firm footing on the river bottom,
and, according to one of the sources, walked across to the opposite bank,
using their trunks as snorkels.[12]

As Hannibal was fighting his way over the Rhone, Scipio landed
at Massilia. As a precautionary measure, the Roman commander dispatched three hundred of his best cavalry to scout the area to the north.
Hannibal sent his own detachment of five hundred Numidian horsemen south, also as a precaution. Within a few miles, the two cavalry
contingents encountered each other and engaged. The fighting was

particularly fierce until Hannibal's cavalry broke off the encounter and returned to report the presence of the Romans. When word spread through the camp that the Romans were nearby, Hannibal's soldiers instinctively began to mobilize for battle.

Hannibal, however, had other ideas. He refused to react to developments in the field, keeping his primary objective, at the forefront of his thinking. Italy was his objective and he wanted to reach it with as much of his force intact as quickly as he could. Engaging the Romans at this point, even defeating them, would gain him nothing but a short-term boost to the morale of his army—a moment of euphoria. There was no strategic value to a fight at this point in the campaign. A loss to the Romans could mean the end of his campaign, while even a victory would result in losses of manpower and material, which would hamper if not cripple him later in Italy. He decided, to the disappointment of his soldiers, to avoid a battle with the Romans and focus on getting over the Alps.

At that moment, a delegation from the Boii, a tribe who had been fighting the Romans in the Po Valley, arrived, led by their chieftain, Magalus. They had just crossed the Alps and their arrival distracted the soldiers from their disappointment over not engaging the Romans. The Boii had come to inform Hannibal that the war against Rome in Northern Italy had begun and that they were there to guide his army over the mountains. Their arrival reinforced Hannibal's decision to avoid confronting Scipio's army and to proceed directly over the Alps. What the Roman presence at Massilia did achieve was to cause Hannibal to alter the route he intended to use to reach Italy.

The most direct route from the southern reaches of the Rhone River to Italy is due east, slightly inland from the Mediterranean coast, across a flat plain, and then into a low range of mountains known as the Alpes Maritimes. Most of the route is through relatively wide valleys, making for an easy passage through what is today Provence. The Romans would eventually build their main road from Italy to Spain along this same route, and two thousand years later, Spanish, French, and Italian engineers would construct their superhighways, the AutoRoute and AutoStrada, there.

Even this route was not without risk. The greatest danger was at the outset, because it would take Hannibal and his army perilously close to Massilia and the probability of a confrontation with the Roman army. The terrain in the wide valley just north of Massilia is flat and suitable for the type of large-scale set battle that Hannibal would have wanted, at this point in his campaign, to avoid at all costs. Even if he would bypass the Romans at Massilia, the danger resurfaced when his army reached another Greek city along the route, Nicaea, or modern-day Nice. Nicaea had been founded by the Greeks and could easily be reached from Massilia by ship, allowing the Romans to be in place and waiting for Hannibal when he arrived. Even if he could avoid the Romans at Nicaea, more danger lay in the mountains behind the city. Although those mountains are the lowest in the Alps and the easiest to cross, the tribes who inhabited them, known as the Ligurians, were so ferocious that the Romans were unable to pacify them until the reign of the emperor Augustus, nearly two hundred years later. To celebrate the subjugation of these tribes, Augustus had a massive temple erected on a mountain pass above modern-day Monaco, known as La Turbie. The temple has been restored and offers stunning views of Monaco below, as well as the sea and the Alps to the north.

However, Hannibal decided to avoid this route and move his army rapidly north along the east bank of the Rhone River in an effort to lose any Roman force that might try to follow. Once free of the Romans, he intended to turn due east and cross the Alps by several available passes. When Scipio learned that Hannibal had crossed the Rhone, he must have been incredulous at his speed and realized that he had seriously underestimated his adversary. It was now apparent that Hannibal's objective was Italy, and Scipio realized that he had to be stopped or at least delayed. By the time Scipio and his army reached the site of Hannibal's camp at the Rhone, it was too late; Hannibal and his army were gone. The choice Scipio now faced was whether to try to overtake Hannibal or be waiting for him in Italy when he came down from the Alps. Following Hannibal, Scipio decided, would be a mistake, as he already had a significant head start and Scipio's army lacked suitable clothing and equipment to cross the Alps. Scipio followed the more prudent course: he returned to Massilia, sent his army to Spain under the command of his brother Gnaeus, and prepared to return to Italy and raise a new army.

As Hannibal's army moved north along the Rhone, stories began circulating among his soldiers about the dangers in the Alps. With each telling, the stories grew more ominous. There was the prospect of a long march into unknown territory, the fear of ambush by hostile tribes in the narrow mountain defiles, the dangers inherent in climbing the mountains, numbing cold, starvation, and the specter of death from the elements. All these began to have an adverse impact on the morale of men already worn down by months of marching and fighting. Hannibal now faced the possibility of a mutiny. The army was called into general assembly, and, with the Boii at his side, Hannibal addressed his soldiers to dispel their fears and infuse them with a renewed sense of courage and resolve. He opened with a rhetorical harangue: "What sudden fear is this among you, the men who followed me from Spain on our mission to destroy Rome and set the world free? What fear among you, who made your way over the Pyrenees and fought the wild tribes there? What fear among you, who crossed the waters of the mighty Rhone to defeat the warriors who waited for you on the other side? Now when you have the Alps nearly in sight, when you are at the very doors of the enemy you stop and falter? What do you think the Alps are? They are nothing more than high mountains and no heights are insurmountable to men of determination!"

Hannibal's speech is similar in tone and content to one Alexander the Great gave to his army when it mutinied on the shores of the river Beas in India. When rumors about a great desert ahead of them and a crocodile-infested river a mile wide (probably the Ganges) caused them to refuse to go on, Alexander tried to rally them. He told his soldiers he set no limits to what men of ability could accomplish, and they responded by telling him that a great leader knew when to quit—forcing Alexander to turn back for the first time in his career.

Then Hannibal turned and pointed to Magalus and his men. "How do you think they got here—you think they flew over the Alps? They crossed, with their women and children following, and you, brave men with nothing more than your weapons to carry, are afraid!" Magalus addressed the assembly and to build their confidence told the soldiers how his people, already at war with Rome, were waiting to join them on the other side of the Alps. He acknowledged that sections of the route would be difficult, but not impassable. There would be ample supplies of food along the way, as well as guides to lead them. Finally, Hannibal exhorted his soldiers to steel their hearts and march forward. Theirs, he promised, was a noble crusade to bring freedom from oppression to the Italians and the chance to line their pockets.[13]

Hannibal succeeded in motivating his soldiers and infused them with renewed enthusiasm—but in the weeks ahead, his words would ring hollow. The army would lose its way. Hungry and cold, the Carthaginian column would struggle to find a way over the snow- and ice-covered peaks that lay ahead while being constantly shadowed by mountain tribesmen tracking them like wolves in winter following their prey. In the weeks to come Hannibal would lose more men to the mountains than he had in fighting all the battles and crossing all the rivers on his long march from Spain. It was now late summer and he was anxious to push forward with all speed and cross the Alps before winter set in.

CHAPTER III

Over the Icy Peaks

O F ALL HANNIBAL'S accomplishments, nothing quite resonates like his passage over the Alps. It was not just audacious, it was unimaginable. The crossing eclipses even his spectacular victories in later battles against the Romans. Although it is often cited as an example of leadership at its best, it also accounted for more casualties and losses than any of the battles that followed. The feat can be viewed as a stunning success, an example of a leader overcoming nature by the sheer force of his determination, or a colossal failure when measured in terms of the cost in human life. In biographies of Hannibal and in histories of the Punic Wars, authors tend to gloss over this part of the story, preferring to focus instead on his battlefield victories in Italy.

The Alps are a natural barrier between France and Italy—stretching over two hundred miles from majestic Mount Blanc in the north to the Mediterranean Sea in the south. They begin as a relatively low range of mountains (three thousand to four thousand feet) just east of the Rhone River, gradually building in height and steepness until they attain their full measure of majesty (twelve thousand to fourteen thousand feet) on the Italian frontier. At the frontier, there is a dramatic change in their contour as they suddenly end in a precipitous drop from the dizzying heights straight down onto the level plains of Italy below. Seemingly a solid wall of rock, snow, and ice between France and Italy, the Alps have a series of depressions or passes which run east to west between their highest peaks. These passes[1] provide the only way over the peaks and make for a convenient division of the range into sections. The lowest and most southern section is called the Alpes Maritimes, beginning at the Mediterranean Sea behind the city of Nice and ending at the Col de la Bonette, at nine thousand feet, the highest pass in the Alps with a hard surfaced road over it. North of the Alpes Maritimes is the section known as the Cottian Alps—named by the Romans after a Ligurian ally, King Cottius. This section is centered on two passes, the Mount Cenis and the Montgenevre, both well-travelled routes over the mountains between Italy and France. The Alpes Graiae, or Greek Alps, are the next section located between the Mount Cenis pass and Mount Blanc. This is the range that the legendary Hercules allegedly crossed on one of his adventures. The final range is the Alpes Penninae or Pennine Alps, which extend from the Swiss frontier and the upper Rhone valley to the most northern and western portions of Italy.

Scholars are generally of the opinion that Hannibal passed over the Cottian Alps, which begin in the Rhone Valley in an area of relatively low mountains known as the pre-Alps or the Alpes du Dauphine. Once over this first low range, Hannibal would have descended into a series of valleys before starting his second and final climb over the higher mountains, the Hautes Alpes, on the frontier with Italy. The only way over the mountains is to follow valleys. Their riverbeds afford level footing, provide ample sources of drinking water, and eventually lead to streams on the mountainsides. These streams in turn lead to passes, which are the only practical way over the peaks. The sources of the streams begin at the highest elevations, where the snows begin to melt and then cascade down the mountainsides. Streams become rivers and the rivers, over millennia, have formed long transverse valleys as they find their way to the Rhone. But even following rivers can be risky, because it is easy to become confused and lost in a labyrinth of blind valleys along the way. Valleys often contain gorges, narrow passages where there is a risk of being trapped and swept away by the torrents of water, mud, and rocks that periodically surge from the heights, destroying everything in their path—something the author has witnessed firsthand in the valley of the Queyras.

There are four principal rivers that flow from the higher elevations of the Alps and make their way to the Rhone. The farthest north is the Isere, which begins as a stream in the glaciers of the high Alps near the Val d'Isere and enters the Rhone as a sizable river at the city of Valence. This riverbed is the preferred choice among historians who have speculated on the route of Hannibal. Below the Isere is a smaller river, the Drome, which begins in the pre-Alps or the Alpes du Dauphine and flows into the Rhone just south of Valence. Another even smaller river just south of the Drome is the Aygues, which also begins in the pre-Alps and enters the Rhone just north of the city of Orange. Neither the Drome nor the Aygues leads directly to passes in the high Alps. The last and longest of the four is the Durance, which begins as a series of streams on the slopes of the highest mountains on the Italian frontier and flows southwest through a broad valley before it reaches the Rhone just south of Avignon. Ruling out the coastal route to Italy because of the risk of encountering the Roman army at Massilia, Hannibal's best choice among the four options would have been the Durance. The river leads to one of the lowest and easiest passes over the mountains— the Col du Montgenevre. But that route, in its initial stages, had to be avoided as well, because it still brought Hannibal's army perilously close to the Romans.

In searching for a way over the Alps, Hannibal had no choice but to move farther north along the Rhone than he perhaps originally intended. Then, once he had lost the Romans, he could turn east and make his way into the upper reaches of the Durance River, near the modern French towns of Mont Dauphine and Guillestre. From there it is an easy passage into Italy by way of the Montgenevre—a pass that is less than six thousand feet, and today a principal truck and car route between France and Italy.

The ancient sources indicate that after Hannibal left his crossing point on the Rhone he marched north along the eastern bank of the river for four days in an attempt to lose the Roman army he feared might be following. Based on accounts of the expeditions of Alexander the Great in Asia and Julius Caesar in Gaul, events which bracket Hannibal in time, his army could probably cover ten to fifteen miles a day under ideal conditions. Even allowing Hannibal and his army the more conservative figure of ten miles a day, leaving from the vicinity of Arles would have brought them to a point along the Rhone close to what is today the French city of Orange. Historians speculate that land travel, especially in the interior regions of France, might have been fairly easy because roads were relatively well developed.[2] Those roads followed the river valleys through the mountains and then, through a system of sharply graded pathways, some eventually reached the passes.

On the fourth day, Hannibal and his army came to an area along the Rhone simply referred to in the manuscripts as the "island"—a triangular body of land that resembled the Nile Delta because it was low-lying, subject to seasonal flooding, fertile, and densely populated. The main river that bordered the "island" was clearly the Rhone, while the identity of the second remains uncertain. Polybius, writing in Greek, named this second river the Iskaras or Skaras, while Livy, writing in Latin, called it the Arar or Araros. The tribe that occupied the island was the Allobroges, a generic name for tribes that inhabited a wide section of Gaul from the Rhone River to the Alpes du Dauphine and were loosely bound together by language and custom. This tribe had recently lost its king, and his two sons were contending for the throne. The elder, Brancus, claimed the throne by right of primogeniture, while the younger, whose name is never given, was threatening to depose his brother if he declared himself king. The tribe was on the verge of civil war. According to Polybius, Hannibal sided with the older brother and then used his army to drive the younger one and his followers from the area.[3] Livy, on the other hand, maintains that Hannibal played a much more conciliatory role, serving more as a mediator with the assistance of the tribe's elders.[4] Either way, the dispute was settled in favor of Brancus, and to show his gratitude the new king provided clothing, weapons, and supplies for Hannibal's soldiers suitable for the journey ahead of them. Then he furnished an armed escort to guide them as far as the foothills of the Alps.

From the island, Hannibal turned east and began his trek following this second river for ten days and covering about a hundred miles. The march was uneventful and relatively easy until the column reached the foothills known as the Alpes du Dauphine, where the escort provided by Brancus left to return home. The terrain became more difficult in these higher elevations, and the column was now being shadowed from the heights above by local tribes that might have allied themselves with the younger brother of Brancus.

While the Alpes du Dauphine only rise to a height of between four and five thousand feet, they are still a formidable obstacle. The farther the column moved east, the higher the mountains became and the slower their progress. More tribesmen began to appear on the heights above them. When Hannibal's scouts reported that a particularly narrow gorge lay ahead, he became concerned. That night, exaggerated reports of the dangers ahead circulated through the camp, causing apprehension among the soldiers. The scouts further reported that the tribesmen shadowed the column by day but returned to the comfort of their villages at night. That gave Hannibal an idea. He ordered a larger than normal number of campfires to be built just before dusk, so that when darkness fell the tribesmen would think the camp was settled for the night. The tribesmen withdrew to their villages, and Hannibal slipped out of his camp with a force of lightly armed infantry. They scaled the heights over the gorge and positioned themselves above the ledges usually occupied by the tribesmen during the day. Just after daybreak the Allobroges returned, unaware that Hannibal and his men were lying in wait. The army below broke camp and slowly began moving into the gorge. Once in, the walls seemed to close around them and an ambush seemed certain. By late morning, the vanguard had cleared the gorge and begun to climb to an adjacent pass.

Initially the tribesmen only watched as the column slowly threaded its way into the gorge and then began to move up a track leading to a pass. The track eventually became a narrow ledge with a precipitous drop to the river on one side and a sheer wall on the other. In places, the column had to move nearly single file along the ledge. As the Allobroges watched the column struggling along the ledge, they could no longer restrain themselves. They began screaming and hurling their spears. Their cries echoed and re-echoed through the gorge as they purposely wounded horses with their arrows, causing them to rear out of control. The animals, maddened by pain, either lost their footing and fell off the ledge or pushed blindly ahead, shoving men and animals over the side. Casualties began mounting as panic and confusion took a greater toll on Hannibal's soldiers than the spears, arrows, and rocks raining down on them. Watching from above, Hannibal continued to restrain his soldiers, even though they pleaded with him to allow them to relieve the pressure on their comrades. But Hannibal hesitated, fearing an attack at this point would only add to the confusion on the ledges below and increase the casualties. Finally, when the Carthaginian column was close to breaking apart, Hannibal ordered the attack. Within a short time the heights were swept of the enemy, and the column slowly regained its cohesion. The remaining elements were now able to climb out of the gorge and make it over the pass safely. Even the most experienced and battle-hardened among the mercenaries were shaken by what they had been through. Only when the last of the soldiers, horses, and pack animals had been brought through safely were the elephants led along the ledge and over the pass. Hannibal's tactics were similar to what Alexander the Great had done over a hundred years before when the defenders of the Persian capital Persepolis trapped his army in a gorge and began inflicting heavy casualties. Alexander led a small contingent of soldiers up and over a mountain at night, coming down on the enemy just before dawn and winning the day.

Not far from the pass, Hannibal's scouts came upon a town that belonged to the Allobroges. It was largely deserted as most of the inhabitants had fled to the forests and higher elevations. When the scouts entered, they discovered some of their compatriots, who had been captured while foraging days before, and enough grain and cattle to supply the army for three days. The town was burned, and as a result the other tribes in the area allowed Hannibal's army to pass through their territory unhampered.

Where was Hannibal's army ambushed? Based upon this author's research, it is doubtful it was along the Isere River route—a popular choice among scholars. Having traced the route, the author found that it leads to the Alps without any particularly difficult gorges to march through or passes to climb. There is no place along this valley the author could find that corresponds to the conditions Hannibal encountered. The only possibility is the Gorges de la Bourne, which can only be reached by leaving the Isere at the town of St. Nazaire-en-Royans and following a smaller river, the Bourne, due east. The gorge is admittedly an ideal site for an ambush, but why would Hannibal have left the easier and safer Isere route to follow the more difficult Bourne? Just beyond the gorge is a second smaller gorge, the Gorges du Furon, but no second

gorge is mentioned in the ancient sources. Nor could the author find a
mountain pass near the gorge. The Bourne route eventually leads back
to the Isere River at Grenoble.

A few miles south of the Isere is a more likely possibility—the Drome.
This river enters the Rhone just north of the modern town of Le Pou-
zin, in an area that closely resembles, even today, what could have been
the island mentioned in the manuscripts. But the Drome does not lead
to the frontier with Italy. Its riverbed leads east, paralleling the D93
highway, but only as far as the pre-Alps. It does, however, come very
close to the Durance River at one point, and Livy mentions that Hannibal eventually reached a river named the "Druentia"—a Latin name
that is tantalizingly close in spelling and sound to the modern name
Durance.[5] While Hannibal would have avoided the lower reaches of the
Durance where it flows into the Rhone near Arles for fear of encountering the Romans, farther north the river would have been a safer and
easier route to Italy.

Along the Drome River route is the Gorges des Gas, which leads
directly to a nearby pass, the Col de Grimone, accessed today by a roadway, the D539. The gorge and pass are less than sixty miles from where
the Drome flows into the Rhone, a distance Hannibal's column could
have covered in the ten days the manuscripts say it took to reach the
ambush point. Although the manuscripts also tell us there were times
when the column lost its way, sometimes simply "wandering," either because of the treachery of the native guides with them, or when they
would not trust the guides, "their own blindness."[6] Often they had to
guess at the route and then retrace their steps when they entered valleys
that offered no exit.

After following the gorge for a few miles, the roadway narrows considerably, not far from the village of Glandage. Once through this defile,
there is a long climb to the Col de Grimone, a pass at four thousand
feet. From there, it is an easy descent to the small town of La Faurie,

some fifteen miles away. This town might have been the one looted and burned by Hannibal's army. From La Faurie, it is twenty miles to the Durance River at Tallard and from there an easy march of less than sixty miles along the level valley floor to the Italian frontier by way of the Col du Montgenevre.

Once Hannibal and his army entered the Durance River valley at Tallard, the route would have been clearly marked and relatively safe. The valley is wide and passes the modern towns of Embrun and Mont Dauphine. As the column entered the valley, a delegation of elders from the surrounding tribes approached, bearing branches as symbols of peace and promising Hannibal his army could pass through their territory in safety. Although Hannibal cautiously accepted their gestures of peace, he demanded hostages to guarantee their word, provisions to feed his army, and guides to lead them over the final barrier of mountains. The elders agreed; hostages were turned over, guides designated, and large quantities of supplies provided. Despite their assurances of friendship and their willing compliance with his demands, Hannibal remained skeptical. His army had survived a particularly bad time, which made him reluctant to accept overtures of peace and friendship from these mountain tribes at face value. While the elders had been very accommodating and were quick to comply with his demands, Hannibal suspected there was treachery afoot, but at the same time, he was careful to avoid any slight that might provoke them to attack.

As the column moved northeast along the valley and reached what is today the fortress town of Mont Dauphine, they were horrified by the view that unfolded before them. The ancient sources describe "a dreadful sight before their eyes; high peaks covered with snow and all around them everything stiff with cold." They faced the highest and most formidable mountains in the Alps; a barrier so high it seemed to touch the heavens. These mountains were like nothing they had seen so far on their journey, and the sight brought back a hundredfold the fear that had gripped them when they first reached the Rhone.[7] The peaks in this part of the Alps can rise to nearly fourteen thousand feet, and they stand like immovable, unassailable giants—daring anyone to scale their heights. Yet unknown to Hannibal and his army at this point in their journey, they were less than fifty miles from Italy.

Livy tells us that the people who inhabited these high mountains were "ragged and unkempt, more horrible to look upon than words can tell." Another Roman, Pliny the Elder, writes that many of these mountain people suffered from a disfiguring condition that made them grotesque to look upon,[8] and the Roman Diodorus describes them as living "a hard and luckless life" in huts or caves and because of constant climbing, hard work, and little food they were thin but muscular.[9] Only "half-civilized" and barely able to sustain themselves, the Greek geographer Strabo recounts how they supplemented what little they had by attacking and plundering wealthier villages and towns at the lower elevations where people lived relatively comfortable lives. When they raided, they were without pity, killing not only all the males they found, but also any pregnant women whom their priests divined carried male children within them.

It was now late September or early October; Hannibal was anxious to press ahead as conditions in the higher elevations were deteriorating and becoming more dangerous as each day passed. The longer the delay, the more likely the column would be caught in bad weather. At that point, Hannibal made one of the most disastrous tactical decisions of his career, and at the same time the one that put him in the history books. At the urging of the guides offered by the elders, he led his army away from the safety of the wide valley floor of the Durance at Mont Dauphine and into a narrow gorge known as the Comb du Queyras. These guides assured Hannibal this was a quicker passage over the mountains, and the Boii in Hannibal's entourage, probably not familiar with the area since they crossed into Gaul by one of the lower and easier passes at the southern end of the range, could not object. The Comb du Queyras is an ominous place, where Druid priests held ritual human sacrifices—hurling young virgins from its cliffs into the river below.[10] Even in summer, when the sun is high overhead, the gorge is covered in dark shadows. Torrents and streams cascade down its cliffs, and today a narrow roadway, suspended over the swift and turbulent river below, clings precipitously to its walls as it follows the bed of an old Roman road.

Suspicious of his guides and concerned by the gorge, Hannibal tightened the formation. When the soldiers marched through territory where they felt secure, they moved in a more relaxed fashion. But in times of uncertainty, Hannibal moved the cavalry and the elephants to the head of the column and positioned the lighter infantry on the flanks to protect the baggage train and the civilians. Last in the column was the heavy infantry, which served as a rear guard under the direct command of Hannibal. As the column moved toward the gorge, the elders who had offered Hannibal their most sacred assurances of safe conduct were dispatching messengers to the outlying tribes with a call for armed men. The call was answered as men crawled out from their crags, caves, and hovels, all with one mind—to ambush the column and loot the baggage train of its weapons, horses, clothing, and food. On the wide, flat expanses of the valley floor, the elders knew their men were no match for Hannibal's cavalry, his elephants, and his infantry. But an ambush in the gorge was something that gave them the advantage and was more conducive to their style of fighting.

The entrance to the gorge is narrow, so only a few soldiers at a time could get through. This slowed the column, causing it to back up for a considerable distance. Once in the gorge, soldiers found themselves moving along a narrow pathway with a steep wall on one side and a swiftly flowing river on the other. Concealed in the heights, the tribesmen were positioning themselves and waiting their chance to strike.

They waited patiently as the column below moved deeper into the gorge. Behind the column, another force of Gauls shadowed at a distance, while at the far end, where the gorge opened into a small valley, a third force was assembling to massacre any survivors who might escape the ambush. The column moved slowly and apprehensively as the sides of the gorge closed in on them. Soldiers became silent as they glanced nervously at the heights above. At the front of the column, the Boii scanned the cliffs looking for any sign that might indicate an ambush, while the local tribesmen who were guiding the column became increasingly restless as they looked for an opportunity to escape before the carnage began. The hostages, like lambs being led to slaughter, marched dutifully in line, bound to their captors and meekly awaiting whatever fate had in store for them.

At one place, midway through the gorge, the track became so narrow and the walls of the cliffs closed in so tightly that Hannibal's men were only able to walk three or four abreast, "with one foot on land and the other in the river." The walls on either side were so high that even at midday they blocked the rays of the sun. The first attack came as the baggage train was passing through this section and the rear guard under Hannibal's command had just entered the gorge. The Gauls had stockpiled small boulders and rocks at key points along the ledges, to be rolled down on the column. The tribesmen charged the rear of the column and Hannibal ordered the heavy infantry to turn in formation and face them. The attacking Gauls were stopped by a solid wall of extended spears and interlocking shields. While the heavy infantry under Hannibal's command held the Gauls at bay, they could not help those who were already deep in the gorge as rocks and debris rained down on them from the cliffs above. The roar of the falling rocks blended with the terrified shouts and cries of those below who were powerless to shield themselves.

Unable to find shelter from the hail of death, soldiers and civilians alike pressed themselves against the walls of the gorge in desperation—walls which offered little or no protection. The cries of the wounded and dying were smothered by the noise and confusion around them. Officers in the line tried their best to maintain order and encourage the ranks to keep moving ahead as debris and the bodies of the crushed and mutilated, men and animals alike, blocked their path. As bodies and debris piled up, they choked the narrow river passage, yet the waters pushed their way through, indifferent to the slaughter going on as their color changed from the mineral green of pristine mountain streams to the blood-red of the wounded, dying, and dead.

After the boulders and rocks had done their damage, the Gauls let loose with an unrelenting barrage of arrows and spears. Wounded animals reared out of control, thrashing out and causing as much injury to those around them as the weapons of the Gauls. The slaughter in the gorge continued for hours, sometimes lighter in one area and heavier in another. In one place the attack was so concentrated that the tribesmen descended to the floor of the gorge and separated Hannibal and his heavy infantry from his cavalry and elephants at the front. The light infantry and the baggage train suffered the most, while at the front of the column many of the elephants became uncontrollable in the confined spaces as the Gauls from the heights above did everything in their power to torment them. Eventually their handlers regained control and used them to clear the pathway ahead of debris. The defile became a killing ground of unfathomable horror, a murderous gauntlet. Finally, the vanguard broke free onto a wide expanse in the valley ahead. When the tribesmen who were waiting for the survivors to exit saw the elephants emerge, they retreated in fright. Once the bottleneck was broken and cleared, the greater part of the column was able to extricate itself and regroup. By late in the day, only the last elements in the column were still being subjected to attacks, and Hannibal worked his way to the front, where he took command of the vanguard.

The losses resulting from the ambush raise questions about Hannibal's ability as a leader. Why would an experienced commander have allowed himself to be drawn into such an obvious trap? Not once, but twice. Even some of the ancient commentators expressed surprise that a man of Hannibal's experience and rank would have allowed his army to be placed in such a vulnerable position. Livy comments that Hannibal "nearly succumbed to the very tactics in which he excelled"—outthinking and outmaneuvering the enemy.[11] Was Hannibal careless? Was he too anxious to get over the last barrier before the passes were sealed by snow and ice for the winter and thus allowed the Gauls to lure him in with the promise of a quick passage over the mountains? Did Hannibal underestimate the Gauls and their potential to mount such a sustained, fierce, and effective attack along the length of the gorge or did he find himself up against an exceptionally skilled rival commander who managed to get the upper hand? The Gauls were particularly effective in guerilla warfare, and after the Punic Wars ended, the Romans would engage them in a series of long campaigns that lasted until Julius Caesar pacified them in the middle of the first century B.C. Finally, Hannibal, because of his youth—he was not yet thirty at the time—might just have made a mistake, a tactical miscalculation that cost him almost half his army.

When the vanguard of Hannibal's army broke out of the defile, they regrouped around a massive rock on the valley floor. They climbed over every part of it they could, hiding in its fissures and caves and building a crude defensive barrier against what they feared would be another attack. All through the night, soldiers, civilians, and animals, dazed and wounded, slowly made their way to the rock, and it was well into the next day before stragglers finally stopped coming. The location of that rock has figured prominently in efforts by historians and adventurers over the last two centuries to pinpoint the gorge and valley through which Hannibal passed. Only the dead and seriously wounded were left and there was nothing Hannibal could do for them. Unable or unwilling to risk sending a rescue force back into the gorge, he had no choice but to leave them behind. While the dead were beyond pain, it was the wounded who were to be pitied as the Gauls vented their anger on them over Hannibal's escape.

By late in the second day, Hannibal had the column on the move once more and heading due east along the valley floor. There was no going back into the gorge and no way of knowing if there would be a way out of the valley ahead of them. For the moment, the Gauls were occupied in the gorge, stripping the bodies of the dead of any armor, weapons, or valuables they could find. As the column moved forward, smaller attacks against sections of the baggage train continued until a defensive perimeter was established using the elephants and the cavalry to protect the flanks of the main column. Hannibal was now moving blindly as the guides provided by the Gauls had either been killed in the fighting or run off. The hostages who survived the carnage were executed in retaliation. The column was now alone, hurt and demoralized, trapped in a valley from which they worried there might be no escape.

Where did the second ambush happen? The sources are clear it took place in "a steep and precipitous defile through which a river ran," where the Gauls held the heights above,[12] and the column was forced to march along a narrow track hemmed in by walls of rock.[13] We know that Hannibal and his column marched for three days, probably thirty to forty miles, after he sacked the town of the first mountain tribe that had ambushed him. Hannibal could easily have covered that distance to the Comb du Queyras. At Mont Dauphin, the valley of the Durance divides. To the left, it continues past the fortified heights of Mont Dauphin, then Briancon, and by the Col du Montgenevre into Italy. To the right is the entrance to the Combe du Queyras, a treacherous, seven-mile-long gorge. The gorge opens into a small valley, which continues for another fifteen miles before it ends in a cul-de-sac framed by a ten-thousand-foot-high wall of precipitous rocks, snow, and ice dominated by Mount Viso, at fourteen thousand feet, the second highest peak in the French Alps.

A small but turbulent river, the Guil, flows through this valley into the Comb du Queyras, and finally reaches the Durance. It begins as a series of streams from the melting snows on the slopes of Mount Viso, which converge at the base of the mountain and form the river, which flows rapidly through the valley. When the river enters the gorge, it become a torrent until it exits, calms, and reaches the larger and slower-moving Durance at Mount Dauphine. This small river can suddenly turn so violent, that several times in the last century it has devastated the valley, destroying villages, bridges, and hamlets along its banks. The author witnessed its destructive power firsthand in the late spring of 2000 when the valley had to be evacuated. Avalanches, which can be equally destructive, are frequent and have made parts of the valley so dangerous that the French government has designated them zone rouge—meaning no one can live there during the winter months.

The valley floor is relatively level, and while not nearly as wide as the valley of the Durance, it has more than sufficient space for an army to pass. But once in, the only way out is by the highest and most difficult pass in the Southern Alps, a narrow ledge nestled in the arms of Mount Viso, known as the Col de la Traversette. The Traversette lies on the current border between France and Italy, and this is probably where Hannibal crossed into Italy.

As the column moved forward along the valley floor, the only resistance it now encountered came in the form of sporadic attacks against sections of the baggage train and the killing of stragglers who lagged too far behind to be protected. The Gauls avoided engaging the main body of the column, since Hannibal's cavalry and elephants could easily reach any section under attack. Even the scouts who moved ahead of the column encountered only light resistance, and by late in the day they had reached the end of the valley and climbed to the top of the pass. Midway up the mountainside, between the valley and the pass, on a wide stretch of level ground fed by multiple streams, they established a base camp and waited for the remainder of the column to reach them. By the end of the day most of the soldiers had reached the camp and by nightfall the entire army was settled in. The ground on the side of the mountain had a light covering of snow, which was quickly cleared before the tents were erected and the fires started. For the next two days, the column remained in this makeshift camp, resting and tending to its wounds.

The army had suffered a terrible mauling in the gorge, soldiers were exhausted, many were wounded, and despair could be seen everywhere in the ranks. Provisions were in short supply, most having been lost in the fighting, and what remained was rapidly being consumed. Only water was plentiful since there were several streams on the mountainside and the snow, which was everywhere, could be melted. Starvation, coupled with exposure, now took over where the Gauls had left off— moving in first among the wounded and taking the weakest. Then it began to affect even the hardiest among the soldiers. Animals that had been wounded or died were quickly butchered and eaten. The suffering and hunger darkened the mood of despair, a despair that was reflected on the somber and gaunt faces of thousands huddled around the campfires.

Anxious to see the pass, Hannibal was among the first to reach it, taking in the view of Italy that unfolded before him—a view which even today takes the breath away. Visible below was the Po River and in the distance the vast plains of northern Italy. Over the last five months, Hannibal had led his army over a thousand miles, fighting for nearly every mile just to reach this spot—the last barrier to Italy. While his army was weak, it was still intact, and what now remained was to get the soldiers, horses, and elephants down from this mountain and into Italy as quickly as possible with a minimum of casualties.

The engineers began to prepare a pathway from the base camp to the summit and then to plan their descent. Because of the nature of the Alps, climbing to the pass from the French side is relatively easy compared to the descent into Italy. The climb, while steep in some sections, is generally gradual, with no difficult passages. The author has done it on multiple occasions, with a full pack, in less than three hours—admittedly under perfect conditions—while his close friend and guide, Bruno Martin, can do it in half that time. The descent into Italy is another matter entirely. There is nothing gradual about it—it is steep and treacherous, almost vertical in some sections. It is so treacherous that before Hannibal could reach the valley floor in Italy, he would lose nearly as many men as he had in fighting the Gauls.

The soldiers rested while the engineers worked on stabilizing the approach to the pass by widening it. When the grading was completed, they were gradually moved to the pass above. Hannibal was waiting for them with words of encouragement. He urged them to take heart and continue, pointing out the view of Italy below and describing the long-awaited rest that awaited them in the lush valley below. He inspired as many as he could with his optimism and explained to all who had the strength or the inclination to listen how close they were to the end of their ordeal. After this, he promised, it was "all downhill" and after "a fight or two," the Romans would surrender, the war would be won, and they would all go home rich, famous, and contented.[14]

The worst was far from over. The descent into Italy would be fatal to many, especially those worn out from the fighting, weak from hunger, drained by despair, or just unlucky. Men and animals would be lost in alarming numbers on the ledges before the army would once more feel level ground beneath its feet. Death was far from finished with them, and what the Gauls had not completed in their ambushes, nature would try to finish on this mountain. Periodically, small bands of Gauls appeared, seemingly from out of nowhere, to attack sections of the struggling column, and then withdrew just as quickly, disappearing into the rocks and crevices from which they had so unexpectedly emerged.

As the engineers worked on grading the descent, they discovered what appeared to be a narrow path just below the pass that was partly covered by snow. During World War II, sections of this track were purposely destroyed by the French to prevent its use by invading Italian and German soldiers, and after the war, to discourage smugglers. The going was slow and tedious, made worse by intermittent falling snow, wind, and numbing cold. A fresh layer had settled on top of the old snow from the previous winter, and while the first elements of the vanguard could pass easily over it, those who followed quickly found they were in trouble. The fresh snow, trampled by those who had passed first, turned into a slush that quickly froze into a layer of ice.

Soldiers began to lose their footing. A stumble could result in a slide, and a slide often could not be arrested because a falling body on the steep slopes gains momentum quickly. If a slide could not be arrested within seconds, there was little to be done to stop a man or an animal from going over the edge. At ten thousand feet, there is nothing to hold onto. The unlucky or careless ones who stumbled and slid clawed desperately around them to find anything that might stop their slide to the certain death that awaited them below. Pack animals, burdened with what remained of the supplies and equipment, would often drive their hoofs through the soft top layer of snow and become stuck in the layer below. As they struggled to free themselves, driven by their panic and whipped by their handlers, they would fall, snapping their brittle legs and sealing their fate.

With the engineers leading the way, the column worked its way slowly down the eastern face of the mountain. The farther they descended, the more difficult the pathway became, and accidents occurred with increasingly fatal frequency. Men and animals were swallowed by the yawning black chasms below them. For any who slid to the end of a precipice and teetered there, rescue was often impossible. They had to be left lying by the edge until, weakened by exposure or despair, they simply gave up and slipped into the abyss. After having descended only a few hundred feet below the summit, the column suddenly came to a halt. The track ended—destroyed by a landslide and taken away vertically for several hundred feet. Try as they might, the engineers could not find a way around. As word of what happened was passed back along the column, some soldiers began to panic while others lapsed into so deep a despondency that they simply gave up and, falling upon their packs, waited for death to come for them.

When word reached Hannibal, he worked his way to the front, re-assuring the soldiers in line as he passed that it was only a temporary obstacle. When he reached his engineers, all agreed the only solution was to create a new ledge above the old one. Initially they made progress because they could obtain footing in the fresh snow, but they reached a point when the footing became too treacherous because of the angle of the slope, and the column was forced to settle in for the night. Each soldier had to make the best of where he stood. Some were able to turn back, going over the pass and then down to the base camp where the horses and elephants were kept. Nearly thirty thousand men were on the mountain, praying to their gods that the weather would not worsen or the Gauls attack. When temperatures fell that night, death came once more to carry off the weakest in body and spirit.

Construction of the new ledge came to a stop when the engineers encountered a large rock that blocked their progress. So much time and effort had been involved in chipping out the new track that they had no choice but to find a way to dislodge it. The size, weight, and position of the rock made moving it impossible, so they set about to destroy it, using a process which has been utilized by farmers for centuries to clear their land. The engineers would render the rock friable. A relay was set up that stretched back over the pass and down to the tree line. In the heavily forested slopes, dead wood was collected and trees felled. The wood was hauled as far as possible by elephant, horse, and mule and then passed along from there by human relay to the engineers working on the other side.

The engineers used the wood to build an enormous fire around the rock and fed it all through the night. Aided by a favorable wind which fanned the fire, the rock became hotter as the hours passed. When the rock was sufficiently heated, the soldiers passed along their rations of sour wine, which the engineers poured over it. Sour wine is essentially vinegar, and its acetic content caused the hot surface to develop multiple fissures. The engineers then set to work with iron picks and in short order destroyed enough of the rock to continue creating their ledge.[15]

Once the rock had been disposed of, the work went quickly. Within a day, the vanguard of the column was able to safely reach the valley floor in Italy, and by the next day the track had been widened sufficiently to enable the horses and the supply train animals to be led down. It took three more days and nights for the main part of the column to reach the Po Valley below—a descent that under ideal weather conditions the author has done in less than two hours. When it was over, nearly thirty thousand men, horses, pack animals, and elephants had been taken over the pass and then brought down on the Italian side. But the cost was high. Hannibal's army sustained more casualties than in any of the multiple river crossings and battles they had fought in the five months since leaving Spain. When the soldiers were assembled and a final count was made, the magnitude of the losses was shocking. Hannibal had crossed the Rhone River nearly a month earlier with thirty-eight thousand soldiers and eight thousand horsemen.[16] Now he was down to twelve thousand Africans, eight thousand Spanish, and a small number of mercenaries. His cavalry numbered six thousand, but miraculously, all his elephants survived. The highest number of casualties occurred in the two ambushes and in climbing over the last pass—all this happening in the short space of approximately two weeks.[17]

In Italy, everything was green, the climate was temperate, and the food plentiful. The inhabitants on this side of the Alps, according to the sources, enjoyed a better quality of life than their unfortunate cousins on the French side. Hannibal's soldiers established a base camp at the foot of the mountain and turned the starving animals out to graze on its lower gentle slopes, lush with vegetation. Thousands of feet above the camp, work continued for two more days as the track was widened enough to lead the elephants down. The army remained in camp, but recovery was not easy for men who had endured weeks of deprivation. They found it, at least in the initial stages, to be difficult both physically and psychologically. Hannibal's soldiers "had come to look more like beasts than men,"[18] and the sudden change from hard labor and exhaustion at the higher elevations to leisure and rest on the lower slopes, from hunger to plenty, from filth to clean living, affected them in a multitude of ways, not all of them positive.[19]

While the crossing of the Alps has been traditionally regarded as Hannibal's greatest feat, or at least the one that placed him in the history books and immortalized him in the popular imagination, it can just as easily be classified as one of great failure. The fact that Hannibal made it over the mountains and to Italy tends to overshadow his losses. The Alps are a dangerous place—even today they claim on average some two hundred lives a year according to French authorities. But as this author has learned from firsthand experience, despite their imposing presence, they can be crossed quickly when weather conditions are stable. The author has gone over the Traversette, into Italy, and back to France well over twenty times during the last few years, admittedly under ideal conditions. It is possible to reach the pass from the French side in three hours, enjoy the view, descend to the Italian side in another two hours, have a substantial lunch of pasta and sausage at a nearby farmhouse, then reclimb the pass and return in time for a late dinner—all in one long but fulfilling day.

Hannibal's losses crossing the Alps hobbled his army and perhaps even compromised his ability to defeat Rome in the end. He lost close to half his army, and to replenish their numbers he now had to recruit among the less dependable Gauls in northern Italy. Now the war between Hannibal and Rome would begin in earnest and in the end it was a war that would be decided not by ability and courage, but by the passage of time and the crunching of numbers—neither of which were in Hannibal's favor.

CHAPTER IV

Crushing the Romans

T HE WAR IN Italy would last for nearly sixteen years. The first
phase was a two-year period from 218 until 216 B.C. that would
see Hannibal winning spectacular battlefield victories in rapid succession. It was the apex of his career and a time when it seemed all but certain that Rome would be crushed in this war. Then, as happens in war,
things changed. Hannibal lost his momentum and a slow hemorrhage
set in. The nemesis of Rome stopped winning every battle and was
eventually driven to and confined in southern Italy until he was recalled
to North Africa in 203 B.C. Any one of Hannibal's victories during that
initial two-year period should have been enough to have brought the
war to an end or at a minimum forced the Romans to the bargaining
table. That did not happen. Instead the Romans absorbed their losses,
put more men into the field, and continued to resist—unresponsive to
Hannibal's overtures to end the war.

What made Hannibal initially so formidable a force on the battlefield? The key to his success is found in his ability to think outside
the confines of conventional strategy—rather than be locked into the
proverbial box, as were so many of his adversaries. When it came to tactics, Hannibal improvised and did the unexpected. Time and again he

demonstrated the brilliance that earned him his place as one of history's greatest commanders. In nearly every battle he faced superior Roman numbers, but by doing the unexpected and taking calculated risks, he did exactly what his enemy thought could never happen and turned disadvantage into victory. At the same time he was a commander who engaged in meticulous planning—making sure logistics and the elements of psychology and nature had been taken into careful consideration and utilized to their maximum benefit. Hannibal thought and planned before he took action, and that repeatedly gave him the advantage over his more impulsive and impatient adversaries. It was Hannibal who always chose when, where, and how to fight—not his enemy.

Following his descent from the Alps, Hannibal rested his army for nearly two weeks in the Po Valley west of modern-day Turin. His army was in poor shape, his soldiers suffering from hunger, exposure, and the psychological impact of having lost nearly half their number. But at the lower elevation, where the climate was temperate, where men and animals were protected from the elements and food was plentiful, the soldiers recovered rapidly, regaining both their strength and spirit. The respite was a bonus given to Hannibal because while the Romans knew he was coming, they were not sure where to find him. They were probably aware of the major passes which he could have used, such as the Montgenevre, the Mont-Cenis, or the Little St. Bernard, but a remote pass like the Traversette must have been completely unknown to them. All the Romans knew for certain was that Hannibal was coming into northern Italy, somewhere, and soon.

Scipio left Massilia praying to his gods that Hannibal and his mercenaries would perish in the mountains—either from starvation and the elements, or at the hands of the Gauls. When he arrived at Pisa, he began to worry that Hannibal might just succeed in crossing the Alps. With authorization from the senate, Scipio raised a new army and led it north to Placentia and Cremona, where he intended to integrate his soldiers with the remnants of the legions already garrisoned there. As Scipio was moving into northern Italy, Hannibal began moving his army east along the Po River and into the territory of a large tribe called the Taurini. The Taurini were at war with the Insubres, another tribe of Gauls who had allied themselves with Hannibal. In an effort to persuade the Taurini to stop fighting and join him as an ally, Hannibal sent emissaries to their principal stronghold—probably the site of what is today Turin. The Taurini rebuffed the overture and Hannibal laid siege. Within three days his soldiers had breached the walls. All the surviving defenders had their throats cut, while the women and children were parceled out as slaves. It was a psychological move intended to make an impression on any other tribes in the area who might be undecided about joining Hannibal or considering resisting him. The quick defeat of the Taurini and their harsh punishment had the intended effect, as tribes began to send emissaries to pledge their support.

Hannibal needed the Gauls, both to supplement his depleted army and to supply him with provisions. Several tribes had promised to join him, both before he crossed the Alps and after his defeat of the Taurini, but few delivered more than assurances. While the Gauls were quick to boast about their bravery in battle and the numbers of soldiers they would provide in the field, many of their leaders began hedging their bets, waiting to see the outcome of the first clash between Hannibal and the Romans before committing to either side. They stalled in sending Hannibal reinforcements and supplies, while a few others blatantly reneged on their promises. While they no doubt feared Hannibal, especially after his quick defeat of the Taurini, they counted on the Roman army in the area to keep him occupied.

As Scipio moved west along the Po River looking for Hannibal's army, he began pressing many of the Gauls who lived along the route into Roman service. The area was already rife with anti-Roman sentiment and had been that way since the Romans waged a brief war against the Gauls a few years earlier and established colonies at Cremona and Placentia. Scipio's presence exacerbated an already volatile situation, and all the Gauls needed was a sign that Hannibal could defeat the Romans on the battlefield for them to join him en masse. At this point in the war Hannibal was looking for more than a decisive victory against a Roman army. He wanted to send a shockwave from one end of Italy to the other, a message to the cities and tribes, especially those in the south, that Rome was not invincible and that a new age was dawning. Hannibal counted on defections from the Roman confederation having a domino effect, beginning with the Gauls in the north and then moving at a rapid rate as far as the Greek cities of southern Italy and even onto the islands of Sicily, Sardinia, and Corsica. This was his initial strategy for the war, and he needed a big win to put it into play. He chose to provide that sign at a small tributary of the Po River, the Ticinus.

Hannibal was concerned when he learned that Scipio had reached northern Italy so quickly. Only a few weeks earlier Scipio had been at Massilia, and now he was at the head of an army and closing rapidly. But the army Scipio had with him was not of the same quality as the one he had commanded at Massilia. That force had been sent on to Spain under the command of his brother, Gnaeus Cornelius, and what Scipio now led was an army composed of recently conscripted recruits— farm boys mostly, from throughout Italy and with little idea of what they were in for.

At the outset of the Second Punic War, Roman armies were not the well-drilled and skilled legions that would conquer the ancient world in the centuries to follow under leaders like Marius, Pompey, Caesar, Antony, and Augustus. They were divided into legions of anywhere from four thousand to six thousand men, conscripted from throughout Italy and then further subdivided into maniples of between three hundred and four hundred. Each maniple was organized into three ranks or lines for combat and commanded by a centurion or master sergeant.

The first rank was disposalable element, composed of younger, less experienced and more impoverished recruits, who engaged the enemy and attempted to break its forward progress. If they failed, the second line, consisting of older, more experienced and better equipped soldiers, would engage while what was left of the first retreated through their ranks. The third line were the most experienced, well-equipped veterans. They were committed to the battle at a crucial moment to turn its tide. The soldiers in each line fought in a staggered arrangement, like a checkerboard square, so that during a battle the first line could retreat behind the second if needed, and the second either advance or retreat behind the third, without disrupting the cohesion of the entire maniple. This arrangement had been the standard operating procedure of the Roman army for the last century, and while simple in design and effective against enemy armies of lesser skill, it proved ineffective against the tactics and resourcefulness of Hannibal.

Roman armies were commanded by consuls, men who had been vetted by the senate and elected by the citizens of Rome for a one-year term of office with the responsibility of conducting a war. The consuls were first and foremost politicians, not professional soldiers. They came primarily from the patrician class, the Roman aristocracy, and the advancement of their political careers was their primary concern. Military command for them was a means to an end—a stepping stone. Success in Roman politics, with all its status and lucrative rewards, depended on victory on the battlefield and a return to Rome in triumph. Victory translated into popularity, and the spoils of war provided the funds to buy votes and influence elections through the sponsorship of public entertainment—feasts, games, and circuses. Votes meant election and reelection to the highest and most prestigious offices of the Republic.

Most of the soldiers who made up the infantry in the Roman army were farmers from towns, cities, and tribes allied to Rome and known as the *socii* and *amici*—allies and friends. They were bound to Rome by treaty and relatively free to govern themselves depending on their degree of cooperation. This loose system of alliances gave Rome a vast reserve of manpower, and manpower became the decisive factor in the war with Hannibal. By the time of the Second Punic War, nearly every part of the Italian peninsula, except for the far north and parts of Sicily, had come under some form of Roman oversight or control, usually through treaty, but in some cases by outright conquest and annexation. This system of alliances gave those who actively cooperated with Rome—in terms of providing money, supplies, and armed men—increased benefits such as Roman protection and often a lighter tax or tribute liability. The remainder of the infantry and the cavalry was composed of Roman cit-izens, those who had answered the call to duty in time of crisis and usually served on the second and third lines. Military service, or *dilectus*, as the Romans called it, was a sacred duty of every citizen.

Scipio's soldiers joined the garrisons already posted at Cremona and Placentia, but those garrisons, even though they were composed of more experienced soldiers, were in a demoralized condition. They had been defeated by the Boii and the Insubres a few months earlier, and Scipio found himself leading inexperienced, nervous recruits and demoralized veterans. It was a poor mix, both militarily and psychologically. Scipio's soldiers were frightened of Hannibal—his reputation as the man who had destroyed Saguntum, brought an army over the Alps, and defeated the Taurini preceded him. Scipio had no time to train his soldiers and build their confidence, all of which made him apprehensive about his chances of success in the first encounter with Hannibal; nevertheless, he pushed hard along the Po valley to find him.

A second Roman consul, Tiberius Sempronius Longus, was on his way through Italy with an army to reinforce Scipio. Sempronius had been posted to Sicily earlier in the year with orders to prepare for an invasion from North Africa, but when word reached the senate that Hannibal was in the Alps, those orders were changed. Sempronius left

Sicily and marched his soldiers from the extreme southern tip of Italy to Ariminum (Rimini) on the Adriatic coast in just forty days. From there, he moved northwest to reinforce Scipio and meet the threat from Hannibal. Until Sempronius reached him, Scipio was left to deal with Hannibal as best he could.

Scipio crossed the Po and established his camp on the banks of the Ticinus (Ticino in Italian) just twenty or so miles southwest of modern-day Milan and somewhere along the eastern bank of the river between the modern villages of Pavia and Vigevano. Scipio determined Hannibal was in the area somewhere on the other side of the river and prepared his soldiers for the battle to come with an exhortation—a traditional commander's speech before a battle, intended as a morale booster to energize his troops—a standard practice in the ancient world. Scipio's army needed it. Most of his soldiers probably had little real understanding of why they had been called away from their farms and villages to march across Italy and fight this North African. His reputation as the invincible master of battlefield tactics and his fierceness in combat were well known in Roman military and political circles. Hannibal had amazed Scipio by his rapid crossing of the Alps, and now the Roman consul had to prepare his largely green recruits to engage him.

Despite what must have been Scipio's high personal regard for Hannibal as a commander, he chose to denigrate him and his army before the assembled Roman soldiers. He explained that the enemy they would face on the battlefield the next day was one their fathers had already defeated in the First Punic War. The soldiers in Hannibal's army were but the "shadows of men, wasted by hunger and cold, filthy, bruised and crippled by the rocks and cliffs of the Alps, muscles stiffened by the cold, bodies numb, weapons broken, horses lame and feeble."[1] They had lost two-thirds of their number crossing the Alps, and even when they had their full strength on the banks of the Rhone River weeks before, they showed no stomach for combat and had chosen to flee into the mountains rather than stand and fight. Victory in the battle to come, Scipio told his men, would be so easy that the credit should go to the Alps, which had done their work for them beforehand.

Then Scipio went on to recount how Hannibal had broken the truce of the First Punic War and treacherously destroyed Saguntum. He portrayed the Carthaginian as nothing more than "a young upstart, a criminal—drunk with ambition." The peroration of the speech was one that leaders have resorted to for centuries to motivate their soldiers to fight an invader—protect their property, the honor of their wives, and the lives of their children. Despite what he had told his soldiers, in the privacy of his tent that night Scipio must have been concerned about his chance for victory. Hannibal was a formidable adversary directing experienced mercenaries. Scipio, like most Romans, was superstitious and believed that victory was the result of divine favor—so he paid careful attention that night to rituals and omens. That night a swarm of bees descended on the consul's tent and a wolf made its way into the camp, killing several soldiers who crossed its path. For a superstitious man these were bad signs.

A few miles to the west, Hannibal prepared his men for their first encounter with the Romans. He had his soldiers form a great circle into which several captured Gauls were placed. The Gauls were offered the opportunity to fight each other in individual combat, with the winner in each exchange given the choice between his freedom to return home or the opportunity to join the army. The losers would be freed from their captivity by death. It was Hobson's choice. With no alternative, they fought each other with bravery and spirit—something which impressed the assembled Carthaginians. When the last of the combats had ended, Hannibal explained to his soldiers that the contests had not been staged to entertain them, but to illustrate the gravity of their own situation. They were far from home, and there was no avoiding the Roman army that lay ahead of them. Returning to Spain was not an option, as the Alps behind them were sealed by winter's snow. South of them toward Genoa lay the Ligurian Sea—which they had no ships to cross. Like the Gauls who had just fought, their survival depended on their courage and skill. There was no turning back—no retreat. Defeat would mean slavery or a cruel death and an unmarked shallow grave in Italy, while victory would mean money—enough to make each man a king in his own right—as well as slaves, fame, and glory. Every soldier who excelled on the field of battle, Hannibal promised, would be given tax-free land of his choosing in Italy, Spain, or Africa, and any who wished could become citizens of Carthage. It was a highly enticing prospect for men who had so little in life.

To further build their morale, Hannibal recounted their long journey from Spain and enumerated the many tribes they had defeated along the way. He recognized and praised individual soldiers from among each of his contingents, his North Africans, his mercenaries, the Celtic allies from Spain, and his own countrymen from Carthage. He praised the Gauls of Northern Italy as those who had recently joined him to free their land from an arrogant and rapacious race intent on enslaving them—this battle and the war to be fought were to strike a blow for freedom everywhere.[2] Hannibal then reminisced about his youth, recounting how he had been raised in the army camps of Spain and grown to manhood among his veterans. He had learned the art of war under their watchful eyes, and it had been they who had voted him their commander upon the death of Hasdrubal. Hannibal concluded his speech by reminding his men that the Romans they would face on the field of battle were green recruits and a few veterans who had already been beaten by the Gauls months earlier. Scipio and his soldiers were strangers to each other and no match for fearless men who had crossed the Alps. He urged his soldiers to steel their hearts and look upon death with contempt. Then Hannibal, the man who the ancient sources tell us had no fear of or respect for the gods, prayed aloud to Baal Hammon for victory, and with his right hand, smashed the skull of a lamb which had been laid upon a hastily constructed altar. The army roared its approval and prepared for battle.

Scipio's army, camped on the eastern bank of the Ticinus, constructed a temporary bridge over the river and a palisade for protection. Then they moved to the far shore of the river, looking for Hannibal.

Despite the extensive pre-fight rhetoric of its commanders, the first clash turned out to be little more than a brief skirmish in the level fields that today form a triangle between the modern towns of Lomello, Vigevano, and Pavia. The cavalry clashed initially, and Hannibal's Africans quickly dominated the open ground, inflicting a decisive defeat over the less skilled and inexperienced Romans. During the skirmish, Scipio was wounded, and when he fell from his horse, the Carthaginians closed in on him like wolves on wounded prey. At the last second Scipio was miraculously snatched from death by his seventeen-year-old son.[3] Sixteen years later, that same boy, now a man and in command of a Roman army, would defeat Hannibal in North Africa and end the war. The young Scipio drove his horse into the midst of the startled Carthaginians, scattering them long enough to rescue his father and escape. The Romans retreated to Placentia, where they awaited the arrival of Sempronius. The defeat, though far from a major loss, still reinforced the apprehension with which the Romans viewed Hannibal and set a psychological tone for the much larger battles that were to come. Hannibal quickly became a larger-than-life figure for the superstitious Romans, a battlefield commander with superhuman qualities, who could not be defeated by mere mortals.

As news of Hannibal's victory spread, the Gauls sent emissaries to pledge their support, but once again, while they promised much, they delivered little in the way of reinforcements and supplies. Critically short of food, Hannibal sent contingents of his cavalry to capture a Roman grain depot at Clastidium, some five miles south of the Po River, near the present town of Casteggio. The Roman commander of the garrison was from Brundisium in southern Italy and when confronted willingly turned the depot and its garrison over in return for four hundred gold pieces and a place in Hannibal's army. The commander and his soldiers became the first of the "Italian allies" to defect and join Hannibal.

Hannibal established his camp five miles from Placentia and each day sent elements of his African cavalry to the plains in front of the Roman camp to taunt, insult, and provoke them to combat. Scipio, still convalescing from his wounds, ordered his soldiers to remain safely behind their palisades while they awaited the arrival of Sempronius and his army. The bravado of Hannibal's cavalry impressed many of the Gauls who were serving with the Romans as auxiliaries. Their admiration grew daily, and coupled with their underlying resentment of the Romans who had pressed them into service, eventually reached the point where they decided to go over to the Carthaginian side. Waiting until the early-morning hours, slightly over two thousand Gauls deserted, but before they crossed over to Hannibal, some of them decapitated several Roman sentries on duty as well as some soldiers they found sleeping nearby. Stuffing the severed heads into sacks, they proudly presented them to Hannibal as symbols of their allegiance.

Immediately after the Gauls deserted, Scipio moved his army south to a more secure site in the hills overlooking the east bank of another Po tributary—the Trebbia. Fearing the advantage that Hannibal's cavalry and elephants had over his army on level ground, Scipio moved his army into the hills. To further fortify the area, the Romans dug a wide ditch several hundred meters in front of the camp, erected a palisade

behind it, and waited for Sempronius to arrive. The site of this second
camp probably lies in the area around modern-day Pieve-Dugliara, just
a mile north of the village of Rivergaro and reachable today along the
Strada Provinciale 28 roadway to Placentia—an area the author can-
vassed extensively in researching this book.

When Sempronius arrived, he was eager to fight. Even though he
had experience leading Roman armies, he was foremost a politician,
and what he wanted was a quick victory over Hannibal that would advance his career and his reputation. Nothing mattered more to a man
of his position in Roman society. To reach and remain in the highest
offices, leading members of the nobility needed to win *fama et gloria*—
fame and glory—by the performance of great military victories in the
service of the *Populi Romani*—the Roman people. Sempronius's term
of office as consul was coming to an end, and he wanted to end it with
a victory worthy of his ego. Impetuous and domineering, Sempronius
was the opposite of the naturally cautious Scipio.

As it was late December and weather conditions had begun to de-
teriorate, Scipio argued that the prudent course of action would be to
avoid any contact with Hannibal. The nights were long and the days
cold, with intermittent snowfall. Scipio favored keeping the army in
secure winter quarters where they had ample supplies of food, a defensive advantage, and his soldiers could recover from their defeat at
the Ticinus. He believed the consular armies needed to integrate, im-
prove their skills, adjust to their new command structure, raise their
confidence levels, and synchronize their efforts before they could engage
Hannibal. Hannibal was not an adversary to be underestimated. Given
time, Scipio was confident the Gauls, with no prospect of fighting or
opportunities to loot, would become bored and return to their towns
and villages for the winter. Then, without allies, Hannibal would be
reduced to foraging the barren countryside for supplies. When the time
was right, perhaps in early spring, depending on the weather, the legions

could leave the security of their camp, refreshed and confident, to hunt a weakened Hannibal.

Sempronius would not hear of it. For him there could be no delay; the idea of resting in camp all winter and enduring months of inactivity ran contrary to his impatient personality and the impending Roman election schedule. Using Scipio's wounds as a reason, Sempronius took command of both armies, which now numbered some sixteen thousand Romans, twenty thousand auxiliary troops or "allies of Rome," and about four thousand cavalry. He ordered them to prepare for battle. Hannibal had established his camp on the west bank of the Trebbia, probably on the grounds of what is now the Croara Country Club, just off the Strada Provinciale 40 and about a half mile from the river. His army had grown to an estimated forty thousand men, counting his new allies. The opposing armies were evenly matched in terms of numbers, but the Romans were inexperienced, suffering from low morale because of their recent defeats, fearful of the unreliable Gauls living in their camp, and confused by a leadership divided between an impetuous Sempronius and a cautious Scipio. What the Romans did enjoy was a secure defensive position, which Sempronius was preparing to compromise.

Hannibal, unaware that Sempronius was intending to come out and fight, began to formulate a plan to draw the Romans out of their camp and onto the plains, where they would be most vulnerable to attack by his cavalry and elephants. First, he sent his cavalry into the countryside to plunder and burn the towns and villages of the Gauls who were loyal to Rome. The Gauls in response pressured the Romans for assistance and Sempronius sent out cavalry contingents. According to plan, Hannibal's cavalry gave way at each encounter, and this had the cumulative effect of building a false sense of confidence among the Romans and making Sempronius even more anxious to engage.

As was his inclination, Hannibal carefully reconnoitered the area between the Trebbia and the open areas near his camp. He found his battlefield and next to it a sizable ravine that was thick with scrub and brush. In the dim light of overcast winter skies, especially with the possibility of rain or snow falling, Hannibal believed he could hide a contingent of his soldiers and they would go unnoticed by the advancing Roman legions caught up in the excitement of the battle and focused on the enemy in front of them. Then, at a crucial point in the fighting, these troops would emerge from hiding and attack. The plan depended on two elements for success; keeping this small force hidden in the ravine and luring the Romans out of their camp and across the river onto open ground. While Hannibal suspected Scipio was probably too cautious to be drawn out, Sempronius might not be.

Shortly before dawn, on the day Hannibal had selected to implement his plan, he sent his African cavalry across the river to the Roman camp. It was cold and a light snow had begun to fall. They began to taunt the Roman sentries in a manner carefully orchestrated to provoke Semporonius into sending his soldiers out of camp before they had time to prepare. Hannibal's tactic required Sempronius to react in anger to the taunts, not think. While Hannibal's horsemen were baiting the Romans, his soldiers on the other side of the river were preparing for battle; readying their weapons, donning their armor, consuming their morning meal, and even taking the added precaution of coating their bodies with oil as insulation against the cold. Then, when they were ready, they moved into position.

Much earlier that same morning, Hannibal had dispatched a contingent of one thousand infantry and an equal number of cavalry under the command of his younger brother Mago to hide in the ravine near the river, where they waited patiently for events to unfold. Sempronius took the bait and ordered his troops onto the field. First the cavalry and then the infantry, in disarray and without any clear plan, began chasing the Africans. The Africans knew exactly what they were doing as they feigned a frightened retreat and drew the Romans farther away from the safety of their camp and toward the river. Sempronius, caught up in the emotions of the moment and tasting victory, ordered the entire Roman camp into battle.

The Romans went onto the field without breakfast. They charged after the Africans, fueled by an adrenaline rush brought on by the illusion that they would win the day. All Sempronius could see were Africans fleeing, and he was certain that victory was his. Scipio, confined to his tent by his wounds, saw it differently and worried about the outcome. The African cavalry rode at a measured pace just fast enough to allow the Romans to keep up a short distance behind them. Then they crossed the river, reaching the far bank of the Trebbia. Once the Roman infantry entered the river, the cold and swiftly running water was a shock to their systems. While the water was only chest height, because of the cold it was numbing. They struggled to reach the far bank as their energy began to wane. Having already run nearly a half mile in their armor before they even entered the frigid water, they had to climb out of the river, waterlogged, cold, tired, and hungry to continue forward and fight.

Positioned well back from the riverbank and drawn up in battle order, Hannibal and his army waited. With his African cavalry covering the flanks, Hannibal arrayed his infantry, composed mostly of Spaniards and Gauls, in a wide line facing the advancing enemy. Behind this line he placed his elephants and his most experienced mercenaries. As the Romans came out of the river, their pace slowed and, exhausted, many began to falter. Hannibal's cavalry, which had baited the Romans in their camp and led them across the river, then wheeled around and charged back on the Roman flanks, inflicting heavy casualties. As the advancing Roman infantry engaged the Carthaginian line, the African cavalry shifted their attack from the flanks to the rear of the Roman army. At that point, the elephants were driven forward—but with mixed success. Initially they caused the Romans to panic until lightly armed skirmishers, throwing darts at the eyes of the elephants, caused them to turn back on their own soldiers. As the frightened elephants turned to escape their torment, Romans stabbed them with spears in the area just below their tails, where the skin is soft and tender, driving the beasts mad with pain. Several fell, fatally wounded. Seeing what was happening, Hannibal ordered the remaining elephants to be removed from the battle line and repositioned at the flanks, where they could be used more effectively working in tandem with the cavalry.

With both sides now fully engaged, Mago and his troops emerged from hiding. The psychological effect of their sudden appearance threw the Romans into confusion. The Roman flanks were already hard-pressed by the combination of Hannibal's elephants and cavalry, and with Mago's forces attacking them from the rear, the Roman army began to come apart. It was now late morning, and the light snow of the early dawn hours turned into a cold driving rain. A contingent of ten thousand Roman soldiers pushed through the Gauls holding Hannibal's center and escaped to reach Placentia—some twenty miles to the north and east.

The desertion of this large contingent of infantry weakened an already faltering Roman line, and a disordered retreat to the river began. Hannibal now held not only a tactical and psychological advantage over Sempronius, but a numerical one as well. As the Romans retreated, many were killed by the pursuing African cavalry or trampled by the elephants. By midday the rain had become so heavy that Hannibal ordered his army to break off the pursuit at the river and return to camp. His soldiers were exhausted, but elated. The Trebbia was their first win against a Roman consular army, and it was not just a victory, it was a slaughter. Hannibal had brilliantly utilized tactics, terrain, weather, and psychology to defeat Sempronius. Carthaginian losses were minimal as most of the casualties were sustained by the Gauls—a scenario that would be repeated over and over during the Second Punic War.

The battle at the Trebbia illustrates a successful tactic Hannibal would use consistently against the Romans for the next decade—until it was turned against him in North Africa. That tactic was envelopment.

Hannibal would place his less reliable and more expendable troops, the Gauls and Spaniards, in the center of his battle line to absorb the first assault of the Roman infantry and sustain the greater number of casualties. Then, when the center of his line began to fail, at just the right moment, he would commit his experienced and disciplined mercenaries to the battle, while using his cavalry on the flanks, to turn the tide in his favor. It was a tactic that the Romans succumbed to time and again.

At the Trebbia, Hannibal captured a considerable number of prisoners, who were quickly divided into three groups; Romans, Italians, and Gauls. The Romans were treated harshly—confined and put on short rations—while the Italians and Gauls were fed and sent home to their families without having to pay a ransom. The psychological impact was enormous. The Romans were devastated as they watched their elated and grateful allies fed and freed. As they were released, Hannibal told the prisoners to carry home with them his message; he had come to Italy to wage war against Rome, not against the Italians and Gauls. His purpose was to free Italy from Roman domination, and he welcomed those who wanted their freedom to join him. It was all part of his strategy for breaking apart the Roman confederation

Sempronius and the ailing Scipio led the battered remnants of their army to the safety of a larger fortified Roman camp at Cremona. Hannibal apparently allowed them to retreat in safety, even letting them pass within a few miles of his camp, perhaps because his men were so exhausted from fighting that he was hesitant to risk another encounter. Once the Romans reached Cremona, they settled in for the winter while Sempronius left for Rome to oversee the elections for the next year and explain his defeat to the senate. Hannibal remained in his camp that winter (218/217 B.C.), waiting for the supplies the Gauls had promised. When those supplies were not forthcoming, he sent his cavalry into the countryside to plunder their towns and villages. It was a cold winter, and all the elephants died but one.[4] Scipio waited out the winter at Cremona, unable or unwilling to move against Hannibal.

When word of the defeat reached Rome, there was fear mixed with anger. The senate demanded to know how two Roman consuls and their armies could be defeated by an African and his mercenaries. Sempronius blamed the weather—the snow, rain, and cold. Then he recounted how, at great personal risk, he had avoided the African cavalry who were ravaging northern Italy to make his way to Rome and report to the senate. Initially the senate accepted his version of events, but as the details of the battle emerged and the magnitude of the loss settled in, the mood became less accepting and more critical of his leadership.

Even though Sempronius had fallen out of favor, he was not censured. Rome was short on generals, and he was appointed proconsul or acting consul for the forthcoming year and ordered to return to the area of Cremona and Placentia as commander of the army there. Gaius Flaminius, a plebeian, and Gnaeus Servillius, a patrician, were elected consuls with a mandate from the senate to raise additional troops and elicit more help from the Greek cities of southern Italy and Sicily. The total number of Romans under arms in the spring of 217 B.C. came to nearly one hundred thousand divided into eleven legions. The expense of raising, equipping, and paying those soldiers was accomplished in part by devaluing the currency—reducing the percentage of bronze in the coins used to pay the soldiers and suppliers. The gold and silver reserves of the Roman treasury would be dangerously diminished during the next several years, so much so that the coinage was further debased and taxes increased to help pay for the war. Currency devaluation and increased taxes were met with anger and resistance, both from the Romans who had to pay them and from their Italian allies. While devaluation of the currency was generally welcomed by those who were in debt, usually the small farmers who bore the main burden of conscription, it was not popular with the wealthier patrician class who owned the debt.

Not all the legions raised that spring were sent to fight Hannibal. Two were already in Spain under the command of Scipio's younger brother, and Scipio was reassigned to join them as a proconsul—a consul whose elective term had expired but who was appointed by the senate on a temporary basis. One legion was stationed on the island of Sardinia and two were sent to Sicily. Two were held in reserve for the possible defense of Rome, while two were dispatched to northern Italy to reinforce what was left of the two legions under the command of Sempronius. The strategy for fighting Hannibal was revised. The Apennine Mountains, which run north to south through central Italy like a spinal column, were to be utilized as a natural defensive barrier to prevent Hannibal from reaching Rome. From the north there were two main routes leading toward Rome, and an army was stationed on each side of the mountain range to guard them. Flaminius established himself at Arretium (Arezzo), just south of where Florence is today, to control the central passes of the mountain range there, while Servillius moved east to Ariminum on the Adriatic coast to block any attempt by Hannibal to come around the northern edge of the range and down the much flatter and easier eastern coast of Italy.

By the spring of 217 B.C., Hannibal was ready to move into central Italy. His army was larger and better equipped than the one he had crossed the Alps with months earlier, although he still regarded the Gauls who had joined him as unreliable and even treacherous. While Hannibal needed them to offset the Roman advantage in manpower, he regarded them with so much suspicion that at times he feared for his own safety. As he moved about his camp and even on the march he used a multitude of disguises to thwart any attempts at assassination.[5] Hannibal donned a variety of wigs and apparently used makeup to alter his appearance. Foremost in his mind must have been the memory of his brother-in-law's murder at the hands of a Gaul. The Gauls, in turn, had not failed to notice that their new leader had placed them, along with their Spanish cousins, on the front lines at the Trebbia, and that they bore the greatest number of casualties. All the fighting between the Carthaginians and the Romans so far had been in their territory, and their tribes had suffered from the looting and burning carried out by both sides. The Gauls were anxious to move south to begin their own looting at Roman and Italian expense.

Hannibal had two routes to the south open to him. The first was directly over the western side of the Apennine Mountains and into Etruria. The second avoided the mountains altogether and followed the Po Valley east to the Adriatic coast and then south—a much easier route for a large army to follow because the terrain tends to be flat and wide, making for easy marching. For some reason, Hannibal chose the mountain route, which leads to speculation that he might have intended to rendezvous with a Carthaginian fleet on the west coast at Pisa. There is no precise location reported in the manuscripts where Hannibal crossed the Apennines, beyond the report that he crossed by a little-used road and once over found himself in a sizable swamp or marsh. There are three possible routes the author located, leading from the western side of the mountains into central Italy. The first and most unlikely follows the Trebbia River to its source, then crosses relatively low mountains and comes down to the sea at Genoa. A second follows the Po Valley to Parma, then crosses the mountains to arrive at La Spezia—also along the western coast of Italy, but farther south than Genoa and closer to Pisa. Neither of these ends in or near a marsh. The third route runs from Bologna directly over the mountains and comes down just northwest of Florence at Pistoia. This route is, even today (SS64), a little-used but treacherous road over a relatively low pass and could well be the one Hannibal used. Hannibal made two attempts to cross the Apennines in the early spring. A snowstorm far more violent than anything they had experienced in the Alps forced the column back, but they were able to make a successful crossing a week or so later.

South of Pistoia, some twenty-five miles west of Florence at Fucecchio, is a large area of marshes caused by the periodic flooding of the

Arno River. As Hannibal's army entered these marshes, he ordered the Gauls moved to the middle of the column—wedged between his African infantry and Numidian cavalry. It was a security precaution. The Gauls, Hannibal had found, were incessant complainers about conditions on the march, often malingering and frequently prone to deserting when the going became difficult. When the advanced elements of Hannibal's army entered the marshes, the footing was good since the water was only ankle deep. But for those who followed, it became difficult because the already soft ground was further softened by the thousands of soldiers and animals who passed along ahead of them. The marching slowed to a crawl as the army took four days and three nights to slog its way through; they were continually on the move, often without adequate periods of sleep. Soldiers could rest for only a few hours each night and then, to keep out of the brackish water, many lay on the corpses of animals. Horses went lame when their hoofs rotted from continually being immersed in water. Men and animals died when disease spread through the column in the form of a fever. Hannibal developed an infection in one of his eyes, and according to sources a bloody discharge coverd his face and cheeks. Because he had neither the time nor the inclination to have it treated, he lost sight in that eye. Or perhaps it was the treatment at the time, which in many cases might have been worse than the disease. Hannibal rode on the last surviving elephant, a massive Indian beast named Syrus, although because of the infection he often had to be carried on a litter.

Emerging from the marshes, the army entered Etruria, a prosperous area, and then moved east toward Faesulae just outside of Florence. There Hannibal began gathering intelligence on other routes south. Moving away from Pisa, indicates that the Carthaginian fleet may have been prevented from reaching the port, and Hannibal was compelled to change his plans. Again, we are at a loss to know exactly what his plans were and if he in fact intended heading toward Rome.

From Faesulae, Hannibal's army moved south along the Val di Chi-ana, west of Arretium, by a route selected to avoid the Roman army commanded by Flaminius. While the sources give lengthy profiles of both Hannibal and Flaminius at this juncture in the story, assessing their personalities and strategies, they do not describe in any detail Hannibal's route from Faesulae to Arretium. They tend to make rather vague references to the route, with descriptions such as "fertile Etrus-can plains" and "the mountains of Cortona"—references which are far from clear. The assumption is that Hannibal simply followed the most direct route south, using the Etruscan roads that existed at the time—routes that would have allowed the fastest progress and were most likely to meet the supply needs of the army. On the other hand, those routes would also have been the ones most carefully guarded by the Romans. Along the way, Hannibal turned his troops loose on the local popu-lation. They plundered the prosperous towns and villages, murdering, raping, and pillaging. Hannibal made no attempt to restrain them, as this was a move calculated to draw Flaminius and his army away from the security of their camp at Arretium and onto a battlefield. Like Sem-pronius, Flaminius was impulsive, and Hannibal was sure that he would be unable to restrain himself as he watched the countryside burn.

How Hannibal managed to slip past the Roman army at Arretium remains a mystery. While the direct road to Cortona was probably guarded by the Romans, Hannibal could have marched east of Arre-tium and then turned south under the cover of the hills that surround Castiglion Fiorentino and Cortona. In that way, he might have moved past them without their knowledge. This would have brought him to the north side of Cortona. Another possible route that bypasses Arezzo starts at Anghiari to the northeast and then moves south and east of the hills that encircle Castiglion Fiorentino and Cortona. The terrain along that route is difficult even today for an SUV to cover much less for an army on foot.

Nor is it clear from the sources how both armies moved from Cortona to Lake Trasimene, the site of the next battle. The most direct route today runs from Cortona south to Ossaia and Terontola, then to the western edge of the lake. There is another possible route, a more remote road that also runs south and then east from Cortona through the Pergo valley and then through Piazzano, to the village of Sanguineto and on to the lake. The area between Sanguineto and the lake is where many contemporary historians believe the next battle took place. The ancient historians refer to Arretium and Cortona as towns along the most direct route to Lake Trasimene; but it is uncertain that is the route Hannibal took. What is certain is that Hannibal reached the lake ahead of the Romans, having succeeded in somehow slipping past them at Arretium.

During this time, an interesting episode is reported by the Roman poet Italicus, although it is regarded with skepticism by modern-day scholars. Envoys from Carthage apparently managed to reach Hannibal in central Italy and present him with the demand that his young son be included in the ritual sacrifice to the god Baal.[6] Hanno, the perennial enemy of the Barca clan at Carthage, maneuvered the senate to demand Hannibal's only son as one of that year's victims. Imilce, Hannibal's wife, mounted a frenzied lobby against the order, and the senate, fearful of Hannibal's wrath should they sacrifice the child without his consent, sent the envoys to obtain it. Hannibal replied that his son must be spared to carry on the fight against Rome should he be killed; in place of the child, Hannibal offered to slaughter a thousand Roman soldiers in the upcoming battle to appease the god. Hannibal's son, according to the same source, was born just as he was leaving Spain for Italy, placing him within the age range which archaeologists and forensic experts have determined is correct for the victims of sacrifice at Carthage. How the envoys managed to reach Hannibal in central Italy remains puzzling and leads to speculation that the story may have been fabricated by Italicus two centuries later, for dramatic effect.

When reports reached Flaminius that Hannibal was plundering the
countryside, he exploded into a blind rage and ordered his army to mobilize. The officers around him cautioned against attacking Hannibal
until they had formulated an effective strategy—the defeat of Sempronius at the Trebbia being foremost on their minds. But Flaminius, like
Sempronius, was more concerned with a quick victory and his image at
Rome than with listening to reason. He was under considerable pressure from the senate, which wanted to see a Roman commander who
would take the initiative in the war. Flaminius set off, following the
pillars of black smoke rising from the burning villages and towns, but
Hannibal avoided him and began moving south, in what appeared to be
an alarming move toward Rome.

Once Flaminius took the bait and started following, Hannibal suddenly turned east, just south of Cortona, moving toward the area of
Lake Trasimene, the present-day boundary between Tuscany and Umbria. There he led his army into a narrow plain enclosed by hills on
one side and the large lake on the other. Access to the plain, known
as the Tuoro, is through a defile known as the Borghetto pass on the
northwestern shore. On one side is the lake; on the other, foothills
leading to Monte Gualandro. Access to the site today is easy following
the Strada Statale 73/75 highway, which runs from Siena to Perugia,
but two thousand years ago, the passage through the defile might have
been considerably more narrow than it is today, given how much the
shores of the lake have receded over time. A reexamination of the Trasimene battle site based on recent topographical assessments indicates
that the coastline of the lake may have been much closer, thus restrict-
ing even more the area where the fighting took place. The plain extends
for about a mile or so until it is once more enclosed to the east. The
Romans would have to enter the pass and once on the plain would
be severely constrained in their ability to maneuver. It was here that

Hannibal set his trap for Flaminius. Hannibal placed contingents of his African and Spanish troops at the eastern end of the plain and concealed his Iberian and Carthaginian cavalry at the western end. His best infantry were positioned in the foothills overlooking the pass. By dawn the next day, all Hannibal's forces were securely in position and hidden from view.

Early on a June morning in 216 B.C., Flaminius led his troops into the defile. They moved slowly, enveloped in a thick fog that extended over much of the plain between the foothills and the lake. The fog was so thick and clung so low to the ground that the scouts Flaminius sent out could barely see more than a few feet in front of them. Cautious, they turned back, but Flaminius, anxious to engage Hannibal, ordered the column to keep moving, even blindly, through the defile and onto the plain. Once the greater part of the Roman army was on the plain and the fog began to lift, Hannibal launched his attack from three sides. The poor visibility, coupled with the element of surprise, threw the Romans into confusion, preventing them from making the crucial shift from marching order to battle formation. There was chaos in their ranks, and in the space of three hours, thousands of Roman soldiers were killed. Most were cut down while they were still in marching order, unable for the most part to even draw their weapons because the attack came so swiftly and at such close quarters. It was a slaughter, and the Romans who escaped the initial carnage fled into the waters of the lake, where, encumbered by their armor, they tried desperately to swim away. Those who did not drown tried, with hands raised and pitiful cries for mercy, to surrender. As the Romans begged to be spared, the African and Spanish cavalry drove their horses into the shallows and cut them down where they stood, like so many reeds in the marches. This was no longer a battle, it was a massacre—*un sanguinoso*—a bloodbath, lending the name Sanguineto to a nearby town.

Flaminius had marched his soldiers to the slaughter. It was tactical incompetence, and the ancient sources agree the Roman army was "betrayed by their commander's lack of judgment."[7] He was easily recognizable because of his armor, and the Gauls overwhelmed him. Among those who surrounded Flaminius was Ducario, a chief, who cried out to his compatriots as he beheaded the consul: "Here is the man who decimated our armies, pillaged and plundered our fields and sacked our city (Milan). Now, I, Ducario offer him as a sacrifice to the memory of our people who were massacred."[8] Ducario was from the tribe known as the Insubres, and he had played a leading part in the early resistance to the Roman invasion of the Po Valley. The capital of the Insubres, Milan, had been sacked by the Romans several years before and many of its people killed. It was the custom of the Gauls to decapitate their enemies and keep the heads as trophies.[9] The headless body of Flaminius was stripped of its armor, which went to Ducario as his prize, and then cast upon the mounting piles of dead and dying. When the Roman soldiers saw the head of their consul carried as a trophy by the triumphant Gaul, they lost the heart to continue the fight. Hannibal gave orders to find the body after the battle so the consul could be given a proper burial—but to no avail. The fighting was reportedly so fierce that even when an earthquake shook the region with such force that towns and villages were severely damaged,[10] it was barely noticed by the combatants.

A vanguard of nearly six thousand Roman soldiers had entered the plain and nearly reached the other end when the attack happened. They managed, through a combination of hard fighting and luck, to regroup on a hill at the far end of the plain, and as the early morning fog lifted by late morning, they saw below them what was left of their army. Leaving the hill, they moved to a nearby Etruscan village, where they spent the night. The next day, Hannibal sent a subordinate, Maharbal, with a contingent of cavalry to surround the village. The Romans, hungry and despondent, asked for terms, and Maharbal agreed to spare their lives and allow them to return home. But when the Romans were taken before Hannibal, he refused to honor Maharbal's promise, claiming that his subordinate had exceeded his authority. Hannibal railed against Rome, and when he finished his tirade, agreed to spare their lives in return for ransom.

When the bodies were counted, nearly fifteen thousand Romans had been killed. Pits were dug to burn the dead, probably to prevent disease. At least one of those incineration pits is still visible today, covered by an iron grate in the area of the battlefield. An equal number of Romans were taken prisoner, while another ten thousand managed to escape and eventually make their way back to Rome. Prisoners who were identified as Italians were freed to return home. Hannibal addressed them before they left, telling them he had come to Italy with the sole purpose of freeing them from Roman oppression. If the sources can be believed, Hannibal's casualties were remarkably light in comparison with the Roman losses; thirty of his officers were killed in the fighting, and fifteen hundred of his soldiers—most of whom were Gauls. Funerals were held to honor the dead, and afterward the weapons and armor of the Romans were distributed among the Africans and Spaniards, who came, with their captured shields, helmets, body armor, and weapons, to resemble the very enemy they were fighting.

When news reached Rome that the legions had been defeated at Trasimene and Flaminius killed, panic spread through the city. As soldiers who had escaped from the battlefield slowly began returning over the next several days, the women of Rome, often in groups, ran frantically from one gate to the other, tearing at their hair in anguish, looking for husbands, brothers, and sons who had been with Flaminius, or at least news of them. Crowds assembled at the foot of the Capitoline Hill, demanding explanations from the senate of why their army had been defeated and reassurances that Rome was safe from attack. The magistrate in charge of the city, the praetor Marcus Pomponius, addressed the crowd from the steps of the senate house just before sunset with a taciturn official pronouncement: "We have been beaten in a great battle." Saying no more, he turned and abruptly walked back inside. There was widespread fear throughout the city that Hannibal would be at their gates within days.

From the walls of the city, the women of Rome kept vigil day and night, watching the roads to the north for survivors to appear. As the occasional stragglers drifted in through the gates, they pressed them for news of their loved ones. Rumors of enemy sightings and an impending attack spread, and when it seemed things could not get worse, word arrived that a cavalry detachment of four thousand men, sent by the consul Servillius to support Flaminius at Trasimene, had been ambushed and slaughtered to the last man. The senate remained in continual session from sunrise to sunset each day to debate the next course of action. Rome was in crisis, and in times of crisis the Romans traditionally turned to a dictator to save them. The dictator was the most prestigious and powerful executive office in the Roman administrative hierarchy. Normally, he was appointed by the consuls, but Flaminius was dead and Servillius isolated in the north. Quintus Fabius Maximus was elected by the *comitia centuriata*, the assembly of all Roman citizens; the rich and the poor, the powerful and the weak, came together in their hour of desperation and turned to one man to save them. The powers of the senate and the consuls were suspended for six months. Fabius was entrusted with the defense of the city and was given the keys to the treasury and a mandate to conduct the war against Hannibal as he saw fit. His first course of action was to fortify Rome against attack.

Fabius was fifty-eight at the time of his appointment and nearly thirty years older than Hannibal. His nickname was "Verrucosus," or wartface, and he was an experienced commander who had fought against Carthage in the First Punic War, been elected consul in 233 B.C. and 228 B.C., and granted a triumph by the senate for his campaigns against the Ligurians in northern Italy. Normally, a Roman dictator chose his own deputy, called the Master of Horse, but in a political accommodation to unify the patrician and plebeian classes behind the war effort, Fabius was pressured to accept Marcus Minucius Rufus, a plebeian who had been elected consul in 221 B.C.

Following the victory at Trasimene, Hannibal's officers expected him to march directly against Rome, less than a hundred miles away. But Hannibal had other plans that ran counter to their expectations. Despite resistance from his officers, he turned his army away from the road leading to Rome and headed south and east toward the city of Spoletium (Spoleto). Why Hannibal refused to march on Rome after his victory at Trasimene is a question that has vexed historians for centuries. In hindsight, many believe that if he had, the city would have fallen and the war concluded with a Carthaginian victory. But taking Rome might not have been Hannibal's objective or even possible. The city was protected by a wall, first constructed in the middle of the sixth century B.C. and then substantially fortified after the Gauls nearly sacked the city in 390 B.C. By the third century B.C., Rome's walls were the thickest, highest, and longest defensive barrier in Italy, stretching for nearly seven miles and enclosing over a thousand acres.

To lay siege to a city that size would have required a large amount of engineering equipment and substantially more soldiers than Hannibal commanded. A siege in ancient times is estimated to have required a ratio of ten soldiers to counter every defender manning the walls, vast quantities of supplies, and lots of time. The machines to knock down or undermine thick stone walls would have to be large and heavy—cranes, battering rams, movable towers, and powerful catapults. Because Hannibal had nothing like that with him, the equipment would have to be built, and that alone would have kept his army tied down for months. A siege would have transformed a war of mobility into a static one that carried the risk of neutralizing the military advantage Hannibal had secured after his victories at the Trebbia and Trasimene. Then, there was the additional problem of supplies. The army had to eat, and food would have to be collected and brought in from the countryside on a regular basis. As food and supplies were consumed by the army, the farther out into the countryside the foragers would have to go to find new sources. Finally, a long siege posed a substantial risk that the embers of revolution Hannibal was fanning among the Gauls, Italians, and Greeks might cool and even extinguish if the conflict were confined to Rome. With their short attention spans and no prospects for looting, the Gauls might become bored, pack up, and head back north, while the Italians and Greeks in the south might just decide to hedge their bets, remain neutral, and await the outcome of the siege.

It seems that Hannibal's intent in this war was to fracture the Roman confederation, not to destroy Rome—at least not immediately. His objective was to recalibrate the balance of power in Italy by substantially diminishing the influence of Rome, putting it on a par with the other city-states. In turning south, Hannibal was counting on his army becoming the catalyst for a general insurrection that would sweep the country, not a battering ram to take down city walls. Insurrection, he hoped, would spread through Italy like a firestorm, ignite passions for freedom and strengthen his army with new allies, and bring Rome to its knees or at least to the conference table. As Hannibal's army moved south, his soldiers plundered the countryside, just as they had in Etruria and Tuscany. In a particularly vicious act, Hannibal ordered all adults his army encountered be killed. Ten days after leaving Trasimene, they reached the Adriatic coast in the region of Apulia—carrying so much loot they could barely transport it all. The army that Hannibal proclaimed to be a force for popular liberation had become a horde of criminals devouring everything in their path.

Rome's dictator, Quintus Fabius Maximus, was a cautious man with a very different temperament from Sempronius and Flaminius. He was restrained and calculating in formulating his plans and developed his strategy with considerable forethought. Fabius believed Hannibal and his army were too formidable a force to take head-on—Sempronius and Flaminius had shown what a fatal mistake that could be. So, he settled on a plan to shadow Hannibal at a safe distance, believing that time and attrition, coupled with Rome's vast reserves of manpower and resources, would all work, slowly but invariably, in her favor. The way to defeat Hannibal, Fabius was certain, was to put several Roman armies into the countryside to move against any cities and towns which defected from the confederation. As a result, Fabius hoped, support for Hannibal would slowly diminish as it became evident he could not be everywhere to protect the cities, towns, and villages that joined him from Roman reprisals. The price of defection would become too costly. Without adequate supplies and reinforcements, it would only be a matter of time before Hannibal's Gauls left him and his mercenaries dwindled through desertion, disease, and death. The Roman navy, to an effective degree, controlled most of the coastal areas around Italy and would be able to intercept reinforcements arriving from North Africa or Spain. Only then, when Hannibal's army was worn down sufficiently, isolated and starving, would the Romans converge on it for the final battle.

But the strategy of Fabius did not play well among the Roman people who were filled with anxiety and impatient for an end to the war. After a few months, his caution earned him the derisive title of "cunctator" or delayer and from the floor of the senate, as well as the marketplaces, he was called a coward. Romans referred to him pejoratively as "pedagogus" because they said he followed Hannibal around the countryside like a slave who carries the books of his master's children to and from school. Only later, after the disaster at Cannae and when time demonstrated the value of his strategy, was the title "cunctator" transformed into a participle of praise. Until then, Fabius went about his duties, bearing with dignity the criticisms and insults hurled at him by those he was striving to save.

Along with the election of Fabius as dictator, the senate ordered the elder Scipio to join his brother in Spain and take command of the armies there. The senate hoped that eventually those armies would bring Spain under Roman control and then an attack could be launched directly against Carthage. Rome had the economic resources and the manpower to conduct major operations in three theaters simultaneously—Spain, Italy, and Africa—and Fabius believed that all that was needed to make this plan succeed were time and the patience of the Roman people. The Romans would have to tolerate Hannibal's presence in Italy for another year or two, a virus in the Italian body politic, not strong enough to kill but potent enough to weaken and even incapacitate the patient. Given sufficient time and denied a host, Fabius was sure the Carthaginian virus would die on its own and the patient recover.

From Apulia on the Adriatic coast, Hannibal moved into the interior of Italy—the wealthy province of Campania, which the Romans called the Ager Falernus. His intent must have been to impress several important cities and towns there, among them the wealthy and powerful Capua and Neapolis (Naples). There were smaller cities and towns in the area, like Sinuessa, Cumae, Puteoli, Nola, and Nuceria—all of which would come to play important roles in Hannibal's campaign over the next ten years. In Campania, one of Hannibal's confused the town names Casinum and Casilinum. That took Hannibal off his intended course by miles, and when the mistake was realized the guide was crucified—adding to the Roman portrayal of Hannibal as a cruel barbarian.[11]

In Campania, Fabius held the higher ground, but Hannibal demonstrated his contempt for his Roman adversary as he burned towns and ravaged the villas of the wealthy Romans. He ordered his soldiers to spare those villas which his informants told him belonged to Fabius and his family. Consequently, Fabius was compelled to explain to the senate in Rome as well as his officers in the field that he had not made any deals with Hannibal. At the same time, Fabius continued to resist being drawn into a battle, which he was sure to lose because of the superiority of Hannibal's cavalry. The Greeks and Italians who were allied with Rome saw that Hannibal was effectively in command of the countryside. Many of them were anticipating a spectacular battle to occur at any time, but what they saw instead were the Romans cowering in the hills and Hannibal ranging everywhere unopposed.

Somewhere on the plain between the River Volturnus (Volturno) and Mount Massicus, just north of Capua and south of Pietravairano, occurred one of the most bizarre episodes of Hannibal's campaign in Italy. Fabius was shadowing the Carthaginians as they moved through Campania, avoiding any confrontations by always maintaining a safe defensive position. The Roman commander was sure Hannibal would eventually return to Apulia for the winter months, for while Campania was rich in vineyards and orchards, wine and apples would not sustain Hannibal's army. What he needed were substantial quantities of grain to feed his soldiers, which was more plentiful in Apulia. In anticipation of that move, Fabius secured the main pass over the mountain range that separated the two provinces and waited.[12]

When Hannibal realized Fabius had blocked his return to Apulia, he ordered torches made from the pine knots and dry kindling which could be found on the ground seemingly everywhere. The torches were tied to the horns of some two thousand cattle, which Hannibal's soldiers had pillaged from the surrounding farms and villas and then, under cover of darkness, a contingent of slaves, protected by soldiers, drove them up the hillside toward the pass. When the torches attached to their horns were lit, the animals quickly became unmanageable, they scattered over the hillside. Shaking their heads in panic and causing the torches to burn more vigorously. The soldiers in Fabius's camp believed they were being attacked by Hannibal's army, led by several thousand torch bearers. The Romans guarding the pass thought the hillside was on fire and in a panic deserted their posts. During their escape, they came across some of the cattle and realized too late that they had been tricked.

Fabius, weary of a trap, refused to order a counterattack and kept his soldiers in camp, partly because he was at a loss to know exactly what was happening and because he was resolved to keep to his original strategy and not risk engaging Hannibal in battle. While the Romans remained in their camp, focused on a hillside filled with panicked cattle, Hannibal moved his army quickly over the pass and into Apulia.[13] The episode with the cattle further reinforced the growing belief among the Italians and Greeks of southern Italy that Hannibal could outsmart and outmaneuver the Romans whenever he wanted. Fabius was criticized by his officers for having allowed Hannibal to escape—something which added to their suspicion that he might be in collusion with Hannibal since his family estates in Campania had been spared.[14] Fabius was ordered to appear before the senate in Rome to explain his failure in Campania and address the allegations of collusion with Hannibal. Appearing before the senate, Fabius maintained that the people of Rome should not be critical of him but thankful that the Roman army had not been defeated and was still intact. That explanation was not well received by the senate and, in fact, became the last straw. Wealthy and influential senators were angry because their estates were being burned and looted in Campania while the properties of Fabius and his family remained untouched. Rumors of collusion between Fabius and Hannibal spread throughout the city, and added to the anger of the people who were already critical of Fabius for having allowed Hannibal to escape.

As Fabius's term as dictator came to an end, two new consuls were elected for the forthcoming year, 216 B.C.: Lucius Aemilius Paullus and Gaius Terentius Varro. They had campaigned for office pledging to destroy Hannibal and his army in a decisive encounter, yet neither man had any experience fighting him. Their election was confirmation that the people and the senate of Rome had tired of Fabius. The senate authorized funding for the raising of the largest army in Roman history, eighty thousand soldiers,[15] to be placed under a system of joint command. Paullus and Varro were ordered to move south at the head of the new army, find Hannibal, and in a direct attack, overwhelm his mercenary army with massive numbers. As Paullus and Varro marched out of Rome to the cheers of the people, Fabius warned of their impending doom with the prediction, "If Varro drives straight into battle as he has pledged to do, there will be another loss more terrible than Trasimene."[16]

In Apulia, Hannibal quartered his army for the winter in the town of Gereonium—an area rich in grain. Then, in the late spring, he moved his soldiers south about seventy-five miles and established a camp at Cannae, a deserted fortress a few miles from the sea that was being used by the Romans as a grain storage facility. The area was filled with fields of ripening crops, especially early summer wheat, and it was here that Hannibal decided to give the Romans the fight they were looking for. By the summer of 216 B.C. (late July) the massive Roman army, composed mostly of new conscripts and Italian allies, arrived in the area. The consuls established their camp on a broad plain on the north side of the Aufidus River (now called the Ofanto). Paullus and Varro shared a dual command—an unusual and, as events would prove, a competitive and ineffective method. They alternated command on odd- and even-numbered days and thus no consistent strategy ever developed between them. Drills and tactics depended on who was in command and his prevailing mood. Serious signs of friction began to develop between the two, which became particularly acute and then fatal when the battle commenced.

Paullus was the more cautious of the two and Varro the more impetuous. They paralleled in many respects the personalities of Scipio and Sempronius at the battle of the Trebbia. Paullus respected Hannibal's ability and recognized the advantage his cavalry would have on the wide plains, while Varro was impatient for a quick and decisive win and believed nothing could survive an onslaught by his massive army. When Paullus urged moving the Roman camp into the safety of some nearby hills, Varro insisted they remain on open ground and prepare for the assault he planned to launch. Varro derived a sense of security from the large numbers of his soldiers, and he was openly critical of Paullus in front of the other officers—maintaining that he had come too heavily under the influence of his friend and mentor at Rome, Fabius. Varro prevailed and the Romans stayed where they were while Hannibal, who had initially camped on the south side of the river, now crossed over and established himself directly opposite the Romans.

Over the next several days, both camps were busy preparing for battle. Then, just before dawn on the second of August, 216 B.C., Varro ordered the army to cross to the south bank of the Aufidus. Once on the other side, they turned to face west, their backs to the sea. Paullus, with about sixteen hundred cavalry, commanded the right wing, which was positioned along the river; the infantry were massed in the middle; and Varro took command of five thousand Roman and allied cavalry on the left wing. While this was the standard Roman formation for the deployment of troops in battle, Varro deviated slightly when he ordered the infantry to tighten their ranks. This move compressed the line and restricted the ability of the soldiers to maneuver. The battle line now became narrow and very deep. It was Varro's intention to use an overwhelming concentration of force, a wedge, and burst through the Carthaginian center. That force would be so massive, eighty thousand Roman soldiers pushing forward, that it would simply destroy anything in its path—it was, so Varro thought, unstoppable, and all Hannibal's superior tactics, his cleverness, and the vaunted fighting skills of his mercenaries would have no bearing on the outcome. This was to be a battle, Varro believed, that would be decided by numbers alone.

In response, Hannibal began to deploy his forces, moving his army back across the river and then placing forty thousand infantry and ten thousand cavalry into position facing the Romans. On his left wing, along the river and facing Paullus, Hannibal positioned his Spanish horsemen under the command of Hasdrubal. On his right wing, facing Varro, he placed his Numidians, his best cavalry under the command of his nephew, Hanno. The infantry moved into position between the two wings of cavalry in a long, slightly convex line. Gauls and Spaniards made up most of the first line, while behind them and slightly to either side Hannibal positioned his heavily armed African infantry and other mercenaries. Hannibal and his brother Mago commanded from the center.

The Roman line advanced directly into a hot southwest wind known as the Volturnus (Libeccio). Hannibal had purposely positioned his army so that the Romans would have the wind and the dust in their faces. At the clash of the two lines, Hannibal's Gauls and Spaniards absorbed the initial Roman onslaught, but as the intensity of the attack increased and the full force of the massive Roman line was brought to bear, they began to give way. Then, either by design or circumstance, Hannibal's line began to bend inward at the center, slowly forming a pocket that drew in the Roman vanguard. The Carthaginian army came to resemble an amoeba as it encircled and began to devour the hostile Roman cell within. The more deeply the leading edge of the Roman mass pushed into this pocket, the more densely packed it became. The African heavy infantry, equipped since Trasimene with Roman armor, shields, and swords, were nearly indistinguishable from their adversaries, but Hannibal held them back from the fray, moving them to either side and allowing the Roman army, which resembled a wedge, to penetrate deeper and deeper into the line of Spaniards and Gauls, who slowly but valiantly gave way. What the Romans—from the commanders to the foot soldiers—mistakenly believed was a successful offensive was a slowly unfurling trap prepared by Hannibal.

As the infantry clashed, cavalry battles were being fought on both wings. The Spanish horsemen under the command of Hasdrubal routed the Roman cavalry. Then they circled behind the Roman infantry and reinforced the Numidians fighting under Hanno on the opposite wing. When both wings of the Roman cavalry were routed, Hannibal directed his cavalry to attack the rear elements of the Roman infantry. The Romans, wedged into a tight pocket, were now surrounded by Hannibal's forces on three sides. They were so tightly packed that the sheer mass of their line made it nearly impossible for most of them to use their weapons. They could only push straight ahead as Hannibal's army of forty thousand enveloped them, and a massacre of unimaginable ferocity and proportions began.

It is impossible to determine how many Romans died that August day. Polybius tells us nearly seventy thousand were killed with only 390 horsemen and three thousand infantrymen escaping the carnage. Some ten thousand were taken prisoner.[17] Livy, on the other hand, maintains that number was closer to fifty thousand killed, twenty thousand taken prisoner, and ten thousand escaping.[18] Varro, the architect of the disaster, escaped with a bodyguard and returned to Rome. Paullus, along with about thirty tribunes and eighty senators—men who could have avoided service because of their status—died on the field. Hundreds of Roman knights, known as the equites and distinguished by their gold rings, died that day as well—their rings pried from their fingers after the battle and taken by the bushel (actually a peck, according to Livy) to Carthage by Hannibal's brother Mago, who poured them out on the senate floor for dramatic effect as he announced the victory at Cannae.[19] "Victorious Carthage measured the downfall of Rome by the heap of gold that was torn from the left hands of the slain Roman knights."[20]

If the sources can be believed, Hannibal's losses at Cannae were remarkably light; four thousand Gauls and fifteen hundred Spaniards.[21]

In service academies from West Point and Sandhurst to Saint-Cyr and even Abbottabad in Pakistan, Cannae is taught as an example of the "perfect victory." Hannibal's victory was so lopsided and the numbers of dead so staggering and out of proportion that historians over the last several centuries have expressed skepticism about their accuracy and believe they were exaggerated precisely to emphasize the magnitude of the Roman sacrifice and the heroic recovery.

Fabius was right—the defeat was even worse than what had happened at Trasimene over a year earlier. Clearly, neither the senate nor the Roman high command had learned from the experience. Hannibal won at Cannae because he had carefully thought through his strategy before the battle began and then coordinated the experienced elements of his army to achieve his victory. The Romans lost because the commanders of their armies, and the politicians at Rome, believed that sheer will and numbers would prevail over careful planning, a well-integrated and coordinated command structure, effective battlefield execution, restraint, patience, and experience.

When news of the defeat reached Rome, a worse panic swept the city than the one that had resulted after the defeat at Trasimene. The wealthy made plans to leave the city, while the poor flocked to the temples and begged the priests to consult Rome's most sacred documents, the Sibylline Books, for divine guidance and protection. The loss of so many men at Cannae allegedly drove the women of Rome to consort with slaves and barbarians so their race would not disappear. In their fright, the people of Rome lost all reason and resorted to human sacrifice to appease the anger of their gods and keep Hannibal at bay.[22] In the central marketplace, the Forum Boarium, or pig market, crowds assembled to watch the sacrifice of a man and woman from Gaul, followed by a couple from Greece. On the surface, the sacrifices might have been carried out to appease the gods and safeguard Rome from Hannibal, but they also served as a warning to the Gauls and the Greeks in Italy of the consequences of deserting the confederation to support Hannibal.

When the Romans recovered their sanity, they turned to the defense of their city. To raise morale, women were forbidden to mourn in public for their husbands, brothers, and sons who died at Cannae, and the senate acknowledged that Fabius had been right in his strategy. All males over the age of sixteen were ordered to report for military service, and two new legions were formed from debtors and criminals who were released from the prisons in large numbers. The Romans enlisted eight thousand slave volunteers, purchased from private owners by the state with a promise to pay their value after the war ended and offering the slaves the promise of freedom for those who survived. The use of slaves as soldiers became increasingly frequent to offset manpower shortages. Hannibal was reduced to using slaves as soldiers in Bruttium in 204 B.C. and in Africa at the battle of Zama in 202 B.C.

Following the battle, Hannibal addressed the Roman prisoners and their Italian allies, but taking a more conciliatory attitude than he had done at Trasimene. He offered to send emissaries to Rome to discuss a peace treaty and their ransom. He explained that he was not making war to annihilate Rome or fighting "a war to the death." Rather he was in Italy fighting for his honor and the freedom of Italians from Roman domination.[23] Hannibal expected that following his victory at Cannae, the Romans would be ready to negotiate a peace, and from this conciliatory speech, it can be inferred that he intended Rome would remain a regional power in Italy, counterbalanced by the Greek city-states in the south.

Hannibal's officers, elated at the victory, begged him to take the initiative and move against Rome immediately. But as he had at Trasimene, Hannibal hesitated. Maharbal, one of the cavalry commanders, argued that his men could be at the city gates in as little as four days of hard riding and Hannibal dining there the week after. But Hannibal remained steadfast in his refusal to march on Rome and Maharbal responded angrily: "Vincere scis, Hannibal, Victoria uti nescis"[24] ("You know how to win, Hannibal, but not how to use a victory"). But Hannibal was unmoved by the criticism and waited to assess the impact of his victory on Rome and on the cities and towns of southern Italy.

Confident that the Romans would ask for an end to the war, Hannibal sent one of his most trusted lieutenants, Carthalo, to Rome, to negotiate on his behalf. The Romans had sustained three major defeats in less than two years, each successively more devastating than the one before, but then reaction was not what Hannibal expected. The Roman senate refused to receive Carthalo or even allow him to enter the city, much less discuss peace and the ransom of prisoners. Sixty years earlier, a victorious Greek king, Pyrrhus, had a similar experience with Roman tenacity and intransigence. After a successful campaign in southern Italy, he offered to negotiate peace terms and allow the Romans to ransom their prisoners. They would never negotiate as long as he remained on Italian soil. So, Pyrrhus simply packed up and went back to Greece, commenting that victory against the Romans was not worth the price. The Roman mentality had not changed, and even now, after the worst defeat in their history and in their darkest hour, they remained steadfast in their resolve to see the war out to its conclusion. When Hannibal received word that the Romans would not negotiate a peace or even ransom their soldiers, he vented his anger on his captives. He repeated on a larger scale, what he had done to the Gauls when his army first came down from the Alps. Roman prisoners were selected for paired combat and made to fight each other, brothers against brothers and fathers against sons. But this time there was no offer of freedom to the victor. In one of these combats, difficult to place precisely in time, Hannibal ordered a Roman soldier to fight an elephant. To the amazement of everyone, the soldier slew the beast and was released to return home. But Hannibal, concerned that word would spread that his elephants could be killed by a single soldier, sent a cavalry detachment to overtake and kill the Roman as he walked along the road.

Cannae was Hannibal's greatest moment as a battlefield commander. He had reached the height of his success against the Romans, but following that victory he would enter a period of long but steady decline, a slow but debilitating hemorrhage, resulting in a loss of initiative and his eventual departure from Italy. The war in Italy would not see another battle of similar magnitude. Hannibal's failure to march against Rome after Cannae saved the republic—but perhaps that was his intention all along. Livy writes that years later, Hannibal regretted not having moved against Rome immediately after Cannae—admitting it was a lost opportunity to win the war. He excused his reluctance by contending that while the victory at Cannae was stunning, the idea of marching on Rome was "too vast and too joyous for his mind to grasp."[25] Interestingly, the Roman poet Silius Italicus, in his epic poem *Punica*, offers a slightly different perspective on Hannibal's emotions after Cannae and the reason he refused to march on Rome.[26] According to Italicus, Hannibal was angry because the gods had given him a victory at Cannae, but not over Rome. Exhausted after the battle, Hannibal fell into a deep sleep in which he only dreamed of a victorious march on Rome. The next day, citing the need for the wounds of his soldiers to heal and warning of the dangers of overconfidence, he ordered the army to remain in camp.

Following Cannae there was no force on the Italian mainland that could challenge Hannibal. He could go wherever he liked, except Rome, and no one could resist him. As we will see in the next chapter, towns and cities once allied to Rome, those in Samnium, Apulia, Lucania, Campania, and Bruttium, now went over to him, and across the sea in Macedonia, Philip V, eager to drive the Romans from Illyria (Albania, Bosnia, and Croatia), concluded a pact of mutual assistance with Hannibal a few months later. But Rome's most important allies, those in central Italy and geographically and culturally closest to the city—Latium,

Umbria, and Etruria—remained loyal, and in the end, that loyalty, coupled with Roman tenacity, saved the republic.

In northern Italy, the Gallic tribes once more began making trouble for Rome. In the late spring of 216 B.C., the senate appointed Lucius Postumius Albinus as praetor and sent him with an army of twenty-five thousand to pacify the area just as Paullus and Varro were entering Apulia in the south, looking for Hannibal. Albinus had been called from retirement because the senate was short of experienced military leaders and Albinus had experience. He had been elected consul on two occasions and conducted successful campaigns against the Ligurians and the Illyrians.

In sending an army to northern Italy, the Romans hoped to pressure the Gauls serving with Hannibal to desert him and return to defend their homes. The army of Albinus moved toward the Roman colony at Placentia, and somewhere along the route the legions passed the edge of a dense forest called the Litana Silva—probably in the area around modern-day Modena. The Gauls had set an ambush at the entrance to the forest where large trees lined both sides of the road. While the trees appeared intact to the casual observer, many had been partially cut at the base, enough to weaken them but not cause them to fall. Once the Roman army was through the defile, the Gauls pushed the trees over, crushing the Romans under them. Then the Gauls moved in to slay any survivors trapped under the fallen trunks and branches. Albinus tried to escape, but was caught and decapitated—his skull carried off to be cleaned, adorned with gold, and used to pour libations at festivals.[27]

Word reached Rome of the massacre at about the same time that the news of the loss at Cannae arrived. Two devastating losses had to be absorbed, and for a period Rome became eerily quiet. Shops closed and people remained indoors. The consul Tiberius Sempronius called for a special session of the senate and urged the Roman people not to lose heart. The senate decided to concentrate all its efforts on defeating

Hannibal in the south and abandoned, for the immediate future, any war against the Gauls in the north. There would be time after Hannibal was defeated, Sempronius argued, to even the score. The senate voted to leave northern Italy, the area known as Gallia Cisalpina, out of any campaign plans for that year, and Sempronius ordered shops in the city opened and public mourning curtailed. It would be business as usual in Rome.

Despite their victory in the forest and the obvious Roman weakness after Cannae, the Gauls never moved south, either to reinforce Hannibal or attack Rome. Even the areas around the Roman colonies at Placentia and Cremona remained relatively quiet until Hannibal left Italy. Then the Gauls, under the leadership of a Carthaginian officer left behind by one of Hannibal's brothers, attacked with a vengeance and sparked a new war.

With the devastating Roman defeats at Cannae and the Litana Silva, the war should have ended, if not in a Carthaginian victory, at least in a truce. Hannibal was confronted by a Roman intransigence and willingness to sustain whatever casualties and devastation it took to see the war through to its conclusion. The Romans would not yield and this confounded the Carthaginian commander who, himself, accepted compromise rarely.

CHAPTER V

The Ebbing Tide

Following Hannibal's rapid and stunning victories at the Trebbia, Trasimene, and Cannae, the conflict entered a prolonged and inconclusive phase. For the next thirteen years, from 216 B.C. until 203 B.C., the war settled down to a long period of indecisive maneuvering and intermittent fighting in southern Italy, with each side vying for control of people and resources. It became a period characterized by innumerable assaults and sieges of cities and towns by both sides, with severe retaliatory actions against the civilian populations, whether warranted by their levels of resistance or not. Hannibal moved against any city or town that remained loyal to Rome or even neutral in the conflict. One was either with Hannibal or against him. Those that did come over to him came under intense military, economic, and political pressure from the Romans. Roman reprisals, which were frequent, widespread, and often highly punitive, forced Hannibal to divide and thereby weaken his army to protect as many of his new allies as possible. In areas where Hannibal was not present, the Romans would go on the offensive against towns and cities that had defected, putting considerable pressure on him to come to their aid. With his limited resources, Hannibal simply could not be everywhere at once and in the end, this,

probably more than any other reason, may account for his failure to
unite the Italians and Greeks of southern Italy and bring the war to a
successful conclusion.

During this phase, Hannibal operated in an area of Italy that
stretched from just north of Naples to as far south as Rhegium and the
Strait of Messina. His army moved across the landscape at will as the
Roman legions either followed him at a safe distance in an attempt to
wear him down or retaliated against any of the city-states and towns
which declared for him. After Cannae, the Romans reverted to a modified form of Fabius's plan: they tended to minimize direct confrontations with Hannibal, recognizing that while they had the advantage in
sheer numbers, they were no match for him when it came to battlefield
tactics and the quality of his fighting forces. The armies of both sides
ravaged southern Italy—the provinces of Campania, Samnium, Apulia,
Lucania (Basilicata), and Bruttium (Calabria). While Hannibal concentrated his efforts on bringing the Greek city-states and the Italian
tribes over to his side, the Romans, in response, tried to prevent their
defection. Both sides used everything from promises, rewards, bribery,
threats, and subterfuge to assaults, sieges, and public executions.

Hannibal needed allies because he had little hope of significant reinforcements from Spain or North Africa. His army was forced to live off
the land, and he avoided, for the most part, seeking battlefield victories.
He did, however, always welcome a confrontation when an impetuous
and overconfident Roman commander was foolish enough to challenge
him. Over the next several years, there would be several smaller battles
fought in southern Italy, but Hannibal's major effort was directed to
bringing towns and cities into alliance with him through either direct
assault or diplomacy.

The Greeks and Italians of southern Italy were often divided among
themselves into pro-Roman and pro-Carthaginian factions. In general, the wealthier, aristocratic elements in these towns and cities were

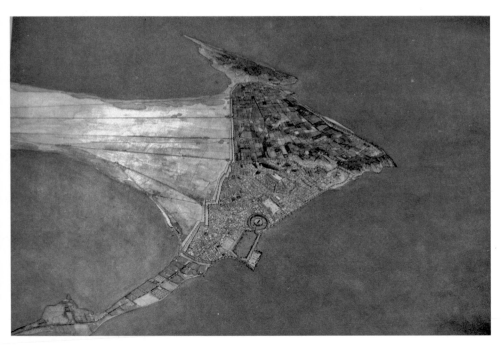

1 and 2: Representations of the ancient city currently on display at the site museum at Carthage in Tunisia.

3: Some of the ruins of ancient Carthage on the Byrsa, the highest point on the site and facing south toward modern-day Tunis in the background. The excavations contain examples of both Carthaginian and later Roman building styles.

4: Excavations of dry dock facilities located at the port of Carthage.

5: The ruins of Saguntum (modern-day Sagunto in Spanish and Sagunt in Catalan) are just a few kilometers north of Valencia. The city was allied to Rome and when attacked by Hannibal became the ostensible cause or pretext for the start of the Second Punic War. The view is looking east toward the Mediterranean Sea. While the walls and buildings date mostly from the medieval period, there are elements in the foundations and many artifacts on display in the site museum which date from the time of Hannibal and the later Roman occupation.

6: Hannibal's Rhone River crossing point at Beaucaire-Tarascon in Southern France.

7: The approach through the Durance River valley to the highest and final Alpine barrier between France and Italy. To the left, following the Durance River, is the easiest route over the mountains, while to the right is the entrance to the treacherous Comb du Queyras and the valley of the Guil—a quicker but more difficult passage.

8: The narrowest spot in the Comb du Queyras and probably where Hannibal and his army were ambushed by the Gauls and nearly annihilated.

9: The massive rock on which Hannibal and his men sought safety after their ambush. On top of the rock is the Chateau Queyras, a fortification designed by the French minister Vauban, the foremost military engineer of the seventeenth century. The Chateau is currently open to the public.

10: The lush valley of the Guil, a cul-de-sac, with Mount Viso looming in the background. Once they entered this narrow valley, Hannibal and his army had no choice but to push ahead and find a way over the mountains and into Italy.

11 and 12: The solid wall of ice and snow that the ancient sources tell us awaited Hannibal and his army at the end of the valley of the Guil. Mount Viso is the second highest mountain in the French Alps, and in this photograph is viewed from the French side with the infamous and treacherous Col de la Traversette nestled on its left. In the foreground is the probable campground used by Hannibal and his army.

13: The author and his students on the final ascent to the Traversette in summer. This pass is one of the very few in the French Alps which has snow on it all year round as described in the ancient manuscripts.

14: The author reclining at nearly ten thousand feet on the ledge of the Traversette after lunch, with his longtime friend and Alpine guide, Bruno Martin, and Bruno's daughter Savirine.

15: The view of Italy from the top of the pass. Using this view Hannibal inspired his men to overcome their despondency and inspire them to continue on to conquer Rome. The Traversette is one of only a very few passes in the Alps which offer such an unobstructed view.

16: The Trebbia River in northern Italy and the site of Hannibal's first victory against a Roman army.

17 and 18: An unusual monument erected on the south bank of the Trebbia by the Rotary Club of the Valli Del Nure e Della Trebbia to commemorate the battle by showing one of Hannibal's elephants with its mahout and soldiers.

19: Lake Trasimeno in central Italy and the site of Hannibal's second spectacular victory against the Romans as viewed from the heights to the north.

20: Cannae the site of Hannibal's greatest victory against the largest army ever assembled in Roman history. Cannae is the apex of the Carthaginian's career as a military commander. The view of the battlefield is looking northwest from the highest point.

21: Hannibal, *victorious at Cannae* is represented holding an inverted captured legionary standard while standing on the shields and swords of the fallen Roman soldiers. The statue is by Sebastien Slodt, the seventeenth century sculptor, and currently on display in the Musée du Louvre in Paris.

22: Temple ruins at Metapontum, an ancient Greek city just south of Tarentum which was allied to Hannibal.

23: Medieval fortifications at modern-day Naples, the ancient Greek city of Neapolis and an important port. Hannibal tried repeatedly to take the city and failed each time because of its imposing fortifications.

24: A second Century, A.D. Roman reproduction of an original Greek depiction of a cavalryman from the third century B.C. at the Naples Archeological Museum. The example gives the reader a good indication of how horsemen both in Hannibal's army and the Roman army would have been dressed and armed.

25: The Metaurus River near Ancona on the Adriatic coast. This unimpressive muddy and slow moving river, just a few miles from the sea, was the site of the most decisive battle of the Second Punic War. The defeat of Hannibal's brother, Hasdrubal, at the Metaurus invariably condemned Hannibal and Carthage to lose the war.

26: The entrance to the double harbors at Tarentum protected by the citadel. While the citadel is medieval its foundations are most probably Greek and Roman dating to the time of Hannibal and even earlier. The port city was crucial for control of the south-eastern Italian coastline and Hannibal needed it to maintain contact with Carthage.

27: The modern Italian town of Crotone and the site of a famous ancient Greek city. In this city, Hannibal and his army were confined by the surrounding Roman armies. Isolated and angry, Hannibal spent his last two years in Italy there, as the focus of the war between Carthage and Rome shifted to Spain and North Africa.

28: A single column looking out to the sea and some scattered ruins of a foundation are all that remain of a once magnificent Greek temple in which Hannibal posted the story of his epic struggle against Rome.

29: A section of the ruins in the ancient city of Gortyn on the island of Crete. Hannibal fled to Gortyn after the defeat of his protector, King Antiochus, by the Romans. It was here, in this remote location in the center of the island, that he sought a brief respite in his never-ending struggle against Rome.

30: Hannibal's castle on the Gulf of Izmit in Eskihisar, Turkey is on the Asian side of the Bosporus and about an hour's drive east of Istanbul. The seemingly abandoned structure is clearly medieval, but, once more, as in other examples in this book, its foundations give evidence of a much earlier even ancient building. While there is no direct evidence to link this castle to the place where Hannibal ended his life, it is in the right location and as any visitor will quickly discern, it fits the mood.

31: The Hannibalin Mezari or Hannibal's tomb is located just a mile from the castle on a remote hilltop. The hard to find Mezari is not really a tomb but rather a monument to Hannibal built in 1934 on the order of Mustafa Kemal Ataturk, the founder of modern Turkey, to commemorate the hundredth anniversary of Ataturk's birth. (Ataturk was born in 1881 and died in 1938, so why the monument commemorates his hundredth anniversary is a mystery to everyone but the Turks).

pro-Roman, and some even had limited degrees of citizenship because of their close ties with Rome through marriage and financial dealings. At the other extreme were the working classes and the peasants in the countryside, those who had no stake in the status quo and saw in Hannibal a chance for a new beginning. Hannibal promised them freedom from Roman cultural domination and economic oppression, and for those who cooperated, there were additional enticements of a new and more prosperous future. For those who refused or hesitated, punishment could be quick and severe—everything from public beheadings to steaming people to death in the public baths.

The Romans were equally harsh in retaliating against those who left the confederation to join Hannibal. Sections of the countryside between the Adriatic and the Tyrrhenian Seas often became a no-man's-land, and control depended on which army was passing through at what particular time and how long it stayed. Hannibal could not draw the Roman legions to fight him on open ground, and at the same time he could not protect all the towns and cities that had declared for him. The Romans, on the other hand, could be everywhere at once. Their manpower reserves and economic resources allowed them to go after those who defected with a vengeance. With multiple armies operating in southern Italy at the same time, they could be in more than one place, forcing Hannibal to continually divide and weaken his forces. The Romans focused on supporting their allies who remained loyal against assaults by Hannibal and punishing those who had defected. Both armies laid siege to towns and cities, burned the countryside, and executed those they suspected of collaboration with the other side. The cost in human suffering and economic loss must have been enormous.

The longer the war dragged on, the greater Rome's chances for victory. Rome had a base of nearly three-quarters of a million men of fighting age to draw upon across Italy, even following the devastating losses in the early battles of the war. The Roman armies had several hundred thousand men under arms doing everything from garrisoning cities allied to Rome to serving in the legions posted throughout Italy, Spain, Sicily, and Sardinia. While the Roman soldiers were not trained and experienced to the level of Hannibal's mercenaries, there were enough of them that Rome could afford to lose ten for every enemy killed and still win the war. The numbers of the Roman legions increased as the years passed, while Hannibal's forces gradually diminished, their numbers reduced thorough death, disease, and desertions. In 215 B.C., the Romans were able to put between twelve and fifteen legions in the field; by 212 B.C., that number had increased to twenty-five—amounting to well over one hundred thousand infantry and cavalry.

In southern Italy, the Romans divided their armies and kept to higher ground on the fringes of the Apennine mountain range. They avoided engaging Hannibal on wide, level stretches of land where he could employ his cavalry and elephants to his advantage. Even with Hannibal's tactical ability, he could not force the Romans onto level ground to fight a decisive battle on his terms. With their multiple smaller armies, the Romans became increasingly aggressive in striking his Greek and Italian allies. Cities under siege or the threat of siege demanded Hannibal come to their aid, and when he could not, confidence in his ability to defeat Rome weakened. Despite Hannibal's tactical genius, he could not overcome the Roman advantage in manpower and resources. The Romans had the resolve to keep up the struggle against him at any cost and refused to compromise.

The Roman navy effectively blockaded large sections of the Italian coastline, preventing a steady stream of reinforcements from reaching Hannibal. Because of their manpower reserves, the Romans were eventually able to carry the war to Spain and Sicily, even while Hannibal occupied southern Italy. War made the republic stronger; its leaders, both political and military, learned from their mistakes and had plenty of replacements to fill the slots of those captured, wounded, and killed.

Rome's Italian allies in Latium, Umbria, and Etruria remained, for the most part, loyal, providing the manpower, money, and supplies needed to continue the war to a successful conclusion. Hannibal was forced to divide his army into smaller units, placing them under capable commanders and sending them out to protect his new allies. There is little reliable information in the sources on the size and composition of his army during these years in southern Italy, but the core of veterans who left Spain with him in 218 B.C. and crossed the Alps must have been considerably diminished after the battles at the Trebbia, Trasimene, and Cannae, despite the light casualties reported in the ancient sources.

Hannibal's army was a mixture of soldiers brought together from the corners of the ancient world and fighting for the spoils of war. They spoke different languages, followed different customs, and worshipped different gods—but the common bond that held them together, at least in the beginning, must have been Hannibal's leadership as well as money. He brought them together, trained them, paid them, and most importantly inspired them to follow him and remain loyal through trying times even when the money was slow in coming. They became unbeatable on the battlefield and remained loyal even as it must have become evident to them, especially in the last few years, that their commander was losing his war. This has come down to us as Hannibal's most admirable quality and testimony to his ability as a leader. Certainly new recruits must have filled their ranks, coming mostly from the Gauls of northern Italy and the Italians (Brutti) and Greeks of the south. Reinforcements, including elephants, were able to reach Hannibal from North Africa on at least one occasion, arriving on the southern Adriatic coast at Locri.

Southern Italy and the eastern part of the island of Sicily were collectively known as Magna Graecia or Greater Greece. They had been colonized by Greeks looking for fertile land and economic opportunities as early as the eighth century B.C. Campania and Apulia were among

the most fertile of these areas and contained some of the most prosperous cities in Italy. Campania occupied a narrow zone between the Tyrrhenian Sea on the western coast of Italy and the Apennine Mountains.
According to the ancient sources, the province surpassed all others in
terms of its natural resources, and even in ancient times it was a favored
holiday resort for Romans because the summer heat was tempered by
a brisk sea breeze. The natural wealth of the area could, in large part,
be attributed to Mont Vesuvius, which over millennia had layered the
land with a rich coating of phosphorus and potash. Campania became
a center of olive and grape production, and its wines, including the dry
and strong Falernian (sherry), were exported throughout the Mediterranean world.

Among the most important cities along the western coast of the province were Cumae, the oldest of the Greek colonies; Neapolis (Naples), a
major port; and Capua, which had been founded by the Etruscans in the
late sixth century B.C. and was the wealthiest of the three. While these
cities were tied to Rome by treaty, each one retained its own language,
form of government, and laws. There were several Greek cities on the
eastern seaboard of southern Italy that were also prosperous: Crotone,
Petelia, Sybaris, Heraclea, Metapontum, and Tarentum. Sybaris, like
Capua, had a reputation for luxury and wealth, and Crotone had been
the home of the mathematician Pythagoras and long a center of culture,
medicine, and science. Tarentum (Taranto) initially had been a Spartan
colony with the best natural harbor on the eastern coast of Italy. Though
prosperous and culturally advanced, the cities on both coasts never joined
together to form a unified political entity. They alternated between periods of cooperation and rivalry, often forming temporary political and
economic networks, but all the while remaining fiercely independent as
city-states, each one loosely connected by culture to its founding city on
the Greek mainland. Some of these cities saw in Hannibal an opportunity to contain if not stifle the influence and control Rome was coming

to establish over southern Italy and an opportunity to play one side off against the other. They would negotiate with Rome and Hannibal, looking for the best deal and then switching sides as events and changes of fortune warranted—something which proved to be a dangerous gambit and often led to the destruction of those who played it.

The interior portions of southern Italy were a world apart from the coastal regions. They were largely undeveloped and inhabited mostly by Italian tribes and clans, among them the Lucanians and the Brutti—a more primitive and considerably less prosperous people. Over the centuries, they came, to varying degrees, under the cultural influence of their Greek neighbors, and some of them adopted Greek styles of architecture, art, religion, and even language. Traveling today through southern Italy, especially along the Adriatic coast, it is easy to see why Hannibal focused on this area. The ruins of Greek towns and cities line the coast and the terrain tends to be flat, wide, and fertile. The lay of the land would have made moving and feeding an army much easier than in the mountainous areas of central and western Italy. In addition, southern Italy was much closer to North Africa by sea, and, along with Sicily, would have made a natural extension to a restored maritime empire for Carthage. At one point Hannibal apparently considered having his army dig a canal across the narrow and most southern section of the peninsula to isolate it from the mainland.

Immediately after Hannibal's victory at Cannae, some of the Greek cities and towns in the area around the battlefield began to defect. The Apulian towns of Salapia (Manfredonia), Arpi (whose ruins are just northeast of modern Foggia), and Herdonia (just south of Foggia, off the autostrada, at the small town of Orta Nova) left the Roman confederation when Hannibal offered them treaties of friendship with Carthage and freedom from Roman taxation and cultural oppression. They were promised there would be no obligation for military service and that they could live in a prosperous new Italy with mutually beneficial

economic ties to Carthage. Hannibal utilized the rhetoric of popular liberation and self-determination. He exploited the political factions within
those cities to his own advantage as he cut deals and offered financial
and military support to whichever factions could be of use to him in his
struggle against Rome. His promises resonated with the impoverished—
the working classes in the cities and the peasants in the countryside.
But in general, the wealthy aristocratic elements in the cities rejected
his call because they were tied to Rome through marriage alliances and
economic arrangements that were more profitable and stable.

From Cannae, Hannibal moved his army west and occupied the
town of Compsa (Conza della Campania), which lay on the boundary
between the provinces of Lucania (Basilicata) and Campania. Its leadership was divided between two mutually hostile clans, the Hirpini and
the Mopsi. The Hirpini supported Hannibal and with his help drove
out the pro-Roman and aristocratic Mopsi. Hannibal garrisoned the
town, using it to store his army's baggage and the massive amount of
valuables and weapons taken at Cannae. Scenarios like what occurred
at Compsa began to play out in other cities and towns in southern Italy
as well. In Salapia, one of the leaders, Dasius, betrayed the city to Hannibal in return for his help in driving out a pro-Roman faction led by
one of his rivals.[1]

At Compsa, Hannibal divided his army into three groups. He sent
one group south into Lucania and Bruttium under the command of his
younger brother Mago, his nephew Hanno, and another of his principal commanders, Himilco. The Bruttians would prove to be fertile
ground for recruitment as they had long resented the Romans and at
the same time were envious of the prosperous Greek city-states along
the Adriatic coast. By joining Hannibal, they saw an opportunity to
remove the Roman yoke and at the same time profit by plundering any
Greek cities that resisted joining him as allies. Mago, Hanno, and Himilco further divided their forces and Himilco undertook to lay siege to

Petelia (Strongoli), a Greek city on the coast. The Petelians were among the most loyal of Rome's allies and they held out for nearly a year, until the siege brought them to a state of starvation, reducing them to eating leather, grass, and tree bark.[2] The defenders managed to send a desperate plea for help to Rome, but the reply was that given their remote and isolated location in the extreme south, they were on their own. Still, the Petelians fought to the last, and when the city was taken, Himilco gave it over to the Bruttians to plunder. Most of its people were killed, and those who survived were sold into slavery.

Using Petelia as an example of what would befall those who rejected an offer of alliance with Hannibal, Mago negotiated agreements with other Greek cities along the southern Adriatic coast and assaulted those that refused or even hesitated. After a short stay in Bruttium, Mago left by ship for Carthage, probably from the port of Locri on the extreme southern tip of Italy, to carry the news of Hannibal's victory at Cannae and ask the senate for reinforcements and money to continue the war. Hanno and Himilco remained in the area and continued to lay siege to towns and recruit new soldiers.

Hannibal left Compsa with his main force and moved once again into the province of Campania to secure a port on the Tyrrhenian Sea. The area around Neapolis constituted a defensive line of fortified cities allied with Rome; among the most prominent were Capua, Acerrae, Suessula, Cumae, Nola, Nuceria, and Casilinum. They were tied together by the Roman highway, the Via Latina, and protected for Rome what was probably her most valuable agricultural region. The area had an accessible coastline with several important ports in addition to Neapolis; the most notable being Cumae (just twelve miles west of Naples) and Puteoli (modern-day Pozzuoli, just a few miles south of Naples). This was Hannibal's second incursion into Campania following his spectacular night-time escape out of the valley using cattle with firebrands tied to their horns.

Neapolis was the prize that Hannibal sought initially. The city had been founded by the Greeks in the sixth century B.C., and its name translates as "the new city." A base there would make for shorter and quicker communication lines with Carthage and provide easier access to reinforcements and supplies from North Africa and Spain. Carthage to Neapolis is a distance of 313 nautical miles. With favorable winds and relatively calm seas, it could be crossed in ancient times in three or at most four days. The voyage from Neapolis would avoid a longer and more treacherous passage from the Adriatic side of Italy and around the often stormy and dangerous southeastern coast of Sicily. When Hannibal arrived and saw the massive fortifications and the sizable Roman garrison protecting the city, he abandoned any idea of a siege and turned his attention to the smaller city of Capua just a few miles to the north.

If he could not take Neapolis, then Capua was Hannibal's second choice. It was one of the largest cities in Italy at the time and very wealthy.[3] According to the ancient sources, its people had been corrupted by the "excesses of democracy" and they set no limit when it came to luxury. Capua, by Roman standards of morality and civic duty, was corrupt because its people had enjoyed so many decades of freedom, they had lost any sense of restraint and discipline. Their wealth was so great that they had access to more than they could possibly want and enjoy. This portrayal of Capua reflects a traditional Roman republican belief that unbridled freedom and extravagance are the ruination of a people. For the Romans of the early republic, what was most desirable was a society of people who were simple living, patriotic, civic minded, religious, and morally upright. That view would change radically following the end of the war with Hannibal, as Rome transitioned from a simple republic to a wealthy empire in the century following.

Capua willingly went over to Hannibal and in so doing provided him with an arsenal of some of the best-quality weapons available in the ancient world. The city was a prosperous manufacturing center which, in addition to making armaments and glass, excelled in the production of perfume. The perfume market or *seplasia* at Capua was recently excavated, and its remains support literary references to the ancient inhabitants' love of luxury. Another indicator of Capua's wealth are hoards of coins that have been found and dated to the period of Hannibal's occupation, 216–211 B.C. The city also produced finished metalwares from iron and copper that were exported all over the ancient world— even as far as Scotland.

Hannibal had demonstrated to the people of Capua that he could annihilate Roman armies on the battlefield, and he promised them, in return for joining him early on in his campaign, a prominent place in the new Italy he was creating. He assured the leaders that their city would become the legal and commercial center of a new confederation of Italian and Greek city-states, and that at the end of the war he would return the Ager Falernus, the fertile river valley that had been taken from them by Rome two centuries before.[4]

The leaders of Capua were clever businessmen and intended to play both sides against the middle to negotiate the best deal for themselves. Before coming to terms with Hannibal, they sent a delegation to the Roman consul at nearby Venusia (Venosa, not far from Compsa), indicating they were open to considering any inducements he might be inclined to offer them to remain within the confederation. In response, the consul reminded the envoys of their city's long association with Rome, the prosperity that had come their way as a result, and the Roman expectation that Capua would honor its prior commitments by contributing men and money in the fight against Hannibal.[5]

The delegation returned to Capua and reported the consul's response to the senate. The senate circumvented the consul, going over his head and sending emissaries directly to Rome to seek a better deal. The emissaries demanded, as a condition of remaining an ally, that one of the two annually elected Roman consuls had to come from Capua. The consuls were the highest executive officers in Rome, and not only did they command Roman armies in time of war, but they administered the state. They were second only to the dictator in their power. Rome rejected the demand out of hand and ordered the envoys to leave the city before sundown. The senate at Capua then sent a delegation to Hannibal, who quickly agreed to everything they asked. To seal the deal, Hannibal assured them Capua would become the most powerful and prosperous city in Italy once the war ended.

Despite Hannibal's promises, the delegation demanded carefully delineated terms as the price for their defection. First, they required that no citizen of theirs would be obliged to serve with Hannibal's army against his will, and second, that Capua would retain its own form of government and laws free from Carthaginian interference or oversight. As a final inducement, Hannibal agreed to exchange three hundred of his most prized Roman captives for an equal number of young men from the aristocratic families of Capua who were serving with the Roman cavalry in Sicily at the time. While these young men were serving officially as Roman auxiliaries, there is some doubt that their service was entirely voluntary. They might well have been kept as hostages to insure the loyalty of their city to Rome.

Capua defected and Hannibal entered the city to a hero's welcome. Crowds lined the streets to see the man who had brought Rome to its knees at Cannae. There is an interesting difference of opinion in the sources concerning the composition of the crowd that welcomed Hannibal that day. One source contends that Hannibal was greeted and escorted into the city by the senators and a crowd of the poor—the rabble, or *turba*, as the Romans called them—while the second source maintains it was the aristocrats with their wives and children who welcomed him.[6] From the outset, Hannibal exerted his authority over the city. He was a tyrant and reputed to have been "naturally short-tempered," and inclined to fits of rage. He displayed the characteristics of a self-centered autocrat from the moment he passed through the city gates. A mob, seeking to curry favor with him, rounded up all Romans in the city, permanent residents, visitors there on business or pleasure, and officials, and confined them to one of the municipal bathhouses. Then the doors were sealed and the prisoners were suffocated, dying in great agony. This story has often been regarded by modern scholars with skepticism because it was reported by Livy, who was markedly pro-Roman and critical of Capua.[7] It was not Hannibal who ordered their deaths; they were killed by a mob. Yet Hannibal never condemned the action. A variation of the story reappears in another later source, which reports that when Hannibal captured the nearby town of Nuceria, he ordered the pro-Roman senators there locked into the baths and steamed to death. These stories might have been invented by the Roman historians for propaganda purposes, to portray Hannibal in the worst possible light, or, conversely, they may well be true.

With the most immediate sources of opposition out of the way, Hannibal's next order of business was to address the senate. Its members prevailed upon him to postpone any serious discussions until later in his visit and spend the day sightseeing in the city. Hannibal, always inclined to get down to business first, but not wishing to offend his new allies, begrudgingly agreed. During his tour, he showed little interest in the usual sights, such as temples and marketplaces, but questioned his guides incessantly about the number of men the city had under arms; the length, height, and thickness of its walls; grain supplies; and how much money was in the treasury.

At the end of the tour, Hannibal was invited to stay in the home of two brothers, the Celeres, who were among the wealthiest and most influential senators in Capua. To honor their guest, the brothers arranged a feast "that tempted indulgence and was to be expected in a city and in a house of such wealth and luxury."[8] Banquets were held throughout the city to honor Hannibal's soldiers. Tables were piled high with

dishes of regional gastronomical splendor, and the wine that Capua was
famous for flowed in unlimited quantities. At Hannibal's insistence, the
banquet at the home of the Celeres was limited to a select few: the two
brothers who hosted the affair, the son of one of the brothers, and a
"distinguished soldier," Vibellius Taurea, foremost among the knights of
Campania. Also present were a few of Hannibal's most senior officers
and a small contingent of his bodyguards.

During the banquet, a plot to assassinate Hannibal surfaced.[9] The
assassin was the son of Pacuvius, one of the Celeres who had lobbied
the senators of Capua to declare for Hannibal. The young man, in opposition to his father, believed passionately that Capua should remain
allied to Rome, and his views had been brought to Hannibal's attention.
Earlier that day, Pacuvius had sought pardon for his son and Hannibal
had given permission for the boy to attend the banquet. That evening
the boy took his father aside, showed him a dagger, and revealed his plan
to stab Hannibal while he reclined at the table. The father was horrified,
and implored his son not to stain the honor of his family by shedding
the blood of a guest and violating the oath of fidelity to Hannibal that
he had made in the senate. Then Pacuvius told his son that the dagger
he would use to strike Hannibal would have to pass through him first.
The father, moved by his love, embraced his son, and, with tears, implored him to recant. He warned him that Hannibal was no ordinary
man but one protected by the gods and powerful bodyguards. He is too
fierce a warrior to be killed by a boy, the father contended, and his armor
is not made of iron or bronze, but the glory he has gained in a life of
constant warfare. The boy, moved by his father's entreaties and a strong
bond of filial respect, cast aside the dagger, and the two returned, arm
in arm, to the banquet.

When Hannibal entered the hall, he initially disapproved of the extravagance of the feast: it was not, he commented to his hosts, in accord
with "Carthaginian military discipline." He reposed on his dining couch

and ate in silence. As the evening wore on, Hannibal began to relax, and settled back to enjoy the singers and lyre-players—slowly allowing himself to succumb to the comforts of Capuan luxury. Later, as the guests turned to pleasures of a more sensual nature, Hannibal began to show a preference for one of the young male singers. According to the sources, Hannibal preferred this young man's company to the sexual debauchery unfolding between the other guests and the female slaves. Unbeknownst to Hannibal, death reclined only a few feet away from him. He had narrowly escaped a turn of events that could have ended his life and altered not only the course of the war, but perhaps the very course of history itself.

The next day Hannibal addressed the senate, and in a pleasant and amicable tone of voice reiterated that when the war ended Capua would be the capital of a new Italian federation and Rome would no longer be the dominant political and economic force in Italy. Following his address, Hannibal took a seat on a judicial panel known as the "tribune of the magistrates." His tone changed from affable to stern as he ordered the arrest and immediate trial of one of Capua's leading citizens, Decius Magius, an outspoken advocate of loyalty to Rome. This man had openly displayed his support for Rome and had been noticeably absent when the other senators assembled with their families to welcome Hannibal into the city. Magius had actively encouraged resisting Hannibal's entry into Capua, even urging his fellow citizens to block the Carthaginian's way with corpses if need be. He protested the murder of the Romans in the bathhouse and openly advocated killing the Carthaginians assigned to garrison Capua. Magius was brought before the tribunal in chains, and Hannibal, acting as prosecutor, exploded in a tyrannical outburst of invective against the accused. The senate sat silently. Hannibal was clearly in charge. When his guilt was announced, Magius called out to the senators, asking rhetorically if this was now what constituted justice for Capuans under their new Carthaginian master.

The plight of Magius resonated with many in the senate, and even more so among the crowd that had gathered outside at the news of his arrest and trial. Hannibal had tried and condemned a citizen in violation of the terms of the new treaty, which specified that a citizen of Capua could only be tried under the city's own laws and by its own magistrates. Magius had not violated any law of Capua, but Hannibal brushed the legality aside and pronounced him too dangerous to be allowed to remain in the city—"a fomenter of insurrection and riots." Hannibal preferred to execute Magius, but given the sentiments of the people, it was a politically dangerous option. Magius's death might further inflame the people and would certainly turn him into a martyr. Anxious to avoid any civil dislocations, Hannibal ordered Magius transferred to a ship bound for Carthage. After putting to sea, the ship was caught in a storm and, blown off its course, made port in Alexandria, Egypt. Magius received political asylum from the pharaoh, Ptolemy IV, and apparently lived out the remainder of his life in Egypt.

Capua would prove to be a double-edged sword for Hannibal. While he had gained an influential and prosperous ally, there is no extant record of any Capuans serving in his army as their Italian neighbors in Bruttium and Lucania did. Hannibal incurred the costly obligation of protecting his new ally from Roman retaliation, which would be forthcoming and harsh. For Capua, the alliance with Hannibal offered some short-term prospects of increased prosperity and the long-term promise of prestige and independence in the ancient world when the war ended. But what actually came to pass was the destruction of the city during the war as Hannibal could not prevent the Romans from eventually exacting their revenge.

Leaving Capua, Hannibal moved south to Nuceria, where he surrounded the city and offered its defenders safe conduct out—if they surrendered without resistance. Then, after they agreed and left the city, Hannibal had them ambushed and slaughtered—his archers killing many of the women and children who were accompanying them as well. When asked why he had gone back on his word, Hannibal offered the same excuse Alexander the Great had when he did virtually the same thing in India over a hundred years earlier. While he had guaranteed the defenders safe conduct out of the city, he had said nothing about what would happen to them once they cleared the gates. Taking control of Nuceria, Hannibal had its senators shut in a public bath and suffocated.[10]

Leaving Nuceria garrisoned, Hannibal moved against several nearby cities, among them Nola, Acerrae, and Casilinum. Nola was a fortress city just east of Naples, and its citizens were divided along economic lines as to which side they favored in the conflict. The prosperous and aristocratic elements in the city were strongly in favor of remaining loyal to Rome, while the common people saw in Hannibal the harbinger of change and the potential for improvement in their lot. Hannibal sent emissaries to negotiate, and the aristocracy, seeking to buy time to arrange for Roman assistance, agreed to discuss terms. The senate secretly sent their own group of emissaries to the praetor Marcellus Claudius at nearby Casilinum to ask for his help while they filibustered the terms with Hannibal.[11] A praetor was the second-highest elected official in the Roman administrative hierarchy and often in command of an army.

Marcellus agreed to help and, avoiding Hannibal, took a shortcut through the mountains, reaching Nola without incident. He arrived at the right moment—beating Hannibal to the city and before those elements among the common people who favored an alliance with Hannibal could overthrow the government. The gates were opened to the Romans, and with the help of the pro-Roman aristocratic faction in the senate, as well as the presence of his soldiers, Marcellus managed to keep the city loyal to Rome. Yet Marcellus was apprehensive. He was suspicious of the common people, especially a young activist named Lucius Bantius, who, while he had fought on the side of the Romans at

Cannae, now agitated in favor of joining Hannibal. Bantius had been wounded at Cannae and buried under a pile of the dead. Hannibal's soldiers found him and nursed him back to health. When he had recovered, Hannibal released him to return home with gifts and honors. As a result, Bantius held him in high regard and encouraged his fellow citizens, especially the poor and working classes, to join the Carthaginian cause. Marcellus, rather than arrest Bantius, undertook to win him over by recognizing and praising his bravery at Cannae and then rewarding him with money. It worked, and while Marcellus succeeded in winning the young man over, elements hostile to Rome remained within Nola.

When Hannibal arrived, Marcellus withdrew his troops within the city walls. He was now caught between the enemy outside and a faction within which could turn on him at any time. He was able to contain the hostile forces within the city, and, at the same time, launch several successful attacks against Hannibal. While Marcellus did not win at Nola, he forced Hannibal to abandon the effort and move against an easier target. With Hannibal gone, Marcellus turned his attention toward those within the city whom he suspected of supporting Hannibal, and over seventy were beheaded.

Leaving Nola, Hannibal moved against Acerrae (Acerra, some twelve miles northeast of Naples). As was his pattern, he sent emissaries ahead to persuade the leaders of the city to come over to his side voluntarily, or at least surrender without a fight. When the people heard Hannibal was approaching, many of them, including most of those responsible for defending the city, escaped under cover of darkness. Hannibal entered the city without a struggle and turned it over to his soldiers to be looted and burned.

The fortified town of Casilinum was Hannibal's next target because of its strategic position at the junction of two important Roman roads: the Via Appia and the Via Latina. Just three miles west of Capua, remains of the ancient city have been excavated to some twenty-five feet below the current ground level. Once again Hannibal sent emissaries to try to negotiate a voluntary surrender of the small five-hundred-man garrison composed of soldiers from the Latin town of Praeneste, just south of Rome. These soldiers had been on their way to fight at Cannae, when word of the defeat reached them and they returned to Casilinum. They garrisoned the town and massacred the residents who showed pro-Carthaginian inclinations. The garrison was subsequently reinforced by another five hundred men from the town of Perusia.

Casilinum was close to Nola, but Marcellus and his army were held in the area by the inhabitants who were terrified that if the Roman army left, the Italian tribes allied with Hannibal would descend on them. Hannibal sent an advanced detachment to negotiate the surrender of the town, or if that failed, begin the assault. The defenders at Casilinum sallied forth from the gates, driving Hannibal's advance force back. When reinforcements arrived, led by Hannibal's famed cavalry commander and critic Maharbal, they too were driven back. Then the main force under Hannibal arrived and launched a relentless assault against the town. According to the ancient sources, Hannibal had trouble motivating his men to fight. Utilizing a combination of sharp rebukes intended to shame them, alternating with references to their bravery at Cannae and Trasimene and promises of gold prizes for those who scaled the walls first, another assault was launched. Still the defenders, heavily outnumbered, held out. They launched counterattacks against Hannibal's army even though his assault force now included elephants, which had arrived from North Africa at the port of Locri on the southern Adriatic coast.[12]

Using his elephants, Hannibal pressed the attack even harder, but to no avail. Mines were dug to try to collapse sections of the defensive wall, and countermines were in turn sunk by the defenders to try to collapse the main shafts of the attackers. Even with his elephants and mines, Hannibal could not take what Livy mockingly referred to as the "little town with its little garrison."[13] In frustration, Hannibal abandoned the effort, leaving a smaller force to keep pressure on the town while he returned to Capua with the rest of the army for the winter. It would not be until the following spring that Casilinum surrendered and Hannibal garrisoned the town with seven hundred of his men.

The winter at Capua ruined Hannibal's soldiers, just as, over a hundred years earlier, Babylon had ruined Alexander's army following their victory over the Persian king at Gaugamela. Easy living was the problem in both instances. While Hannibal's soldiers had been toughened by the hardships of the march over the Alps and in combat in Italy, the "immoderate pleasures" at Capua undid everything.[14] Quartered in plush surroundings, the soldiers consumed too much rich food and drank copious amounts of wine in an environment of continual leisure and debauchery.[15] If food, drink and leisure were not enough, Venus finished the task by sending in an army of harlots.[16]

Hannibal, too, succumbed to the easy living and luxury. The inactivity and debauchery during the winter was a serious failure of leadership on his part, equal perhaps to his failure to march on Rome after Trasimene or Cannae. In the spring, Hannibal left Capua with his army and tried once more to take Neapolis. But he was commanding a different army than the one that had crossed the Alps with him and fought at the Trebbia, Trasimene, and Cannae. Drained by the harlots and the easy living, none of the old esprit de corps among the soldiers survived the winter. On the march, many would give out in both body and spirit; there was constant complaining, and they resembled raw recruits more than seasoned veterans. Desertions increased substantially, and with no place to go, many of Hannibal's soldiers simply drifted back to Capua, seeking out their old haunts. Among those who left and went over to the Romans were some of his Numidian calvalry and Spanish soldiers.

The Romans had recently brought Spaniards to Italy to fight Hannibal, and fifth-column elements apparently managed to infiltrate his army to persuade their compatriots to switch sides.[17]

The only thing that protected Hannibal's army from the Romans now was their reputation. Their attempt to take Neapolis failed a second time, and the sources suggest it was not just the strength of the city's walls, but the easy living the winter before and an army that now suffered from a lack of discipline and enthusiasm for fighting.[18] Apparently, not all of Hannibal's army had spent the winter at Capua enjoying the good life, as units were actively engaged maintaining the siege of Casilinum, which eventually fell that spring when starvation drove the inhabitants to the point of chewing leather and boiling bark to stay alive.[19]

In Bruttium, Hanno and Himilco continued their efforts to bring the Italian tribes and the Greek towns and cities in the area under their control and increase the size of their army. Following the fall of Petelia, Himilco led his army west into the interior against the town of Consentinus (Cosenza)—a town that had remained loyal to Rome but that fell quickly. The Greek cities of Crotone and Locri, farther to the south along the eastern seaboard, fell to Hanno and his Bruttian allies. Only Rhegium (Reggio di Calabria), at the very tip of the peninsula across from Sicily, managed to hold out.

Mago left southern Italy, probably from the port of Locri, which was now under Hanno's control, and sailed to Carthage to announce the news of Hannibal's victory at Cannae and pressure the senate for reinforcements and money. When Mago entered the senate chamber, he poured onto the floor golden rings pried from the fingers of Roman knights slain at Cannae. It was a dramatic gesture, as there were reputed to have been so many rings that they filled nearly four pecks.[20] Mago recounted to the enraptured senate his brother's victories over the Roman consuls Scipio the elder at the Ticinus, Sempronius at the

Trebbia, Flaminius at Trasimene, and Paullus and Varro at Cannae. Two of the five consuls had been slain on the battlefields. Then Mago told how Hannibal had escaped the trap set by the Roman dictator Fabius Maximus in Campania and how not only Greeks, but Italians from Bruttia, Apulia, Samnia, and Lucania had deserted Rome and flocked to their standards—a slight exaggeration designed to win support in the senate. Hannibal, Mago exclaimed, was close to victory, and it was imperative he be given the resources he needed to finish the war: money, soldiers, and grain.

Members of the pro-Barca faction in the senate were ecstatic over the news and turned to their adversaries, taunting them and asking if they now regretted having initially opposed this glorious war to restore the greatness of Carthage. Hanno, the senator who had consistently argued against war with Rome, rose to speak, and the assembly, deferring to his seniority, fell silent. He explained that while he joined the others in rejoicing at Hannibal's victories, he remained skeptical. Only when the war was over would the winner be known and, equally as important, its true cost. Hanno expressed concerned that Hannibal had sent Mago to ask for reinforcements and money to continue a war that should have already been concluded months earlier and should have paid for itself with the spoils of victory. While the golden rings of the slain Roman equites were impressive, they were not enough to cover the cost of the reinforcements and supplies Mago was asking for.

Then Hanno directed his attention to Mago and asked if after each of Hannibal's victories the Romans had sent emissaries to ask for peace. Under forceful questioning, more like cross-examination, Mago was forced to admit they had not. Hanno asked how many Greek city-states and Italian towns, villages, and tribes had left the Roman confederation, and Mago had to admit that not as many had come over to their cause as they would have wished. Mago was forced to concede that the Romans still had considerable resources available to them and could continue the war indefinitely. Hanno agreed that Hannibal had been successful in the short run, but Carthage could not afford a long drawn out conflict against an opponent with such strong resolve and virtually unlimited manpower and resources. Hanno further warned of the vicissitudes of war, pointing out that today's victory could just as easily be tomorrow's defeat—as Carthage had found so painfully in the first war against Rome. Now, Hanno argued, was the moment to take advantage of Hannibal's victories and offer Rome an end to the war on favorable terms. He concluded his speech with a warning to his fellow senators not to become overconfident, for so far, Hannibal had won only battles, not a war.

The senate, elated by Hannibal's recent victories, was in no mood to listen to Hanno's pessimism any longer. His long feud with the Barcid clan had made many in the senate leery of him and tired of his continual complaining. It was the consensus of the senate to give Hannibal the resources to continue the war, and they voted to send Mago back to Italy with four thousand Numidian horsemen, forty elephants, and a large quantity of silver. Then, as Mago was preparing to leave, everything changed. Couriers arrived with news that a Carthaginian army under the command of Hannibal's brother, Hasdrubal, had been defeated by the Scipios on the banks of the Ebro River in Spain.

The Romans had crossed the river early in the spring of 215 B.C. and laid siege to a small town named Ibera. Hasdrubal responded by laying siege to a nearby town, Dertosa (modern-day Tortosa), which was allied with the Romans. The Scipios lifted their siege and moved against Hasdrubal, who met them on a plain near the river. Hasdrubal had two major problems in Spain: the Roman armies, which were pressing him, and increasingly restless and discontented native tribes. Months before, when the senate at Carthage had ordered Hasdrubal to leave Spain and reinforce Hannibal in southern Italy, he warned that if his army left, the country would fall to the Romans. In response, the senate sent another army to Spain under the command of a new general, Himilco, with orders to relieve Hasdrubal and allow him to proceed to Italy.

When the Scipios learned that Hasdrubal would attempt to reach his brother in Italy, they made every effort to stop him—realizing full well that if he succeeded, Rome could lose the war. The brothers concentrated their forces at the Ebro River to stop Hasdrubal from reaching the Pyrenees—the first milestone on his march. They told their soldiers that their families at home were counting on them to prevent Hasdrubal from reaching Italy. Hasdrubal's Spanish soldiers apparently did not have the same level of commitment. Most of them, especially the infantry, preferred remaining home, even under Roman rule, rather than marching to Italy to fight a war for Carthage. When the two armies clashed, the Spanish center gave way, while on the flanks the Carthaginian mercenaries and the Africans made a much more determined effort to hold the line. Still, their efforts were not enough to counter the Roman push through the center. Casualties among the Spaniards were heavy, and once their lines were breached, discipline broke down and desertions increased quickly. The Carthaginian cavalry, seeing their center collapse under Roman pressure, retreated, leaving the crucial flanks exposed. Hasdrubal suffered a crushing defeat and with a small contingent escaped south to Cartagena. That battle turned the tide of the war in Spain. The Spanish tribes that had been undecided now went over to the Roman side, and Hasdrubal had no hope of leading an army to Italy to relieve his brother. In fact, it would be nine years (207 B.C.) before he would be able to leave Spain and lead a relief column over the Alps to reach Hannibal.

In response to the defeat at the Ebro, the Carthaginian senate ordered Mago and his army to Spain and sent a similar-size force to the island of Sardinia to foment a revolt against the Romans there. Had Hasdrubal won at Ibera and subsequently been able to reach his brother, there would have been four Carthaginian armies in Italy by 214 B.C.—those of Hannibal, Hasdrubal, Mago, and Hanno—and the war may well have taken a different course. The defeat at Ibera meant that Hannibal had effectively lost the resources he needed from Spain, and it devalued most of the political capital he had won in Carthage by his victory at Cannae. The Scipio brothers now divided their forces, with Gnaeus taking charge of the ground troops while Publius commanded the navy. They followed a conservative policy of not directly confronting the Carthaginians, but concentrated on winning over or subjugating the Iberian tribes while raiding Carthaginian strongholds and blockading the coast.

Philip V, the king of Macedon, was pleased when he learned that Hannibal had crossed the Alps, and he was even more so when he received subsequent reports of Hannibal's triumphs at the Trebbia and Lake Trasimene. Philip had acceded to the throne in 221 B.C. at the age of seventeen, a young monarch with an aggressive disposition. He was eager to drive the Romans from his northern borders—the area called Illyricum (modern-day Albania, Montenegro, Bosnia, and Croatia) and expand his kingdom south into Greece. Philip saw in Hannibal an ally to help him realize his ambitions, but he was careful to remain outwardly neutral so as not to provoke the Romans who were just to his north or those on the Italian mainland just a short sail from his kingdom across the Ionian Sea. Watching the struggle between Carthage and Rome unfold, Philip waited until after Hannibal's victory at Cannae before he sent envoys to southern Italy to approach him about a formal alliance.

Philip's envoys set sail from Macedon in the early summer of 215 B.C. They avoided the Italian ports of Brundisium and Tarentum because they were heavily patrolled by the Roman fleet, and landed farther south along the coast, just below Crotone, at the Temple of Lacinian Juno. From there, they made their way overland north into Apulia, and, while looking for Hannibal, were captured by a Roman foraging party. Taken to the praetor Valerius Laevinus near Luceria (slightly northwest

of Foggia) for questioning, the most senior ambassador among the
Macedonians, one Xenophanes, managed to deceive the praetor by convincing him that the group was on a mission to negotiate an alliance of
friendship and mutual assistance between Rome and Macedon. Taken
in by the story and impressed with the importance of the mission, Laevinus provided Xenophanes with detailed information on the safest
route to Rome and marked which roads and passes his group should
follow to avoid falling into Hannibal's hands. The Macedonians made
their way through the Roman lines with a safe conduct, and then into
Campania to find Hannibal.

The delegation met with Hannibal and reached agreement on a
treaty by which Philip pledged to send a large fleet of two hundred
ships to ravage the Adriatic coastline of Italy. The army on board that
fleet would then march inland to help Hannibal in subjugating the rest
of Italy. At the war's end, Italy, and all its wealth, would belong to Hannibal who in return pledged to wage war against the enemies of Philip
in Greece. By the terms of the treaty the city-states conquered on the
Greek mainland and the islands that line the Macedonian coast would
become a part of Philip's new kingdom. The terms are interesting because they reveal Hannibal's intentions regarding Rome at the end of
the war. Indications are that he did not intend to destroy the city, only
to reduce its power to a par with the other city-states in Italy.

Three representatives from Carthage were present when Hannibal
negotiated the treaty with Philip's envoys, an indication that Hannibal
might not have had unilateral authority to bind Carthage. They might
have been part of a permanent political delegation attached to Hannibal's army or sent to Italy specifically for the purpose of negotiating
or approving this particular treaty. But if the latter were the case, why
not send them directly from Carthage to Macedon, a much safer venue
for the negotiations than Italy? In any case, the bargain having been
struck, the delegation set out to return to Macedon, accompanied by

the representatives from Carthage. The group made its way south un-
detected as far as Cape Lacinia, where they boarded a ship that awaited
them in a hidden anchorage. While making for the open sea, they were
intercepted by Roman ships and, unable to outrun their pursuers, were
captured and taken to the consul at Tarentum.

Xenophanes tried once more to bluff his way out of the situation by
explaining that his group had been unsuccessful in reaching Rome and
were returning to Macedon when they were captured. When the Carthaginian ambassadors were questioned, their speech raised suspicions.
Their slaves were tortured to extract confessions about the identity of
their masters and the real purpose of their mission. Then the group,
Macedonians and Carthaginians alike, were chained and placed on a
ship bound for Rome. After clearing the Straits of Massena, the ship
put in at Cumae, and the prisoners were sent overland to Rome. When
the senators at Rome learned what had transpired between Hannibal and Philip, they voted funds to raise a fleet of fifty ships and send
them with an army to keep Philip occupied in Illyricum and out of
Italy. Philip had no idea his envoys had been captured, and after several
weeks passed and they failed to appear, he sent a new group. While this
group succeeded in reaching Hannibal and confirming the terms of the
treaty, Philip was now distracted by Roman movements on his northern
borders and their attempts to form an anti-Macedonian league among
the Greek states to his south. The moment had passed, and now Philip
was too preoccupied to support Hannibal. From 214 B.C. until 207
B.C., Philip had plenty of his own problems in Macedon and Greece to
worry about and was little help to Hannibal.

Hannibal still needed a major port, and, frustrated in his attempts
on the western coast around Neapolis, he turned to the southern Adriatic coast, where there were two possibilities: Tarentum (Taranto)
and Brundisium (Brindisi). Brundisium was directly on the Adriatic,
across from Illyricum, and provided quick and relatively easy access

to Greece—but it was garrisoned by the Romans and heavily patrolled by their ships. Tarentum was located some fifty miles farther inland, on the Gulf of Taranto—an inlet of the Ionian Sea. The port had one of the largest and most protected harbors along the entire eastern coast of Italy and had become an indispensable stop for ships moving between Greece and the western Mediterranean. The city had been founded by the Spartans centuries earlier as a place of exile for their women who had consorted with slaves while their men were at war and who were pregnant or had given birth. The city was built on a peninsula that was separated from the mainland by a waterway, the entry to which was guarded by a citadel, as it still is today. With its double harbors for commercial and military shipping, Tarentum was remarkably like Carthage in appearance. The bay was bountiful in fish and hosted one of the richest purple beds in the Mediterranean waters. These beds contained shellfish and snails that excreted a substance from which a precious purple dye could be made. The color was long associated with royalty, and clothes with purple in them conveyed high status in the ancient world. Wool, brought in from the countryside and dyed with the purple from those beds, transformed the city into the main seat of the ancient textile industry in Italy. Even today, as polluted as the waters are, the bay is still bountiful and the city has spread onto the adjacent mainland.

The port's only shortcoming was its distance from Carthage. It was considerably longer than the distance from Neapolis and required sailing around the often treacherous and stormy southeastern coast of Sicily. On the positive side, the port was close to Macedon and the king who Hannibal thought would be his new ally—Philip.

In the spring of 214 B.C., Hannibal moved from Arpi, where he had wintered, to Campania. There he probed the fortifications at Neapolis once more, gave up, and then ravaged the small towns and villages along the coast. During that summer, a small delegation of noblemen from Tarentum made their way to his camp at Lake Avernus, just south of

Naples, with a plan to hand over their city. All these young men had fought Hannibal as allies of Rome, some at Trasimene and others at Cannae. They survived, were captured, and were later released under Hannibal's policy of mercy toward Roman allies. As a result, they held him in high esteem. They explained that Tarentum was garrisoned by the Romans, who were supported by many of the aristocrats with ties to Rome, but the common people hated them both and would rise in revolt as soon as he approached the city walls. Trusting in their assurances, Hannibal moved his army east—some 180 miles across Italy from the Lake to Tarentum. But when he arrived at the walls of the city, no revolt took place. After a few days, Hannibal gave up the idea of taking the port and moved back across central Italy for another attempt at taking Neapolis. Frustrated once more in his attempt to take that port city, he ravaged the countryside and returned to Apulia, where he wintered on the Adriatic coast at Salapia (Manfredonia).

Hanno, with an army of twelve hundred Numidians and seventeen thousand recently recruited Italian allies (Bruttians and Lucanians), made his way north to coordinate with Hannibal, who was moving from Salapia across central Italy, back into Campania. As Hanno and his army passed Beneventum, the Roman praetor Tiberius Gracchus approached the city from the other side with a hastily recruited army of slaves. Gracchus had promised any slave who brought him the head of Hanno his freedom and a monetary reward. During the battle, which was fought just outside the city, the slaves began decapitating every dead body they could find and then running with the severed heads to find their commander and claim their freedom. Most of Hanno's army was killed or captured, or deserted. Hanno managed to escape and reach Hannibal, who now without reinforcements, was forced to return to the safety of Salapia.

Even though Rome had reserves of manpower to draw on, the demands to meet the threat from Hannibal began to stress the free Italian labor market. So many free men, mostly small farmers and laborers, were being conscripted that this resulted in a greater dependence on slaves, especially on the large plantations. There was a constant supply of slave labor to meet the demand, owing to the sale of prisoners of war. The widespread use of slaves began to supplant the use of free hired labor. Thus, small farmers and laborers in Italy, unable to recover from the destruction of their land as a result of the ravages of war and compete with the influx of cheap slave labor, simply went under. This radical altering of the labor pool was one of the lasting effects of the war with Hannibal and would lead to a revolution in the next century. By the end of the war, there were so many slaves in Italy that violent revolts began to occur with increasing frequency. While those revolts were suppressed, an era of enslavement began in Italy on a scale never before seen in the western part of the Mediterranean world and which would become a defining feature of the Roman Empire.

For Hannibal's soldiers, the winter in Salapia was like the one they had enjoyed in Capua. Even the usually stoic and Spartan Hannibal apparently succumbed when he fell under the spell of a local prostitute. According to one ancient source, Hannibal remained faithful to his wife Imilce and, "in spite of his African birth," treated women, especially female captives, humanely.[21] Unlike Alexander the Great and Julius Caesar, with whom Hannibal is often compared, there are few references to his relationships with women beyond these two. Both Alexander and Caesar, at the other extreme, had as many liaisons with other men and women as they had battles.

From Salapia, Hannibal moved his army south, spending most of the summer of 213 B.C. in an area just west and south of Tarentum, where unforeseen circumstances changed his plans. A group of prominent young nobles from Tarentum were being held under a loose form of house arrest at Rome—probably to insure the allegiance of their city. They managed to escape but were quickly recaptured. The senate ordered them scourged, the usual first step in Roman punishment, and then hurled to their deaths from the infamous Tarpeian Rock—a steep cliff on the southern summit of the Capitoline Hill used for the execution of murderers, traitors, captured runaway slaves, and those who had perjured themselves in court. When news of the execution of these young men reached Tarentum, there was general outrage among the people and a conspiracy formed against the Roman garrison there. A group of young men left the city under the guise of a hunting party to find Hannibal. They offered to help him take the city by subterfuge, and in return he pledged that the people of Tarentum would remain free to live under their own laws and would be ruled by their own elected officials. None of Tarentum's citizens would be compelled to serve in the Carthaginian army against their will, nor would the city be required to pay tribute to Carthage or accept a Carthaginian garrison. The Romans living in the city would be imprisoned and held for ransom, sold as slaves, or executed as Hannibal saw fit.

The young men had a simple plan for handing over their city. They would return to Tarentum with cattle and explain to the Roman garrison that they had found them while hunting for game. Then over the next several weeks they would establish a pattern of leaving the city at night, through the same gate, on similar hunting expeditions and returning just before dawn with their kills. They set the plan in motion and, when they returned, each time made it a practice to share a portion of their game with the guards on duty and their officers. After several weeks, their hunting expeditions became so routine that the Roman sentries on duty opened the gate at their approach without question or concern for security.

Hannibal assembled a force of some ten thousand men and hid them in a gorge a few miles from the city. On a night agreed upon, the Roman garrison commander was invited to a dinner party at the home of some prominent Tarentines, where he was plied with wine. The young men, returning from their hunting party, approached the gate before dawn carrying a boar. Just as they passed through the gate, a small Carthaginian force behind them pushed its way in, killing the guards and then opening the main gate to the city. Hannibal's soldiers quickly entered and took control of the streets. Those Roman soldiers who managed to avoid being killed in the initial attack retreated to the safety of the citadel. Once Hannibal was inside, the Tarentines surrendered the city, but the citadel was another matter. Its walls were thick and high, and manned by a garrison that numbered about five thousand.[22] Because the citadel commanded the entrance to the city's harbor, the garrison could be supplied indefinitely by Roman ships, making a long siege out of the question. Hannibal left the problem in the hands of the Tarentines and returned to Campania where the Romans had begun a siege of Capua. Although the loss of Tarentum was a major setback for the Romans, they eventually retook the city in 209 B.C.

The Romans reacted to the fall of Tarentum by laying siege to Capua (212 B.C.). Capua in turn asked Hannibal for help, and he responded by leading his forces once more across central Italy to the walls of the city. There an indecisive struggle took place between Hannibal's forces and the two consular armies that had laid siege to the city. When a third Roman army arrived on the scene, Hannibal withdrew, moving his army back to the Adriatic coast around Brundisium, nearly 250 miles away. There, either unable or unwilling to besiege Brundisium, he returned to Capua the following year (211 B.C.) and made another unsuccessful attempt to relieve the siege. It is difficult to understand what was going through Hannibal's mind as he moved his army, seemingly in haphazard fashion, from one coast to the other, and then back again—failing each time to accomplish his objective.

The country around Capua was open, which would have given Hannibal, with his cavalry and elephants, a tactical advantage over the Romans. But the Romans had constructed double walls, a circumvallation, around Capua and remained securely behind them, ignoring Hannibal's repeated challenges to come out and fight on the open ground. In frustration, Hannibal launched an assault against the outer walls of the Roman encampment, coordinated with an attack from within the city by the Capuans. Both failed, and, in frustration, Hannibal broke off the assault and moved his army north against Rome. While the move might have been intended to draw the legions surrounding Capua away to defend Rome, it failed as the Romans remained within their defensive walls and continued the siege.

With Hannibal gone, Capua was left on its own. With a double wall and three Roman legions surrounding the city, the Carthaginian garrison inside and the Capuans who supported them felt abandoned. The garrison complained that "the Roman as an enemy is more steadfast and trustworthy than the Carthaginian as a friend."[23] Couriers were able to make their way out of the city, carrying messages begging Hannibal for help. Most were captured by the Romans, had their hands cut off, and then were sent back to the city. With supplies running dangerously low and no prospect of help from the outside, Capua faced slow but inevitable starvation.

When Hannibal arrived outside Rome, he took one look at the city's formidable defenses and left. He had neither the numbers nor the siege machinery necessary to breach those walls, and if his intent was to draw off the forces besieging Capua, it failed. When the Romans learned Hannibal was near, initially they feared that he must have destroyed their armies at Capua; otherwise, they thought, he never would have been bold enough to attack them. But Hannibal had played his gambit, and it failed. His decision to march on Rome appears to have been impulsive or born of frustration. Later Roman writers maintained that Rome was saved in 211 B.C. because the gods favored the city and sent a hailstorm to drive Hannibal away.

The prospect of starvation finally drove the Capuans to surrender. The most strident of the anti-Roman senators in the doomed city committed suicide. One group attended a lavish dinner party the

night before the Romans entered, and after a sumptuous feast with copious amounts of wine, the host served poison to his guests in little
dessert dishes—of which all willingly partook. Others died by their
own hands the next day. The Romans occupied the city and set about
arresting those senators they suspected of having sided with Hannibal
and agitated for Capua to leave the confederation. Fifty-three senators
were tried, convicted, scourged, and beheaded, all within the same day.
The inhabitants of the city who survived were sold on the slave markets, while their property was confiscated in the name of the people
and senate of Rome. The senate at Rome ordered the city-state politically dissolved, and Capua was quickly overrun by a horde of Roman
speculators, all looking to profit from its misfortune. Capua fell because
the Romans were persistent in maintaining and pressing their siege—
something that proved greater than Hannibal's ability to rescue the city.
The city was severely punished because in Roman eyes, its people had
been cowardly and duplicitous. They simply had bet on the wrong horse
and lost. Over time, a century or two later, the Roman attitude toward
the city moderated. Capua recovered and prospered, even becoming a
principal center for the training of gladiators. In 73 B.C., it was the site
of the largest slave revolt in Roman history, led by the Thracian gladiator Spartacus.

CHAPTER VI

Unending War

W HEN HANNIBAL LEFT Spain for Italy, he placed his younger
brother Hasdrubal in command of the Carthaginian-controlled
portion of the country. Hasdrubal was tasked with holding southern
Spain, upon whose vast mineral wealth and manpower reserves Carthage depended to fuel the war against Rome. For ten years, Hasdrubal
kept the Spanish tribes nominally under his control and the Romans at
bay. Then in 208 B.C. Hannibal sent word to his brother to bring reinforcements to Italy. Hasdrubal was the equal of Hannibal in all respects:
character, courage, skill, and ability to command. He was, as the Roman
historian Livy commented, "a son of Hamilcar Barca, the thunderbolt,"
and as dynamic and experienced a leader in battle as Hannibal.[1] Hannibal in Italy was trouble enough for the Romans, but now the second
son of the thunderbolt was about to bring another army of mercenaries
and elephants over the Alps to reinforce his brother.

Polybius had similar praise for Hasdrubal, characterizing him as a
brave man, to be admired for his abilities as a commander, and not dis-
missed out of hand because he lost and died at the battle of the Metaurus.[2] Hasdrubal stands out because he kept the Romans at bay in Spain
for ten years, brought his army over the Alps intact, increased its size

with Gauls, and nearly reached his brother. He could see beyond the short-term rewards of victory in battle, glory, and profit and formulated a contingency if things, as they often do, should go wrong. This was something that Polybius found to be a rare and valuable characteristic in leaders of his day.

Both Polybius and Livy praised Hasdrubal for having made it over the Alps with his army—more rapidly than Hannibal, and with significantly fewer losses. It was an accomplishment on a par with Hannibal's but has been overshadowed and relegated to the footnotes of history. Hasdrubal moved quickly through Gaul and over the Alps, due perhaps to better weather conditions. The Gauls probably allowed Hasdrubal, with nearly twenty thousand soldiers and a contingent of elephants, to move through their territory safely, but we do not know for sure if the passage was entirely without difficulties. Hasdrubal reached Italy more quickly than his brother had expected, which may account for the coordination problems that developed between them.

The Roman army was waiting for Hasdrubal at the Metaurus, a river that begins in the heights of the Apennine Mountains and flows east into the Adriatic Sea at Fano, just north of the modern-day port of Ancona. The Romans won that day and their victory was the turning point in the war. The Metaurus is one of the greatest battles in ancient history, yet it has been given remarkably little attention by scholars, overshadowed as it is by Hannibal's crossing of the Alps, and his victories at Trasimene and Cannae. Hasdrubal's defeat and death were significant because they sealed Hannibal's fate in Italy and condemned him to lose the war. The Romans won at the Metaurus because of the competence and effective coordination of the two consuls in command, Gaius Claudius Nero and Marcus Livius Salinator. Of the two, Nero is probably the unsung hero of the battle, and, in some respects, of the Second Punic War. Because of his initiative, boldness, and drive, he turned the tide of the war in Rome's favor and, like Hasdrubal, he has been relegated to history's footnotes. Claudius Nero took a gamble and made a bold move, which deceived Hannibal and defeated Hasdrubal.

The Romans needed competent leaders, one to deal with Hannibal in the south and another to stop Hasdrubal in the north. Many of Rome's most experienced commanders had been killed in prior battles, including the Scipio brothers in Spain. It was the law of Rome that one of the two consuls elected each year to command the armies of the republic had to come from the lower plebeian class and one from the aristocratic patrician class. The patrician candidate for office in 208 B.C. was Claudius Nero, whose descendant some two hundred years later would become the infamous Julio-Claudian emperor. Claudius Nero, whose cognomen or nickname can mean the powerful one or the dark one, depending on the context, was an experienced commander who had fought against Hannibal in Italy and Hasdrubal in Spain.

The plebeian candidate for the consulship was Marcus Livius Salinator, nicknamed the salt man. Salinator had commanded Roman forces in Illyricum but had been censured and then exiled for a term for using his position to enrich himself. Because Rome was critically short on experienced commanders, he was allowed to return and run for the consulship. The two men hated each other because Nero had been one of Salinator's most vocal and strident accusers when he came to trial. After the election, when the senate awarded them their commands and sought to reconcile them, Salinator rebuffed the overture and commented it would be best if they remained enemies. The hope of Rome, now at its most perilous hour since Cannae, rested on two men who detested each other. Salinator took command of the forces in the north, tasked with blocking the Alpine passes through which Hasdrubal had to pass, while Nero was given command in the south against Hannibal. But Hasdrubal, in command of a force now estimated to have grown to some thirty thousand, had moved far more quickly than expected. He came down from the Alps and was on the plains of Italy before Salinator could put his own forces in place to stop him.

In the south, Nero moved his army of forty thousand to Venusia in Apulia, looking for Hannibal, who began playing a game of cat and mouse with his Roman adversary. There were minor skirmishes where Hannibal's soldiers apparently suffered more casualties than the Romans. The fact that Hannibal avoided engaging Nero leads to speculation that his army may have been weakened considerably by this point in the war. Hannibal eventually retreated farther south on the Italian peninsula to Metapontum, where the ranks of his army were increased with new recruits from Bruttium enlisted by his nephew Hanno. Only when his army was reinforced did Hannibal move it back to Venusia, where he waited for Nero to make his next move. Hannibal had become uncharacteristically passive.

In the north, Hasdrubal avoided the Roman army, and instead of crossing the Apennine range by the same route Hannibal had taken earlier, he moved by way of Bologna, directly to Ariminum (Rimini) on the Adriatic coast. Ariminum had been established by the Romans in 268 B.C., shortly before the First Punic War, as the terminus for the recently completed Via Flaminia, an ancient version of a superhighway. The highway led from Rome, over the Apennine Mountains, to the east coast of Italy. At Ariminum, Hasdrubal posed a direct threat, as he was now, by way of the Via Flaminia, less than two hundred miles from the city. The Roman senate, on the advice of Nero, sent an army to block the route. As Hasdrubal moved south along the Adriatic coast looking for his brother, another smaller Roman army, led by the praetor Lucius Porcius Licinius, the pig man, moved into position and began to shadow him from the north.

Anxious to establish contact with his brother, Hasdrubal sent six horsemen south along the coast with orders to find him. Riding day and night, the couriers covered nearly four hundred miles from Ariminum to just north of Tarentum without being detected. Just short of reaching Hannibal, who had retreated to the coastal city of Metapontum, their luck gave out when they came upon a detachment of Roman soldiers who were foraging in the countryside for supplies. Captured, they were taken to Nero, who ordered them tortured until they revealed the details of their mission as well as the size, composition, and route of Hasdrubal's army.

Nero was now faced with a dilemma. Could he trust the information that had fallen into his hands by luck—a gift from the gods—and act on it? Or was this a Carthaginian trick intended to lure him into the kind of trap Hannibal was famous for setting? While everything about these messengers seemed genuine, down to the fact that their horses were worn out from days of hard riding, the year before, a Roman force commanded by Marcellus, one of Rome's best generals, was ambushed on the border between Apulia and Lucania. Marcellus was killed in the fighting, and Hannibal used the consul's signet ring to forge documents in an effort to retake the city of Salapia. The attempt failed when the Roman garrison commander became suspicious about the authenticity of the documents.

Nero put his reservations aside and acted decisively to stop Hasdrubal from reaching his brother. Taking a portion of his army, essentially his best soldiers, he led them north in a forced march to reinforce Salinator at the Metaurus River. Nero's plan was to quickly defeat Hasdrubal and return south before Hannibal even knew he had left. It was a bold gamble with high stakes. If Hannibal learned that Nero was gone and attacked his weakened army in the south, it would be a disaster. Then there was the question of whether Nero's soldiers could be force-marched over such a long distance, fight a major battle, and then force marched back to fight again. How much could human endurance be taxed? Nero sent couriers to Rome to advise the senate to send a legion from Capua to reinforce the soldiers securing the Via Flaminia and then assembled his expeditionary force; six thousand infantry and one thousand cavalry. Marching them day and night, north from Tarentum, through the center of Italy, they arrived where the Metaurus River enters the sea at Fano.

Nero and his army covered the distance in a remarkable seven days. Each soldier carried only the bare minimum—mainly his weapons. Messengers were sent ahead of the army to mobilize the people who lived along the route to prepare food and provide supplies for the soldiers as they passed. In that way, the army could move without being encumbered by baggage, supplies, and camp followers. As Nero's army moved north, volunteers along the route, moved by patriotism and caught up in the emotions of the moment, joined them, swelling their ranks. What Nero was doing went against Roman law. As a consul, he was forbidden to leave his assignment without senatorial permission. Recognizing the potentially devastating consequences of the Carthaginian brothers joining forces or attacking Rome from two different directions, and the need for decisive action, Nero circumvented the law and acted on his own volition.

Livius Salinator, on the other hand, was taking a very cautious approach relative to Hasdrubal and his army. He allowed the Carthaginian army to cross the river and move south along the coast, without engaging them. With the army of Licinius behind him, Hasdrubal camped just a half-mile or so to the north of Livius. Nero arrived with his army late at night and led his soldiers into the Roman camp quietly so as not to raise an alarm among Hasdrubal's sentries. Nero was constantly worried about Hannibal, and despite a long and tiring march, he insisted on fighting Hasdrubal the next day so he could return south as quickly as possible.

The next morning, Hasdrubal awoke to find two Roman armies in front of him and one behind. Overwhelming forces were converging on him at the Metaurus, and this caused him to conclude that Hannibal might already have been defeated in the south. How else could the Romans have been able to bring together so many soldiers against him in the north? Hasdrubal remained safely within his camp and pondered his options. The rest of the day passed without event, as Salinator and Licinius, in spite of Nero's pressure for them to engage in battle, refused to advance on Hasdrubal's fortifications. Nero argued that they could not remain passive, waiting for Hasdrubal to make the first move. All three recognized the urgency of the situation and that time was crucial. Once Hannibal learned that the Roman army in southern Italy was without its commander and weakened in number, he was sure to attack it. The only option open to the Roman commanders was to move quickly against Hasdrubal, destroy him, and release Nero to return south.

Hasdrubal on the other hand had no desire to engage the Roman armies. His mission was to reach his brother with his army intact, so when nightfall came he led them out of camp with the intent of recrossing the river and retreating north as quickly and quietly as he could. Once safely over the Metaurus and well away from the Romans, Hasdrubal planned to try once more to establish communication with Hannibal even though he had only a vague idea of where he might be or even if he was still alive. As the night wore on, Hasdrubal's problems multiplied. His local guides deserted him, leaving him lost in the darkness, trying to find a safe place for his army to cross the swiftly flowing river. A combination of melting snows from the nearby Apennines and spring rains had caused the river to flood, trapping his army on the south shore as his scouts frantically searched up and down the riverbank in the darkness for a place to cross. Many of the Gauls began drinking and in short order became disorderly. Like most Carthaginian armies, Hasdrubal's was a mix of cultures and included the same Iberians, Ligurians, Gauls, and Africans as Hannibal's army.

The first light of morning found Hasdrubal's army in disarray. It was trapped with its back against the banks of the flooded Metaurus, and there were three consular armies converging on it. When the Roman commanders realized Hasdrubal was cornered, they moved their infantry up into position. Hasdrubal's cavalry, the one section of his army that was superior to the Romans and on which he depended heavily, was essentially useless in the confined and hilly countryside around the Metaurus. In a bad position and with no alternative left, Hasdrubal gave up looking for a crossing point and ordered his army to turn and prepare to face the advancing Romans. How many soldiers clashed that day is uncertain, but numbers given by the ancient sources tend, as they usually are, to be underestimated, inflated, or contradictory. The Greek historian Appian, for instance, writes that the Carthaginian force numbered forty-eight thousand infantry, eight thousand cavalry, and fifteen elephants. Livy claims that there were more than sixty-one thousand slain or captured Carthaginian soldiers at the end of the battle and still more who escaped the slaughter. Those numbers indicate an army of far more than Appian's fifty-six thousand. Polybius reported that ten thousand of Hasdrubal's men were killed in the fighting versus only two thousand Romans.

Hasdrubal's army probably numbered thirty thousand including his Gauls, and Livius had roughly the same number. The praetor Licinius commanded an additional two legions, probably ten thousand men, so between them the Roman army might have come to forty thousand including their Italian allies. However, the numbers of the allied contingents fighting with the Romans could have been lower, since some of the confederation members in central Italy, weary with the long and indecisive war against Hannibal, had begun to refuse Roman demands to provide auxiliaries and to pay additional war taxes. Adding Nero's seven thousand troops to the Roman mix, what is certain is that Hasdrubal and his Carthaginians were outnumbered at the Metaurus.

When Hasdrubal's army turned to face the Romans, his right flank, where he placed his best horsemen, was pressed against the river while his left flank was in hilly terrain, which proved to be a mixed blessing. Hasdrubal's most experienced and reliable troops, his African and Iberian infantry, were placed on the right flank as well—the section of the battle line where Hasdrubal now placed all his hope for a victory. The center was composed of Ligurians, who, though not as skilled and well trained as the veterans on the right-flank, could be savage fighters in short bursts of combat. Hasdrubal intended for them to absorb the initial Roman assault and keep his center together until the Africans and Spaniards could turn the Roman flank and carry the day.

On his left, Hasdrubal placed the Gauls, his least reliable soldiers, who would be protected by a deep ravine in front of them and hills behind them. By this point, many of them were, according to Polybius, "stupefied with drunkenness."[3] Hasdrubal had ten elephants, which he used to reinforce the center. However, once the fighting began, the animals quickly became a liability. Frightened by the din of battle, many panicked, and while some charged the Roman line, others turned on their own soldiers. Six elephants were killed and the remainder ran off the field later to be captured or killed by the Romans.

Licinius deployed his infantry directly in front of Hasdrubal's Ligurians, while Salinator took command of the Roman cavalry on the left flank and Nero positioned himself on the right facing the Gauls. The battle commenced with the Roman left flank charging the Carthaginian right, followed by the advance of the Roman center. The outnumbered Carthaginian horsemen fell back while their center held its ground. Finally, overcome by sheer numbers, the center began to give way. Nero tried to attack the Gauls, but the hilly terrain and the ravine made it difficult for his troops to reach them. Then he made a decision that changed the course of the battle. Taking roughly half a legion with him, Nero broke off the attack and led his troops behind the Roman center to strike hard at the Carthaginian right flank. The Carthaginians broke ranks under the assault, and, with Hasdrubal trying in vain to force them back into the fight, their line disintegrated. Panic ensued, followed by desertions. The Romans chased the fleeing Carthaginians, meeting almost no resistance, and according to the ancient sources this is where most of the casualties among Hasdrubal's soldiers occurred. The Carthaginian center, now in disorder, faced a three-pronged attack: Licinius from the front, Livius and Nero from the right. Hasdrubal, seeing that there was nothing more he could do, and presumably doubtful of his own prospects of escape or simply unwilling to be taken captive, charged into the thick of the fighting to meet a warrior's death.

The Romans severed Hasdrubal's head from his body and brought it to Nero as a trophy. Nero ordered it placed in a sack and given to a courier with instructions to ride south, find Hannibal, and throw the head into his camp. This was barbaric and contrary to Hannibal's honorable treatment of Roman officers who had died in battle at Trasimene, Cannae, and even in southern Italy. He had been scrupulous in his treatment of their bodies, giving the dead burial with full military honors and often sending their ashes and personal effects back to Rome. Nearly a decade had passed since Hannibal had last seen his brother, and when the head was brought to him, he recoiled at the sight and groaned. The severed head was the harbinger of worse things to come. The war had turned.

Nero ordered the Carthaginian prisoners executed except the most prominent among them, who could be held for sizable ransom. The success of the legions at the Metaurus filled the Romans with hope and gave them confidence that Hannibal could not remain in Italy much longer. Nero changed the course of the war, forcing Hannibal to retreat into the most southern portion of Italy, Bruttium (Calabria), where he remained isolated until he was recalled to North Africa four years later.

With Hasdrubal's defeat, the war in Italy was essentially lost for Hannibal. Any chance he had of building a force strong enough to even bring the Romans to the conference table was gone. With a Roman naval presence off the coast of Sicily, Hannibal's chances of reinforcements reaching him from North Africa by sea diminished, and the war in Italy became a sideshow compared to the larger conflict that was now being waged in Spain and soon to reach North Africa. With Hannibal confined to Bruttium, the next four years were ones of relative inactivity in Italy—except for a second attempt to reinforce Hannibal which occurred in in 205 B.C.

This attempt was made by Hannibal's youngest brother, Mago, who, like Hannibal and Hasdrubal, was dedicated to the struggle against Rome. Mago was an experienced and competent commander who had crossed the Alps with Hannibal in 218 B.C. and was largely responsible for the victory over the Romans at the Trebbia. He distinguished himself at Cannae and later raised additional troops for Hannibal in Bruttium. Mago was sent to Carthage to report on the victory at Cannae and then to Spain in 215 B.C., where, along with his older brother Hasdrubal and another Hasdrubal, son of Gisco, he conducted the war against the Roman commanders Gnaeus and Publius Scipio (215–212 B.C.). When the Romans launched a major offensive in 211 B.C., Mago was instrumental in their defeat and the subsequent deaths in battle of both Scipios.

In the summer of 205 B.C., Mago left Spain for Italy. Instead of attempting another overland trek and Alpine crossing, he chose a sea route leaving a flotilla of some thirty warships and fourteen thousand soldiers on board. Since Hannibal was confined to the extreme tip of southern Italy on the Adriatic coast, reaching him by sea from Spain would have been nearly impossible. The journey would have been too long and dangerous, both because of the risk of storms and the patrolling Roman navy. Instead, Mago chose to hug the Ligurian coast and landed at Genova (Genoa). From there, he moved overland into northern Italy and, like Hasdrubal, recruited as many Ligurians and Gauls as possible to supplement his army. Since Roman armies controlled both sides of the Apennines and blocked the routes south, Mago and his army remained in northern Italy for the next two years, conducting largely guerilla operations. Then, in the summer of 203 B.C., outside of Milan, the Romans forced Mago into a decisive battle. With a force composed of Numidian and Spanish cavalry, infantry, and elephants, supplemented with Ligurians and Gauls, Mago engaged four Roman legions. During the battle, he was badly wounded in the thigh and retreated to Genova and the safety of the ships that awaited him there.

At Genova, messengers from Carthage were waiting with orders for him to return with his army to North Africa. Mago left behind an officer named Hamilcar with a small force to continue guerilla activities against the Romans in northern Italy. Mago died at sea from his wound, just as his fleet passed the island of Sardinia. Hannibal was confined to a narrow area in Bruttium between the Adriatic coast and what today comprises a series of Italian national parks known as the Sila. Crotone is where Hannibal chose to reside—a Greek city famous for philosophers like Pythagoras and athletes like Milo, the Olympic champion and most renowned wrestler in antiquity. In luxury, cultural refinement, and amusement, Crotone was the equal of Capua, and it was there that Hannibal spent the next two years, 205 B.C. until 203 B.C., while the Romans shifted the focus of the war to Spain and North Africa. Isolated, with one brother dead and another one about to die, his forces considerably diminished in numbers, and resources scarce, Hannibal was no longer driving the war but forced to sit on the sidelines and await developments.

To help keep Hannibal contained, a Roman army under the command of the young Scipio moved from Sicily across the Strait of Messina into southern Italy and captured the Greek port city of Locri, just south of Crotone. The port had been important to Hannibal earlier in the war, and even though he launched a counterattack, he was unable to retake the city. A few miles south of Crotone is Cape Lacinium, or as it is known today, Capo Colonna. Among the sparse ruins on its shores is a solitary marble Doric column that looks out over a vast and desolate sea and gives its name to the present-day cape. That column is all that remains of a once magnificent temple built by the Greeks to honor the goddess Juno Lacinia.[4] Among the most prized treasures of the temple was a column made of gold, which Hannibal allegedly probed to determine if it was solid or merely coated. When he discovered it was solid, he contemplated having it melted and cast into ingots or bricks for his personal use until the goddess came to him in a dream and threatened to take away his one good eye if he dared to desecrate her temple.[5]

It was at this temple, at the end of his campaign, that Hannibal allegedly had a bronze plaque erected. It was inscribed in Greek, the universal language of the ancient world at the time, and in Hannibal's native Punic. On that plaque Hannibal recounted his exploits in crossing the Alps, his battles in Italy, the size of his army, and the numbers of men he had lost.[6] Such tablets, or as the Romans called them, *res gestae*, were commonplace in the ancient world. They were personal monuments of sorts to the ambitions and egos of important men. While Hannibal's tablet has never been found and there are only literary references to its existence, it has given rise to speculation that he had come to regard himself as a king, perhaps the regent of southern Italy, and the plaque was left behind so posterity would not forget his accomplishments, victories, and aspirations.

At the same time, that plaque can be interpreted as Hannibal's tacit acknowledgment that the war in Italy had ended and he no longer had the manpower or the resources to take on the Roman armies. His Macedonian ally, Philip, had failed to deliver, and the last straw came when some eighty Carthaginian cargo ships trying to reach him with provisions were blown off course by a storm and captured by the Romans. The loss of those ships sealed Hannibal's fate, and in 203 B.C. he was ordered to return to North Africa.

When the Carthaginian envoys arrived and relayed the order to return, Hannibal was barely able to contain his rage. He gnashed his teeth and cried out that he had been betrayed, defeated by the aristocratic faction in Carthage, led by Hanno, not by the Romans he faced on the battlefield. He bemoaned that he would fail in this war for the same reasons his father had failed forty years before—lack of support from home.[7] Several towns in Bruttium, seeing the writing on the wall, deserted Hannibal and tried to make their peace with Rome. In response, he dispatched the weakest of his soldiers, those he classified as "unfit for duty," to garrison some of them, which he now held, more by force than loyalty.

In preparation for his return to Africa, Hannibal ordered timber cut from the forests of Bruttium and transported to Crotone for use in building ships. The completed transports would be escorted on their voyage home by a few warships from Carthage that had eluded the Roman navy and made it to Crotone. Hannibal carried out his preparations with "bitterness and regret."[8] He assembled the elite of his army, some twenty thousand of his veterans, who by this point must have been mostly Italians from Bruttium and Lucania, and announced their departure for North Africa. Their response bordered on mutiny. What the ancient sources refer to as a large number refused the order and barricaded themselves in the temple of Juno Lacinia, where they sought sanctuary. Confident that Hannibal would never violate the sanctity of a holy place, they misjudged the man who for his entire adult life apparently had no fear of the gods. Hannibal had the temple surrounded and, according to one of the sources, thousands of rebellious soldiers slaughtered along with horses and pack animals.

The scope of this massacre has often been regarded by scholars as an exaggeration in the ancient sources that probably stems from the reported slaughter of three thousand horses that could not be taken on board the ships to Africa.[9] There certainly may have been mutinous soldiers at that point in the war, and Hannibal may well have had them executed. But the Italian contingents in Hannibal's army were his core, his veterans, and he needed them. By this time, few, if any, of the mercenaries who crossed the Alps with him could have been left. It would be the Italians, those who had fought with him in southern Italy and who were prepared to accompany him to North Africa, who would prove to be his most reliable soldiers in the next and final stage of this long and destructive war.

CHAPTER VII

Return to Africa

HAVING BEEN CONFINED to a small area on the Adriatic coast for nearly two years, Hannibal received orders to return to Africa in the summer of 203 B.C. Even in retreat, he remained a threat to the Romans. If, along with the remnants of Mago's army, he could reach the shores of North Africa, their combined forces could affect the outcome of the war. Yet there is only one scant reference in the sources to an attempt to intercept Mago after he departed Genova and none regarding Hannibal. The Romans had naval forces in Sicily that were active in the waters off the coast of North Africa. Both Hannibal and Mago would have had to slip past them on their way to Africa, yet there is only a brief mention in one source of the senate at Rome ordering the navy to block the Carthaginian departures.[1] That same source, Livy, attributes the failure to even try to stop Hannibal to a lack of determination, and even fear on the part of the Roman naval commanders. As a result, Hannibal and most of Mago's force were able to reach North Africa without incident.

By this point in the war the Romans had shifted their focus to Spain. Scipio, following the deaths of his father and uncle, had taken charge of the Roman forces there and turned the war around. His capture of

Cartagena in 210 B.C., and then a victory at Ilipa, near Seville, in 206 B.C. put Carthage on the defensive. Scipio returned to Rome in 205 B.C. to a hero's welcome. He was so popular that he was elected consul, even though he was legally too young to hold the office. The following year he sailed to North Africa with a newly raised army, and instead of launching an assault directly against Carthage, laid siege to the coastal city of Utica, about fifteen miles to the west.

Outside of Utica in 203 B.C., Scipio defeated a large Carthaginian army under the joint command of Hasdrubal, the son of Gisco, and his African son-in-law, Syphax, which had been sent to lift the siege. Reeling from this defeat, the Carthaginians sent a delegation of their most senior senators to approach Scipio about a treaty. They prostrated themselves before him and acknowledged that while Carthage might have been technically responsible for starting the war, the real cause lay in the ambitions of the Barca clan. In reply to their request for an end to the hostilities, Scipio demanded that the Carthaginians withdraw all their forces from Italy, relinquish Spain and all the islands between Italy and North Africa, hand over their warships and elephants, pay an indemnity of five thousand talents, and feed the Roman army until it left North Africa. The delegation returned to Carthage to report the terms to the senate, which, in response, sent word to Hannibal and Mago to return as soon as possible. The senate then undertook to stall Scipio, who became impatient with the delay and threatened to resume the war. The senate quickly agreed to his terms with the stipulation that a Carthaginian delegation would be allowed to travel to Rome and obtain ratification of the treaty directly from the senate there. It was nothing more than another attempt to gain more time to allow the Barcas to return to North Africa with their armies and resume the war.

The Carthaginian envoys landed at the port of Puteoli, on the gulf of Naples, and then made their way overland to Rome. When they arrived, they were detained outside the walls of the city until the senate agreed to meet with them near the Campus Martius or "field of Mars," a publicly owned area named in honor of the Roman god of war where male citizens assembled every spring to receive their military assignments and every five years to be counted for the census. The mood at the meeting was adversarial. At the outset, the Romans confronted the Carthaginians with their reputation for duplicity and violations of previous agreements. They argued aggressively that there was no point to a peace treaty, since the Carthaginians could not be trusted to honor it once they saw an advantage or a possibility of gain at Roman expense. In response, the Carthaginian envoys pleaded for peace and continued to place all blame for the war on Hannibal and his brothers. They maintained that Hannibal had acted without their express authority when he attacked Saguntum and crossed the Alps to invade Italy—it had all been on his own initiative.[2] The Romans reminded them that, years before, when the Roman ambassadors had protested the attack on Saguntum and given the Carthaginians the choice between war and peace, their senate had enthusiastically chosen war, rolled the dice, and lost. Now they would have to pay the price.

The Carthaginian delegation was left waiting while the Romans retired to debate their course of action. The consensus that emerged was that, with the war in Spain essentially over and Scipio and his army holding the upper hand in North Africa, Carthage was desperate for a settlement. The Romans knew, or at least surmised, that Hannibal and Mago had been sent for and the Carthaginians would resort to any deception to buy time for them to return and relieve the pressure. Many of the senators favored ordering Scipio to continue to press the war in North Africa and refused to consider any accommodation with Carthage so long as Hannibal and Mago remained on Italian soil. A little later, when word reached Rome that Hannibal and Mago had departed, the senate ratified the treaty on the terms laid down initially by Scipio.

When the Romans learned that Hannibal had left, they were ambiv-
alent about his departure. On the one hand, they were glad to get him
out of Italy, and there are indications that with him gone there were
signs of an economic recovery. On the other hand, there was concern
about the impact he and his army would have on the course of the war
in North Africa. To celebrate his departure and insure that the gods
would favor Scipio's campaign in North Africa, games were held and
sacrifices conducted at the Circus Maximus, the chariot racing stadium
and mass entertainment venue situated in the city between the Aventine
and Palatine hills. But the prospect of Hannibal in Africa also worried
the Romans. Scipio was not popular with all the aristocracy, and there
were senators who were skeptical about the outcome when he would
face Hannibal on the battlefield. Scipio was young, and despite his victories in Spain and North Africa, he might not be Hannibal's equal.
Not knowing yet that Mago had died at sea, they feared Scipio could
be facing both Barca brothers in North Africa, experienced commanders who led seasoned veterans. The Barcas had killed several Roman
consuls on the battlefields of Italy and Spain and had as trophies more
captured Roman standards than the Roman armies currently carried.
Nor did the entire senate support Scipio. There was an influential faction that had been traditionally hostile toward his family and wanted
him removed from office and replaced with someone more to their lik-
ing. Quintus Fabius, the former dictator and a respected advisor to the
senate, before he died warned that Hannibal defending his home in
Africa could be a more formidable enemy than he had been in Italy.[3]
Even though Hannibal was out of Italy, many in the senate knew the
war might be far from over.

Factions in the Carthaginian aristocracy had similar concerns about
Hannibal. While there were Romans who worried Scipio was too
young, there were Carthaginians in the senate who argued that Hannibal was too old. While they acknowledged his achievements, they were

concerned because Spain had been lost, and after fifteen years, there was nothing to show for the expense and effort in Italy. The Carthaginian army in North Africa under Hasdrubal and Syphax had been defeated by Scipio just a few miles from the walls of Carthage, and if battles continued to be lost, the outcome of the war was sure to be harsher than the terms that were already on the table. The city could be occupied, looted, and burned. The Carthaginian senate was divided between those who wanted to conclude an immediate peace with Rome to safeguard their holdings, and another, equally influential and vocal faction, which favored supporting Hannibal and continuing the war.

As the Carthaginian flotilla set out to sea, Hannibal looked back at the coastline of Italy, the country he had ravaged for so many years. It must have been a bittersweet moment. Hannibal was young when he crossed the Alps, having just turned thirty, and full of promise now at forty-four he was leaving Italy without even having brought the Romans to the negotiating table much less winning the war. He cursed the gods for his change of fortune, then in hindsight, blamed himself for having failed to march on Rome after Cannae, when his soldiers "were covered with Roman blood from their victory."[4] Hannibal was envious of Scipio because of his youth and success. At the same time, he was critical of him because he had never commanded an army in battle on Italian soil, and now he was in position to march on Carthage. With continual words of self-recrimination and regret, the nemesis of Rome left Italy and sailed toward Africa to write a new chapter in an old book.

A few days later, Hannibal's flotilla landed south of Carthage, somewhere on the coast around ancient Hadrumetum, which today is called Sousse. This was the Barca tribal homeland, and Hannibal established his base camp in the land he had left as a child decades earlier—a land and a people that must have seemed more alien to him than Spain and Italy, where he had lived and fought for so long. Hannibal probably avoided Carthage because of his mistrust of the political

factions there—those who blamed him for the course of the war and
might seek to hold him accountable. Despite his victories and reputation, Hannibal faced the prospect of prosecution, and even crucifixion,
if the senate found fault with his conduct of the war in Italy. As Livy
pointed out, "Hannibal had not been defeated by the Romans, who he
so often slaughtered and routed, but by the Carthaginian senate with its
carping jealousy."[5] With the lessons learned from his father's experiences
in the First Punic War, Hannibal may have decided that he would now
act more in the capacity of an independent warlord in this final phase
of the war than as a general in the service of his city-state.

In the south Hannibal had a considerable buffer between Scipio's
army and his own, allowing him valuable time to organize his forces and
prepare for the next stage of his campaign. The clans and tribes around
Hadrumetum had been loyal to the Barcas for generations, and Hannibal must have been counting on them to augment his forces. Several
of these tribes had come to join him out of concern that if the Romans
were to win the war, their ally, the Numidian king Massinissa, would
dominate most of North Africa and they would lose their independence.[6] So they joined Hannibal, just as the remnants of Mago's army
from northern Italy arrived, bringing word of his death at sea.

With no treaty in place, Scipio turned his army loose to plunder the
countryside to the west of Carthage in a manner similar to what Hannibal had done in Italy for years. Hannibal remained at Hadrumetum
during the winter of 203–202 B.C., even though he received repeated
appeals from the senate at Carthage to engage Scipio. According to the
sources, Hannibal was unresponsive and may even have had his soldiers
out in the groves planting olive trees to pass the time. Whatever his
reasons, Hannibal remained passive for several months, possibly even
as long as a year, before moving his army into the interior of Tunisia
and establishing his camp near a town called Zama. There is little information about the location of Zama, other than references to its being

a five-day march southwest from Carthage, an estimated one hundred miles and roughly the same distance due west from Hadrumetum.[7] Among the possible sites identified over the years by scholars is an area just north of modern-day Maktar. Other possibilities are El Kef and Sidi Youssef, in the same general area but a little farther west and closer to the current border between Algeria and Tunisia.

Military historians have never agreed on the exact location or even the date of the battle between Hannibal and Scipio.[8] Speculation is that it occurred in this general area in 202 B.C. A summer battle is ruled out, given the extreme heat in the desert at that time of year, when temperatures can rise to dangerous levels. The effects of dehydration and sunstroke on the infantry, the elephants, and the horses would have been debilitating. Thus, a date in the autumn, probably between late September and November, is more plausible. In attempting to fix a more precise date, scholars have sometimes looked to the writings of the ancient historian Dio Cassius.[9] Cassius maintained that the battle took place on a day when there was an eclipse of the sun, which alarmed the Carthaginians. Astronomical calculations indicate a plausible date of October 19, 202 B.C., and while there appears to have been an eclipse on that day, further investigation reveals that it probably blocked less than one-tenth of the sun for observers in that latitude. In the heat of battle, it is doubtful that so small a celestial event would have been noted much less been cause for Carthaginian concern.

Scipio moved his army south from the coast and established his camp on a site with an abundant supply of water. Hannibal chose to forego easy access to water for what he considered to be a more secure location and then sent scouts to reconnoiter Scipio's camp. Some of them were apprehended, but instead of being executed as spies, the usual penalty, they were graciously received by Scipio, encouraged to walk around the camp, and make accurate observations of everything they saw.[10] As Hannibal's men were touring the camp, Massinissa made an impressive arrival with six thousand infantry and four thousand cavalry. Scipio was so sure of himself, so confident of victory, that he utilized a clever ploy against the master of psychological tactics. Giving the scouts a tour of the camp, and then releasing them to report back what they had seen, was something Hannibal would have done years earlier in Spain and Italy to rattle his opponent.

When the scouts returned and reported what they had seen, Hannibal sent word to Scipio that he wanted to meet and discuss a solution to ending the war other than by fighting—something Hannibal had never done before in his career. Scipio's ploy had worked. That Hannibal even proposed a meeting could be interpreted as his lack of confidence in his army, or perhaps even in his ability to direct a battle. Scipio was receptive to the proposal, and as their camps were within a few miles of each other, he agreed to meet at a site midway between the two, which afforded an unobstructed view from all directions. Scipio and Hannibal each arrived at the meeting place, accompanied by a small detachment of armed cavalry and an interpreter. The cavalry remained a short distance away as two of history's greatest generals approached each other. Facing each other for the first time, both men initially remained silent, not out of reticence or fear, but apparently from what must have been a sense of mutual respect and admiration.

Initially, each spoke in his native language, but as their rapport developed and they became more comfortable with each other, they may well have dispensed with the interpreters and conversed in Greek. We know from the sources that both men had a working knowledge of Greek, the lingua franca of the ancient world. Hannibal spoke first by taking responsibility for starting the war—a major concession and a conciliatory opening to the negotiations. But instead of continuing in that vein, he began to brag how at several periods during the war victory was nearly in his grasp. Not just a battlefield victory, of which he reminded Scipio he had many, but a victorious end to the war itself. Then Hannibal shifted his approach by becoming complimentary and expressing how pleased he was to be negotiating with Scipio, and not with any of the other Roman commanders, none of whom he considered to be his equal. He praised Scipio for having taken command at a young age, when he was not yet able to qualify for the position, and in avenging the deaths of his father and uncle in Spain. Hannibal complimented Scipio because he had not let vengeance consume him but channeled it into a positive accomplishment. He had the strategic foresight to invade Africa when others thought only of defending Italy. It was a mirror of what Hannibal had done as a young man. He went on to praise Scipio for his ability as a commander by enumerating his recent victories in North Africa and bringing to the gates of Carthage the same fear that the Romans had felt when he was before the walls of Rome.

Then Hannibal began to lecture Scipio about life, and the vicissitudes of war. He concluded with the argument that peace in hand is of greater value and to be preferred to an empty hope of victory. Peace between them now, Hannibal argued, would bring Scipio everything he could want. But if they fought, Scipio would have to accept whatever outcome fate and the gods had in store for him. Unable to let go, Hannibal's ego impelled him to point out how this war was more notable for the Carthaginian victories than the Roman ones. Then he shifted his approach back to praise, this time toward Scipio's family, as he recounted how he had engaged Scipio's father in northern Italy years before. Hannibal acknowledged how they had both lost those close to them because of this war; Scipio his father and uncle, Hannibal his brothers. There was no need to continue the war, Hannibal urged; they could end it now.

Hannibal's words reveal an ego that needed to project strength, confidence, and resolve, while at the same time attempting to hide his fear that his time at center stage was over and this was a battle he might well lose. He continued, noting how much simpler and happier life could have been for both of them if those who directed the affairs of their governments had been able to remain content with what they had and not coveted the possessions of others. If Carthage had only remained content to stay within the confines of Africa, and Rome within Italy, the war and all its suffering could have been avoided—words from the man "for whom Africa was too small a continent." Hannibal mused that while one could criticize the past, no one could change it, and they would both have to deal with the way things were, not with how they would have had them.

Conceding that he was negotiating at a time when Rome clearly held the upper hand, Hannibal reminded Scipio that the outcome of the war had not yet been decided. All that was needed to bring it to an end that benefited both sides without further bloodshed were calm, rational minds and a willingness to discuss and negotiate. Hannibal explained that he saw life now through the eyes of an old man, and old men, aware of the sudden and unexpected changes that fortune can inflict, prefer to follow what is prudent rather than trust in luck. Young men, he lectured the younger Scipio, especially those who have enjoyed good fortune, tend to believe that it will endure forever, and in that belief, Hannibal warned, is their weakness.

Then Hannibal began to outline the terms of a settlement by offering Rome all the territory that was the cause for starting the war, and which Rome now possessed; Sicily, Sardinia, Spain, and all the islands between Africa and Italy (Malta). The terms did not differ significantly from what Scipio had offered to the Carthaginian senate the year before, and remarkably, would be, with some minor additions and adjustments, the terms of the final peace after Hannibal's defeat at Zama. Hannibal conceded that the Carthaginians had been deceitful in past negotiations and often failed to uphold terms they had agreed to. But things were different now. Hannibal was prepared to give his personal pledge to uphold the terms of a peace accord between them. While Hannibal conceded that he had started the war and was successful until the gods became envious of him and reversed his fortune, he assured Scipio that Rome would never come to regret any peace accord which he guaranteed. Then Hannibal moved in to close the deal as he posed the key question: why risk losing everything you have gained so far on the outcome of a battle? By engaging in a treaty now, Hannibal emphasized, Scipio could walk away from the table the winner—with minimal risk. Hannibal's words revealed a man who had accepted that Fortuna, or fortune, the most powerful force in the ancient Roman pantheon, had turned her gaze away from him, but he retained a reputation as an undefeatable commander in battle and with a sizable army behind him remained a formidable threat.

Scipio had remained quiet while Hannibal spoke, listening carefully and taking the measure of the man against whom he had first fought sixteen years before at the Trebbia. Then, Scipio had been a boy of eighteen and held no rank. Now he was the youngest consul in Rome's history and in command of an army facing Rome's greatest enemy. Scipio was considerably less philosophical than Hannibal and not given to long digressions. In his pragmatic manner, he made it evident from the outset that he considered himself to hold the upper hand that day, both in their negotiations and on the battlefield.[11] He reminded Hannibal that times had changed. It was the present, Scipio reminded Hannibal, that mattered, not the past. Scipio pointed out that the Carthaginians had started both Punic wars and to end this conflict he had negotiated with them in good faith. Yet the Carthaginians violated the terms of the agreement when it suited them, because they believed that when Hannibal returned to North Africa he would turn the tide of the war in their favor. Now they were seeking to avoid the consequences of their duplicity.

Scipio pointed out that Hannibal was simply offering to concede what Rome already possessed. The Carthaginians, he contended, did not deserve to have the same terms available to them now as they had before they violated the recent treaty. The time to have negotiated an end to the war on favorable terms had been before Hannibal left Italy, not now. As Scipio saw it, Hannibal had only one option to avoid a battle; unconditional surrender. That would entail, in addition to the original terms of the last treaty, paying an indemnity to compensate Rome for the recent loss of a large convoy of her ships off the coast of North Africa. Those ships had been ferrying supplies from Sicily when they were caught in a storm off Cape Bon and driven ashore. A Carthaginian naval squadron took possession of the transports and towed them back to Carthage, where the people looted the cargo. Scipio had sent a delegation to Carthage to demand the return of the ships and their cargo, as well as an apology for what he considered an act of piracy and a violation of the peace treaty. But the senate at Carthage, emboldened by the prospect of Hannibal's return to Africa, refused. To make matters worse, the Roman ship carrying Scipio's emissaries back to his camp was intercepted by Carthaginian war ships and some of the soldiers on board killed in a skirmish.[12] In response, Scipio demanded additional compensation for their deaths and the mistreatment of his envoys.

In response, Hannibal took a hard line and warned Scipio that they would have to fight and let fortune decide which of them would prevail and whether Rome or Carthage would be master of the western half of the Mediterranean. The meeting ended, and they returned to their respective camps to prepare their armies for battle. The next day the two most famous generals in the ancient world, leading the two most powerful armies from the world's two richest cities, met on a broad plain to do battle. Zama, along with the Metaurus, is among the most underrated battles in history, and yet the outcomes of both these clashes marked the genesis of the Roman Empire and probably helped establish the direction of Western civilization.

The armies that faced each other that day were relatively close to the same size, with the Romans having a slight numerical advantage in cavalry. In addition to his own fifteen hundred horsemen, Scipio had the four thousand horsemen and six thousand infantry brought to him by Massinissa. In terms of infantry, his army was composed of twenty-three thousand Romans and Italians, who, along with the Numidians, brought his total to a little over thirty-four thousand. Hannibal had nearly forty thousand soldiers, among them Ligurians, Gauls, Balearic Island slingers, and Mauritanians, all of whom he placed on his front line. These were the most unreliable elements in his army, and, as in the previous battles in Italy, he intended them to absorb the first wave of the Roman attack and sustain the heaviest casualties. Their sacrifice would make the work of Hannibal's second and third lines easier. Livy refers to the first line as "the scum of every nation," men motivated only by the prospects of money, booty, and slaves.[13]

In front of this line Hannibal positioned eighty elephants to break the Roman assault—the greatest number he had ever used in battle. His second line consisted of Carthaginian and African infantry, while the third was held in reserve to be committed to the battle when Hannibal considered it to be the decisive moment. This last line was composed of seasoned veterans—the Bruttians, the remnants of the mercenaries he had brought with him from Italy. To reinforce them were some four thousand Macedonian heavy infantry who had been sent from Philip. Hannibal purposely held this line apart from the fighting, so when they entered the fray at the right moment they would do so with "strength and spirit unimpaired."

In his usual fashion, Hannibal placed his cavalry on both flanks, Numidians on the left and Carthaginians on the right. But this time he lacked the numerical advantage in cavalry that he had always enjoyed and relied on. Hannibal motivated his soldiers for battle utilizing a combination of fear and self-interest. While the Gauls, Ligurians, and Bruttians hated the Romans, they must also have been enticed to fight by the prospect of the spoils that come with victory. The Numidians, Hannibal's African contingent, were probably fighting for money but also out of fear that a Roman victory would mean enslavement under Rome's ally Massinissa. For the Carthaginians, their motivation had to have been the prospect that a Roman victory would mean they would lose everything. Their city would be sacked and burned, their wives and children who survived carried off into slavery, while victory that day would mean they would regain their commercial mastery of the western Mediterranean world with all the profits that entailed.

As Hannibal addressed his troops, he reminded the veterans of the long years they had fought together in Italy, even though most of them were Italians and recent Numidian recruits—the old core that had come with him from Spain were probably either dead or long gone. He recounted the Roman legions they had defeated in Italy and named the consuls who had fallen before them. Hannibal would stop along the line when he recognized a veteran who had distinguished himself in previous battles, calling out that soldier's name and recounting his deeds for those around him to hear. The problem was, there were very few of those men from the old guard left to honor. Most of Hannibal's soldiers were not of the same caliber as those he had led over the Alps and into Italy. He commanded what must have been a disjointed force of men, many of whom had little experience with him as their commander and with whom there must have been no bond beyond money or fear. Unlike the force of mercenaries Hannibal had led from Spain, he had limited time to train this new army and mold them into anything close to the dedicated, cohesive fighting force he had led onto the battlefields of Italy. What Hannibal had been able to do so effectively in Spain and Italy with his army, he seemed unable to accomplish in North Africa.

In the Roman camp, Scipio followed a similar pattern in preparing his soldiers for battle. He recounted their victories in Spain and in North Africa and explained there was little to fear from Hannibal, an adversary who was but the shadow of the man he had once been. Scipio reminded his soldiers that it was Hannibal who just the day before had come to him seeking peace, not out of a desire to end the war, but out of fear of defeat. Soon, he told his soldiers; they would be enjoying the spoils of Carthage and then returning home to their families—as wealthy, proud, and undisputed masters of the world.[14]

As he positioned his army for battle, Scipio placed soldiers known as the *hastati*, or spear throwers, on the first line. They were usually the poorest and youngest men in the Roman army, those who could afford, if lucky, only modest protective equipment, usually chainmail armor. They were first in battle and bore the brunt of the initial attack. If the enemy overcame the *hastati*, they would come up against the second line, more seasoned infantry, known as the *principes*. These men came from a wealthier class, fought with large shields and swords, and were more heavily armed and more experienced. The third line were the *triarii*, the oldest and wealthiest men in the army, those who could afford the highest-quality equipment. The *triarii* wore heavy metal armor, carried large shields, and fought in a shallow phalanx formation. They were only committed to the battle at a crucial junction, giving rise to an old Roman saying, *res ad triarios venit* (it comes down to the triarii). When the battle lines had been formed, Scipio positioned his Italian cavalry on the left wing and the Numidians under the command of his new ally, Massinissa, on the right.

In drawing up his battle lines, Scipio made an innovative modification that contributed significantly to his victory. Armies at the time were usually drawn up in either the traditional Greek phalanx, a tight formation of soldiers fighting shoulder-to-shoulder with interlocking shields, or in a more relaxed checkerboard fashion, a style that came to characterize the Roman army during and after the Second Punic War. When Scipio saw Hannibal's elephants in the front line, he modified the checkerboard pattern by ordering the second line to position itself directly behind the first, and the third behind the second. This arrangement opened pathways or alleys to the left and right of each file of soldiers that ran directly from the front of the first line straight back to the third. Into these alleys, Scipio interspersed very lightly armed soldiers known as *velites*. Like the *hastati*, they were among the youngest and poorest but most mobile of his troops. They were nearly naked and armed with javelins. Their function was to harass the enemy at the initial encounter but not stand and fight. They were skirmishers, and once they had done their work, they quickly faded back into the files as the opposing armies closed. Scipio intended for them to give way as Hannibal's elephants charged, moving themselves laterally out of the path of the animals, and then turning to torment the beasts with javelin thrusts to their eyes and rectal areas as they passed.

As the armies engaged, Hannibal ordered his mahouts to drive their elephants directly into the Roman first line. The Roman infantry responded by beating their swords on their shields, and the noise, combined with the blowing of trumpets, panicked some of the elephants, causing them to turn back on their own lines. Others charged forward into the Romans and instinctively took the path of least resistance—directly through the alleys created between the maniples. As they passed, they were tormented by the *velites* and eventually driven off the field.

At first, Hannibal's front line managed to push the Romans back. But eventually the Romans stopped giving ground and held fast. So close were the armies pressed together at this point, that spears were dropped and the fighting became hand-to-hand with swords. Then, at a crucial moment in the battle, Hannibal ordered the Carthaginian troops in his second line to come to the aid of those on the first—but they refused to move forward. As one ancient source phrased it, they demonstrated "a thoroughly cowardly spirit."[15] Apparently Hannibal had little confidence in them from the outset because of their "inherent cowardice" and had probably placed them between his first line and his seasoned veterans in the third in an attempt to force them to fight when their turn came. Without support, Hannibal's front line eventually gave way, and as the soldiers turned to retreat, they found themselves fighting the Romans behind them and the Carthaginians who now blocked their only avenue of retreat in front. Large numbers of Hannibal's soldiers died at the hands of their own, while any who managed to extricate themselves from the fighting and emerge found their escape blocked by the interlocking shields and lowered spears of Hannibal's third line— his Bruttian allies and the Macedonian phalanx.

What was left of Hannibal's first and second lines was eventually pushed out onto the flanks, where they attempted to run into the open countryside. But there was no escape from the carnage, and most were killed or captured by Roman cavalry detachments waiting on the wings for them. The space between the two armies filled with the dead and the dying—the ground soaked in the blood and gore of both men and animals. Corpses were piled up in heaps in a macabre display of con-torted arms, legs, and torsos extending in every direction. The turning point in the battle came when Roman and Numidian cavalry detach-ments, returning from having driven Hannibal's cavalry off the field, attacked his third line from the rear. The level ground gave them every advantage over Hannibal's best infantry, who were now confused and disorganized, fighting their own men in front of them and the Romans behind them.

When the battle ended, over twenty thousand of Hannibal's soldiers were reported to have been killed and an equal number taken prisoner. If the numbers reported in the ancient sources can be believed, the Ro-mans suffered only fifteen hundred killed. With Hannibal's army in dis-array, the Romans moved to plunder his camp. The battle was over, and Hannibal, once the terror of Italy and the nemesis of Rome, deserted what was left of his army. With a few of his closest supporters, he fled across the desert on horseback, riding all that night and into the next day, until they reached the safety of the coast at Hadrumetum. Despite

Hannibal's defeat, the Greek Polybius found no fault with his actions at Zama, nor did he question the competence of his command.

According to Polybius, circumstances and fortune simply did not favor Hannibal that day, as he had come upon an adversary who was his equal. Polybius believed that Hannibal did everything possible to avoid fighting at Zama. He attempted to negotiate a settlement, and when that failed and he was forced to fight, he acted to the highest standards in the way he deployed his army. But the Roman army at Zama was not like those Hannibal had faced in Italy. This army and its commander were more experienced and better trained than those Hannibal had slaughtered at the Trebbia, Trasimene, and Cannae. The Romans had come a long way in sixteen years of war and learned their lessons the hard way. What Hannibal faced at Zama were disciplined, experienced soldiers led by a new breed of commander, one who thought and acted like a professional soldier, not a politician.

In analyzing the battle of Zama, the primary question is why did Hannibal lose? Was it because he held back his best troops, his Italians and the Macedonian phalanx, while the rest of his army was being cut to pieces? This was not consistent with his usual tactical modus operandi. With the Roman army engaged with his first line and their cavalry off the field, why didn't Hannibal drive his third line of fresh and experienced veterans into the fray while executing the lethal cavalry flank attack or envelopment he was famous for in Italy? Was he too distracted, contending with a mutiny in his Carthaginian second line? Why did he allow the Romans to control the flanks—the most important position in a battle?

Hannibal appeared uncharacteristically passive at Zama, leaving the initiative to Scipio. He took a defensive posture by engaging in a traditional slugfest of attrition. His inclination to maneuvers and the employment of innovative strategies, moves that once defied convention and gave him the advantage over larger armies, was not in evidence, despite the praise of Polybius. This was clearly not the same general who had commanded at the Trebbia, Trasimene, and Cannae over a decade before.

After plundering Hannibal's camp, Scipio returned his army to its base at Utica. There, he dispatched an emissary to report his victory to the senate in Rome and prepared his army to march on Carthage. He sent half his force by sea and the remainder overland. Scipio was aboard the flotilla, not far from Carthage, when a ship "laced with woolen fillets and olive branches of supplication" intercepted them.[16] On board the approaching vessel were ten of the most prominent citizens of Carthage, who had come to beg for mercy. Scipio ordered them to return to the city and wait until he established his camp nearby at the site of modern-day Tunis, the capital of Tunisia. In an attempt to help the Carthaginians, the son of Syphax attacked the Roman camp with a sizable force of infantry and cavalry, but the Romans drove them back into the desert from where they had come.

The Carthaginians sent a second delegation to Scipio, this time thirty of their leading citizens, begging an audience to discuss terms. Their reception was hostile, because, "the memory of their treachery was still fresh." Scipio held a council of his closest advisors to discuss his response, and the consensus that emerged was that Carthage should be destroyed. When Scipio's advisors began to discuss in detail what an assault on the city would entail, the magnitude of the undertaking and the probable length of the siege became sobering. Political considerations also had to be accounted for. Despite his success on the battlefield, Scipio was not popular with all the political factions in the senate at Rome, and he suspected he might be replaced. If that happened, his successor could reap the credit for winning the war without ever having fought a battle. With these considerations in mind, the decision was made not to lay siege to Carthage but to end the war immediately on relatively lenient terms.

The Carthaginian envoys were called to Scipio's quarters where, once more, they were sharply rebuked for the duplicity of their people, and then the terms of a remarkably lenient peace were laid out before them. Carthage would be allowed to remain an independent city-state—free from Roman military occupation. Its citizens would retain their own form of government and continue to formulate and live under their own laws. Carthage would retain control over all those territories she held in Africa before the war began, and all Roman prisoners, deserters, and runaway slaves were to be returned. All Carthaginian warships, except for ten, were to be turned over to the Romans, along with all the remaining war elephants. Carthage was prohibited from waging war anywhere in the ancient world without the permission of the Roman senate, and Massinissa would be awarded territory in North Africa as delineated by Rome. Scipio's soldiers were to be fed and paid a salary by Carthage for a minimum of three months or until envoys returned from Rome with ratification of the treaty. In the meantime, a truce was in place, but not a peace treaty. A hundred hostages, all between the ages of fourteen and thirty, were chosen by Scipio from among the leading families of Carthage and surrendered to guarantee compliance with the truce. The Roman ships that had been salvaged by Carthage were to be returned and their owners compensated for lost or missing cargo. Finally, Carthage was to pay an indemnity to Rome of 10,000 talents in equal annual installments over a fifty-year period—considerably more than the 2,200 talents imposed at the conclusion of the First Punic War in 241 B.C.

The envoys returned to Carthage to present the terms to the senate for ratification. Hannibal was summoned from Hadrumetum, probably to account for his defeat and explain why the war had been lost. When he returned to Carthage and reviewed the terms, Hannibal urged the senate to accept them and put its trust in Scipio. When the terms were announced to the people in a public forum, they were initially met with disapproval. Speaker after speaker took the podium to rail against rat-ification. The people were tired of the war, even though it had failed to touch most of them directly. They complained over the additional taxes and assessments imposed by the government to pay the first installment of indemnities due to Rome.

Hannibal, present in the assembly, became so agitated that he forc-ibly pulled one speaker from the dais in frustration, and the crowd reacted angrily to his action. There were shouts that Carthage was a democracy—where people had a right to express their views. When Hannibal took the podium, he responded to a bevy of taunts, but calmed the crowd by explaining that he was a soldier and not accus-tomed to the "excessive freedoms of city life." He had been away for nearly forty years waging war to protect their freedom and needed time to accustom himself to the "conventions, laws and customs of civil life and public discourse."[17] Hannibal commanded great respect, and the crowd responded favorably to his apology. They listened attentively as he explained the reality of their situation and the fairness of Scipio's terms. They accepted his criticism that people only seem to feel the misfortunes of war when they impinge on their purses. There is no sting more painful, he commented, to people who are wealthy, comfortable, and secure than the loss of their money.[18] Hannibal turned the crowd in favor of peace on Roman terms that day, and with few options open to them, the popular assembly and then the senate approved them.

At Rome matters began to unfold just as Scipio had feared. Elections for the consulship were held, and one of those elected for 201 B.C. was Gnaeus Cornelius Lentulus. Lentulus, with support from senators who were critical of Scipio, maneuvered to have Africa assigned to him as his province. Ambitious men were seeking appointments so they could partake of the final victory feast at little personal risk. There was money to be made in North Africa, and Lentulus calculated that with the major fighting over, he could claim the final victory and its rewards with minimal risk. Even if hostilities resumed, he believed they would do so only on a limited basis. The financial and political rewards far outweighed any risks. But the attempt to assign him Africa was defeated in another political venue. Scipio's supporters circumvented the senate and went directly to the popular assembly to have it grant Scipio "imperium"—a combination of political, military, and economic authority over Africa. Now he had sole command over the Roman land forces in Africa and the authority to administer his peace treaty with Carthage. Carthage surrendered its warships, and some five hundred were towed out to sea, burned, and sunk within sight of the city ramparts. Then the Carthaginians turned over their elephants, along with four thousand Roman prisoners, deserters, and slaves. Scipio had the soldiers repatriated, the deserters crucified, the Italians among them beheaded, and the runaway slaves scourged and returned to their masters.

With his work in North Africa completed, Scipio prepared to return to Rome. Before leaving, he assigned all the cities, towns, and territory held by the defeated Numidian king Syphax to Massinissa and then, crossing the Straits of Messina, travelled overland to Rome dragging the chained Numidian behind his chariot.[19] Crowds lined the route to watch the parade and cheer the man who had saved Italy. Scipio entered Rome to the greatest triumph ever awarded a victorious general. He displayed the spoils of his campaign in Africa and deposited over sixty tons of silver into the treasury after paying a bonus to each of his soldiers. The senate declared a period of thanksgiving, with games and festivals, and Scipio picked up the bill for everything. Of all the honors bestowed on Scipio the greatest was the cognomen or nickname Africanus—a name that reflected his conquest of Carthage and that he would carry for the remaining years of his life. The appellation was a first for the Romans, and it would become an honor every powerful Roman after Scipio coveted and future emperors of Rome would bestow on themselves for their conquests, real or imagined. Whether the title was bestowed on Scipio by his soldiers, by the people of Italy, or by the senate is never made quite clear in the sources.[20] What is evident is that even though Scipio returned to Italy a national hero and probably the most popular political figure in Rome, opposition to him and his family grew—led by a conservative, stridently anti-Carthaginian Tuscan landowner and senator named Cato.

Scipio spared Hannibal from execution or imprisonment, and it is generally conceded by scholars that the senate at Rome agreed due to Scipio's popularity with the people.[21] Sparing Hannibal made Scipio more enemies in the senate. Besides holding Hannibal in high esteem, Scipio had a practical reason for sparing him. There can be little doubt that, among the potential leaders at Carthage, Scipio considered Hannibal to be the most likely to honor his commitments, uphold the terms of the treaty, and make sure the payments to Rome were made in full and on time.

Nothing is known for certain about Hannibal's activities in the years immediately following the end of the war (201 B.C.–196 B.C.). Only two ancient sources report on him during the five years following the peace between Carthage and Rome, and those references are scant and even contradictory. Hannibal seems to drop from sight shortly after the peace, but from one source we learn that he remained head of the army and that, in a vague statement, "with his brother Mago at his side, continued to make war in Africa until 200 B.C." However, we know from other sources that Mago died at sea nearly three years earlier. Nor is it clear in this reference who Hannibal was fighting: Africans or Romans? There is also a reference in a much later source to Hannibal's concern about the effect of idleness on his soldiers, so much so that to offset it he had them plant olive trees. However, since the reference is not tied to any specific year, the planting could have occurred in the year before the battle of Zama, during Hannibal's time in Hadrumetum, or after peace with Rome was ratified. What is certain is that Hannibal seems to have

withdrawn into private life for at least part of this period, and that he
stayed away from Carthage.

The only references found in the main sources to continued Carthaginian resistance against Rome around 200 B.C. concern the actions
of Hamilcar the Carthaginian,[22] an officer who had been left behind
in northern Italy by Mago in 203 B.C. Another source maintains this
Hamilcar was left behind by Hasdrubal when his army passed through
northern Italy in 207 B.C. In either case, he could have been left by
Hasdrubal and then later joined with Mago, but it is curious that his
activities in northern Italy are never mentioned in any detail by the main
sources. This Hamilcar apparently operated in Italy for several years,
raiding Roman colonies like Placentia and Cremona with his army of
Gauls and Ligurians. His army apparently became sizable, numbering
some forty thousand, if the sources can be believed, making it as large
as if not larger than, any of the armies commanded by Hannibal, Hasdrubal, or Mago in northern Italy.

Because the Roman armies in northern Italy were apparently never
large enough to confront this Hamilcar directly, envoys were sent from
Rome to Carthage, demanding his recall or surrender. The best that
Carthage could do, in reply to the Roman demand, was to declare Hamilcar an outlaw and confiscate his family property in North Africa.
This indicates he could have been a rogue operator and not under any
orders from Carthage. Finally, Roman legions, considerably reinforced,
confronted Hamilcar and his Gauls at Cremona, where his army was
defeated and he was killed in the battle along with an alleged thirty-five
thousand of his soldiers—another highly suspect number because it
makes the battle deaths there second in number only to the horrendous
Roman losses at Cannae.

In a later recounting of the battle, the same source has Hamilcar captured alive,[23] and then in a third rendition, he is captured and led in chains
before the chariot of the triumphant Roman commander Cornelius on

his return to Rome.[24] Regardless of Hamilcar's fate, killed in battle or executed, his presence in northern Italy is confusing. It could be interpreted as evidence of clandestine Carthaginian resistance to Rome, a "black ops" operation of sorts, or that he was acting independently— as a warlord of sorts, leading the Gauls. Hamilcar's presence in northern Italy with his army of Roman-hating Gauls could have been a reason for Hannibal, as we will see in the next chapter, to have encouraged King Antiochus of Syria to invade Italy rather than Greece.

The end of the Second Punic War saw the political situation at Carthage change dramatically. A struggle developed between the aristocratic elements that had traditionally controlled the society and the popular assemblies. Traditionally, the most powerful political body at Carthage was called the "order of judges," and it consisted of some 104 of the richest men in the city, who were appointed for life terms. They were so intent on protecting their own financial interests that anyone at Carthage who offended one of them became the enemy of all of them.[25] While corruption and mismanagement in the higher echelons of government were rampant, the judges were so powerful they had been able for years to stifle attempts at reform. They were the oligarchs, those who had made money during the war and were concerned only with lining their own pockets and taxing the poor to pay Rome.

When the first installment of the war indemnity for 199 B.C. came due, it was short, so the Carthaginians sent Rome a debased quality of silver. When the talents were received at Rome and tested by the officials in charge of the treasury, they found that 25 percent was base metal. The Romans, with good reason, were convinced that the Carthaginians were up to their old tricks again. Confronted with their blatant attempt to pay with debased silver and anxious to avoid any resumption of hostilities, the Carthaginian senate quickly made good the discrepancy by further taxing the common people. Popular dissent over the next couple of years reached crisis proportions. Hannibal believed the time had come to curtail the power of the oligarchs, and he reappeared on the scene in 196 B.C.—elected suffete, or chief executive officer, of Carthage by the popular assemblies. The position of suffete was the highest executive office in the government of Carthage and similar to the consulship in Rome. Normally, two suffetes were elected by the popular assemblies to serve concurrent one-year terms directing the administration of the state, just as two consuls were elected in Rome to do the same. Two were elected so that each could serve as a check on the other as they performed certain religious duties and judicial functions, controlled government finances, prepared legislation, and presided over the popular assemblies. Only Hannibal's name is mentioned as suffete for the year 196 B.C.; it is possible that only he was elected, or, if a second suffete was elected, his name was simply lost to history.

Hannibal campaigned by condemning the "haughtiness" of the judges and accusing them of oppressing the liberty and economic well-being of the common people.[26] He entered the political arena campaigning against the privilege and corruption of the very class from which he had come. Although Carthage had always been a plutocracy and the rich had traditionally governed there, the loss of the Second Punic War and the indemnities imposed by the Romans sparked a popular opposition when the oligarchs tried to shift the burden of paying that indemnity onto the backs of the middle class and the poor through a special assessment. The oligarchs had been so blatant in their mismanagement and even theft of public funds that Carthage was in danger of defaulting on its next payment to Rome and thus the reason for the special assessment. State revenues had been consistently mismanaged, stolen, and wasted. The treasury was rapidly being depleted, yet when Hannibal ordered an audit of the tax revenues from landholdings as well as duties collected at the ports, he found the amounts collected were more than sufficient to meet the obligations of the indemnity owed Rome, but they were routinely being siphoned off by the oligarchs. When the information became known, there was a popular outcry, and Hannibal became the champion of those who wanted to break the hold of the oligarchs over Carthage. Hannibal challenged the assessment and argued that excessive taxation at the expense of the people was unnecessary.

It was a charge that resonated with the popular assemblies, and as suffete, Hannibal was given the authority to reform the government and fiscal administration of Carthage, something that brought him into conflict with the oligarchs. While each member of the order of judges had been elected for life, Hannibal pushed a law through the popular assembly that required the annual election of judges and set two-year term limits. It was a radical challenge to the traditional power structure of Carthage, and although it made Hannibal popular with the lower classes, it incurred the animosity of the oligarchs.

The war changed Carthage. While limited democracy had existed there for centuries in the form of the popular assemblies, it was closely regulated by the oligarchs. Following the end of the war the popular assemblies increased their influence in public affairs by taking a stronger stand against the aristocracy. The people demanded more of a say in policy formulation, and the suffete, who presided over them and was elected directly by them, became, especially under Hannibal, their champion. While at Rome, the opposite was happening. The senate, with no basis in Roman constitutional law but because of its effective direction of the war, was coming to dominate the society at the expense of the popular assemblies and acting more and more in the interests of the aristocracy. The Roman senate had existed since the founding of the city by Romulus (756 B.C.) and was initially an advisory body to the Roman kings composed of the hundred richest men in the society. By the time of the Punic Wars, it had increased in size, prestige, and power. The consuls, the heads of the army, and the executive branch of Roman government came from the aristocratic class, and although the candidates for the consulship were selected by the senate, they were elected by the people. They reported to the senate, and at the end of their term, joined it for life. Thus, it was always in a consul's interest to conform to the will of the group he would be joining at the end of his term and the group with which his economic interests were so closely aligned—not the constituency which had elected him. It would be several decades following the conclusion of the Second Punic War before Rome would undergo a transformation similar to the one that occurred, however briefly, at Carthage under Hannibal. That change at Rome came with the rise to power of the tribune—the man elected annually by the Roman lower classes, the plebeians, to champion their cause with the aristocracy and protect their interests in government.

In the short term, Hannibal seems to have instituted some reforms, but owing to the entrenched corruption among the aristocratic class and his subsequent flight into exile, he proved powerless to bring about any lasting changes as Carthage reverted to business as usual. Because Carthage had been spared the ravages of war, the economy was positioned to prosper. The Carthaginians had used mercenaries to do their fighting and had not suffered significant losses of manpower. Over the next ten years, Carthage made significant economic gains in North Africa even though she had lost her overseas possessions to Rome. The money Carthage had spent to fund wars now went into economic development—a phenomenon known as the "revenge of the defeated."[27] Carthage recovered to the point of being able to supply Rome with enough grain to feed the people in Italy as well as the Roman armies fighting in Macedon and Greece.[28] Ten years later, Carthage was able to export over half a million bushels,[29] and by 171 B.C. the amount had risen to over 2 million.[30] So prosperous and rapid was the recovery, that Carthage was able to offer Rome the balance of the indemnity due in one final payment—which the Romans refused.

One area that contributed to the economic recovery was a brisk trade that developed between Carthage and Rome for finished products—the Carthaginians fabricating and selling, the Romans buying. The harbor at Carthage, according to fairly recent excavations, seems to have undergone extensive renovations and even expansion after the end of the Second Punic War—which can only be explained within the context of the economic recovery of the city. There are also indications of significant strides in urban development in and around the city during the period of Hannibal's administration, and it is perhaps more than coincidental, as shall be seen in the next chapter, that he is reported to have undertaken the design of cities for the kings of Armenia and Bithynia.

The aristocrats or oligarchs at Carthage, largely because of Hannibal's reform movement, faced a growing popular discontent and calls for holding them accountable for their corruption and mismanagement of the government. Faced with the prospect of losing their privileged position in the city and having to pay back to the state treasury the funds they had embezzled, a cabal of oligarchs plotted to discredit Hannibal and remove him from political office. A faction in the senate pulled the one chain they knew would alarm the Romans, the prospect of another military threat from Hannibal. They sent word to Rome that they suspected Hannibal was planning to invade Italy again, this time with an army composed in part of Macedonian mercenaries provided by King Philip. They maintained Hannibal was corresponding with King Antiochus III of Syria in an effort to gain financial support for his plan to invade Italy again, and even receiving the king's agents at Carthage.[31] The oligarchs further fueled the fire of suspicion by contending Hannibal was a man of "inherently violent disposition" who believed only war could bring prosperity, and that a people who remained at peace for any extended period would become soft and complacent.

When the matter was debated in the senate at Rome, Scipio rose to defend Hannibal. He objected to what he argued were groundless accusations[32] and advised the senators not to be drawn into the petty squabbles and rivalries of the Carthaginian aristocratic political factions. But Scipio had his own problems at home; there were those in the senate who viewed him as too accommodating when it came to Hannibal. Scipio now found himself the target of a political inquiry into the mismanagement of state funds that had been allocated to him during his campaigns in Spain and Sicily.

In the late spring or summer of 195 B.C., a senatorial delegation from Rome was sent to North Africa under the cover of mediating a border dispute between Carthage and Massinissa. The three senators who constituted the delegation were openly hostile to Scipio and had come to build a case against Hannibal. Before the delegation arrived, Hannibal left Carthage—travelling by horseback south along the coast to Hadrumetum. There he hired a ship and set sail for the island of Cercina, some thirty miles due east off the coast of Tunisia. Cercina was a resupply depot used by ships plying the Mediterranean, and from there Hannibal intended to sail on to Tyre on the coast of Lebanon.

Landing at Cercina, Hannibal was recognized immediately. His reputation had made him a celebrity in the ancient world, and "in every city people were eager to catch a glimpse of him."[33] He explained his presence to the port authorities by contending he was on a diplomatic mission to Tyre. Fearing that word of his location might reach Carthage quickly by one of the ships daily leaving the port and complicate his departure from Cercina, he devised a ploy. Hannibal announced the preparation of a sacrifice to be followed by a great feast—all at his expense. The officers and crews of all the ships in port were invited, and to give the guests shelter from the midday summer sun, he asked the captains to remove their sails and erect them as sheltering canopies during the festivities. The sails from all the ships were taken down—except for those on Hannibal's ship—and transported to the site of the festival. The sacrifice was held and the feasting went on well into the night. Late in the festivities, Hannibal returned to his ship and quickly set sail.

There was not a ship in port that next day that was capable of over-taking him. Crews had to recover from their binge and their ships had to be rigged for sailing again—a time-consuming process. When word reached Carthage that Hannibal was at Cercina, the senate sent two warships to try to overtake him. The judges and the senate declared him an "outlaw," his family property was confiscated, and his homes demolished—perhaps to convince the Roman delegation that the aristocratic faction at Carthage was not a part of any Hannibal plan to resume war.

By the time the Carthaginian warships were at sea, Hannibal had found his first refuge as an exile. The man who for nearly a quarter of a century was the driving force for war in the western Mediterranean prepared to become a humble supplicant at the knees of the eastern Hellenistic potentates. His first stop, as irony would have it, was in the same city from which Elissa, the founder of Carthage, had fled over six centuries before. Hannibal was preparing to begin a new chapter that held little promise for the man who had terrified all Italy and come close to changing the very direction of history.

CHAPTER VIII

Exile

I N THE AUTUMN of 195 B.C., Hannibal left Tyre and moved north along the coast to the city of Antioch—near what today constitutes the tense border between Syria and Turkey. Hannibal was seeking an audience with Antiochus, the sixth king of the Hellenistic state, which had been formed shortly after the death of Alexander the Great in 323 B.C., by his Seleucid successors. Antiochus came to the throne in 223 B.C. at the age of eighteen, and during his first decade as monarch set about to reconquer the lands in the east that Alexander had subjugated a hundred years before and which, over time, had gradually been lost. At the height of its power, the Seleucid empire encompassed western Asia Minor, central Anatolia, Persia, the Levant, Mesopotamia, and parts of what are today Kuwait, Afghanistan, Turkmenistan, and Pakistan. The young king's initial move was against Egypt in 217 B.C. but failed when his army was defeated in Palestine not far from Gaza. Undeterred, Antiochus led his army east into Armenia in 212 B.C., then Persia (Iran) in 211 B.C., Bactria (Afghanistan) in 208 B.C., and eventually reached the borders of India in 206 B.C. Then he turned back, by way of the Arabian Peninsula, reaching his capital at Antioch by 204 B.C. Not satisfied with his conquests in the east, Antiochus looked to Greece and colluded with Philip of Macedon in 202 B.C. Pleased with the scope of his conquests and his prospects for the future, the king bestowed upon himself the epithet "the great"—reflecting his belief that he was the new Alexander for his age.

With the Second Punic War over and the western Mediterranean now relatively secured, the Romans set their sights on the east: Illyria, Greece, and Asia Minor. They declared war on Philip in 202 B.C., a move that proved to be a convenient opening into Greece. Their justification was Philip's alliance with Hannibal during the previous war and the presence of a Macedonian phalanx in action against the Roman army at Zama. In command of the Roman forces in Macedon and Greece was the consul Titus Quinctius Flamininus, a man who had been too young to fight and make a name for himself in the Second Punic War but who was intent on winning glory in the east to rival what had been accomplished by other Roman commanders in the west. Flamininus was determined that he would be to Greece what Scipio had been to Spain and Africa. From a well-known patrician family in Rome and politically ambitious, Flamininus was a philhellene and presented himself to the Greeks as their savior from the tyranny of an avaricious and barbarous Macedonian Philip.

Flamininus defeated Philip in 197 B.C. in northern Greece (Thessaly) at the battle of Cynoscephalae or the "dog's head." In that battle, the Roman legions demonstrated their superiority over the once-invincible Macedonian phalanx with which Alexander the Great had conquered so much of the eastern part of the ancient world. Philip quickly came to terms, and the senate at Rome affirmed the treaty. The following year at Corinth, Flamininus used the setting of the Isthmian Games, athletic competitions that often rivaled the Olympic Games in scope and size, to announce to the world that Rome and he were the guarantors of the freedom of the Greeks.[1]

With Philip out of the picture, Antiochus saw an opportunity to expand his empire into the west. He moved his army north along the western coast of Asia Minor, first taking the great Greek city of Ephesus and then nearly everything else all the way to the Hellespont (Gallipoli). Crossing the Dardanelles, he probed the area of mainland Greece known at the time as Thrace and which today comprises northeastern Greece, southern Bulgaria, and western Turkey to gauge Roman reaction to the incursion. At this point, Hannibal entered the picture, arriving in Ephesus in 195 B.C. seeking an audience with the king, who had just returned from Thrace. Antiochus was at the height of his power and undisputedly the most powerful monarch in the ancient world. Hannibal was looking for a safe haven and a job. The two men were close in age, with Hannibal slightly older, but the king, while recognizing the Carthaginian's reputation as a military leader and his successes in battle, clearly saw himself as the superior. Still, Hannibal had value for Antiochus. There was no one in the ancient world at the time who had more experience fighting the Romans, and having Hannibal in his military entourage might have given the king a psychological advantage. With Hannibal on his side, the Romans might be intimidated and deterred from resisting his invasion of Greece. It was not just a matter of Hannibal commanding an army by the side of Antiochus; it was the threat that the extensive resources of the king could finance another Hannibal invasion of Italy.

For Hannibal, joining Antiochus, even in a subordinate position, presented an opportunity to continue his struggle against Rome. But it meant that he had to be prepared to accept a subservient role in the relationship—something that must have been difficult for a man who had given orders most of his life, not taken them. Both Hannibal and Antiochus were men of considerable ego. Antiochus considered himself a ruler who had conquered far more than Hannibal ever had and at a younger age. Hannibal, on the other hand, had been commander of the Carthaginian forces for nearly two decades and certainly was not given to living in the shadow of another. Would Hannibal accept orders from Antiochus and would Antiochus take advice from Hannibal? Were these two monumental egos on an inevitable collision course?

For the next three years, Antiochus waged what some contemporary scholars have termed an ancient version of a "cold war"[2] against Rome. The first year, 195 B.C./194 B.C., saw Hannibal doing very little militarily, as the king tried several diplomatic initiatives to win concessions from the Romans. Antiochus sent emissaries to Flamininus with a proposal for an alliance in 193 B.C., but contingent on Rome's recognition of him as the sovereign of Asia Minor and Thrace. Flamininus rejected the proposal and warned him to keep out of northeastern Greece or the area known as Thrace—a restriction the Syrian king refused to accept. That same year, Hannibal persuaded Antiochus to fund an expedition to Africa, a variation of modern-day covert operations.

The first step in the plan was to dispatch an agent to Carthage, under cover, to establish contact with the pro-Barca factions in the city. A merchant from Tyre, Ariston, was chosen. If he was successful, then Hannibal, with a force of a hundred warships, ten thousand infantry, and a thousand cavalry, would land on the shores of North Africa and march west against the city, increasing the size of his army with African recruits and conscripts as he went. The plan depended on the pro-Barca factions in the city overwhelming the garrison there and opening the gates to him when he arrived. Should the attack on Carthage fail, the alternative was to abandon the effort in North Africa and sail to southern Italy. Probably landing in Bruttium, he would use his small army to resume guerilla operations against the Romans on Italian soil while, at the same time, Antiochus would launch an invasion of Greece.[3] The intent was to surprise the Romans and confront them with a two-front war.

Once Ariston arrived at Carthage, his visit quickly became the talk of the town. He was brought before the "order of judges" to be interrogated about the true purpose of his presence. Ariston was careful enough not to have any compromising documents on his person when he was apprehended, and he managed to evade direct answers to the questions put to him by the judges. Faced with the prospect of imprisonment and even crucifixion, he took advantage of his temporary release by the authorities while they investigated further to escape by ship. Just as he was leaving, Ariston managed to have a notice posted in a public forum, probably a central marketplace, which implicated many of the judges in the plot he was suspected of fomenting. Using this tactic, he shifted suspicion away from his contacts in the city and onto the highest levels of government.[4]

As a result of Ariston's public disclosure, the judges felt compelled to send a delegation to Rome to explain the matter and at the same time to lodge a complaint against the Numidian king Massinissa for some recent border encroachments. Massinissa also sent an embassy to Rome to present his side of the dispute and to mockingly argue that all Carthage had a legal right to in North Africa now was the small strip of beachfront that the ancient Phoenician queen Elissa had taken from the Numidians by trickery centuries before. The Carthaginians countered that Massinissa had violated the borders established by Scipio in the treaty of 201 B.C. The senate sent Scipio to Carthage, along with two colleagues, to mediate the dispute and further investigate the allegations posted by Ariston.

At approximately the same time, probably the autumn of 193 B.C., the Romans sent a delegation to Ephesus to engage Antiochus in talks. Hannibal was present when they arrived, but his role if any in the official discussions is not evident. What did happen is that during their visit, some members of the Roman delegation revealed to the king's advisors that they were engaged in private meetings with Hannibal.[5] This caused Antiochus to become suspicious that Hannibal was colluding with the Romans and it is easy to conclude that the Romans purposely sought to compromise him in this way. According to Livy,[6] one member of the Roman delegation, the former consul Villius Tappulus, actually engaged Hannibal with the specific intent of driving a wedge between him and the king.

One meeting between Hannibal and the Romans at Ephesus became legendary in Roman literature and has been passed down through the centuries.[7] Scipio Africanus apparently was a member of the delegation, and he encountered Hannibal casually one day in a gymnasium. They spent the remainder of the day together, walking the streets of the city, and their conversation was so pleasant that Hannibal invited Scipio to dine with him that night. Hannibal was Scipio's senior in years and did most of the talking. As would be expected, the two discussed military matters, and inevitably the question came up: Who were the greatest commanders in history. Hannibal replied, without a moment's hesitation, Alexander the Great. For Hannibal, Alexander was first because he had conquered almost the entire eastern part of the ancient world with only a small army, but one intensely loyal to him. When asked who he would consider the second-best general in history, Hannibal named Pyrrhus, the Greek king who had invaded southern Italy and fought the Romans just a few years before the outbreak of the First Punic War. Hannibal admired Pyrrhus not only because of his ability as a soldier and his effective utilization of diplomacy, but also for his ability to know when to cut his losses and quit. In third place, Hannibal offered himself. When Scipio inquired where Hannibal would have placed himself if he had won at Zama, Hannibal replied, again, without a moment's reflection, above even Alexander the Great. It was the subtlest of compliments and one not lost on Scipio. While the story has been a cornerstone of the Hannibal legend throughout the centuries, some contemporary scholars have come to doubt it as they question how Scipio could have been at Ephesus when he was part of the delegation that had been sent to Carthage.[8]

Because of his meetings with the Romans and the resulting allegations of collusion, Hannibal's position at court was compromised. He was excluded from all meetings with the king and his advisors, and it was decided that any future role he would play in a war against Rome would be minor. Instead of directing military operations or commanding one of Antiochus's armies, it was decided that Hannibal would be sent to Africa with a small force to create a diversion while the king launched his invasion of Greece.[9] The idea was apparently at the instigation of a Greek, a representative of the Aetolians named Alexander, who was close to the king. The king, against Hannibal's advice, agreed. The Aetolians were a confederation of tribal communities and city-states in central and western Greece who had lobbied Antiochus to assist them in resisting any Roman incursions. Hannibal argued in favor of an invasion of Italy, not Greece, since it would force the Romans into a defensive posture—protecting their sources of manpower and supply. An attack on Italy, Hannibal urged, would also have a strong psychological effect on its people, by reviving once more the nightmares of the Second Punic War. An invasion of Greece, he contended, would give the Romans a slight logistical advantage over Antiochus since one of their principal ports, Brundisium, was just a short sail across the Adriatic Sea. They could easily supply their armies with reinforcements from that port—an area Hannibal knew well. Alexander considered himself Hannibal's equal when it came to expertise on how and where to fight the Romans, and he had considerable influence with Antiochus. He urged the king to be wary of Hannibal and concentrate on an invasion of Greece instead of Italy.

Initially, Hannibal bore his exclusion from court and subsequent humiliation in silence. As Livy writes, "he was no longer honored at court."[10] Finally, unable to bear the ostracism any longer, he requested an audience to ask the king the reason for his displeasure. Antiochus was direct in his reply. He suspected Hannibal of colluding with the Romans and thus no longer trusted him. In response, Hannibal explained to the king that he would never find, in all his realm, a more loyal or effective ally in his struggle against Rome. He recounted how his entire life, from his childhood, had been devoted to one thing, fighting Rome, and that for nearly four decades he had led a struggle that saw his brothers killed and his family lost. He had been exiled from his homeland and the only life he knew was fighting the Romans—"I hate and am hateful to the Romans."[11]

Accommodation, Hannibal argued, could never be an option with his enemies, and to reinforce his hatred of Rome he recounted to the king the story of the oath he had taken as a young boy. Hamilcar was preparing to leave for Spain and, as was customary in Carthage, he prepared a sacrifice to ensure a safe voyage and a successful mission. Hannibal was brought before the altar of the gods at Carthage, a place where the "horrid rites" of infant human sacrifice were often carried out, and on the altar, he watched as the sacrificial animal was opened and the priests sought an oracle.

At that point, Hamilcar demanded that his son pledge before the gods of Carthage that "with fire and sword," he would reenact at Rome the destruction of Troy.[12] That sacred oath, Hannibal explained, bound him to continue his struggle against Rome throughout his life and at any cost. Even in exile, wherever he might be, if he could find someone to fight Rome, he would be there by his side. There was nothing he would not do, Hannibal contended, if it advanced the destruction of his sworn enemy—Rome.[13] If what Antiochus wanted was accommodation with Rome, Hannibal advised, then he should look to others. If he wanted war, then he could find no better or more loyal advisor and ally. Antiochus was moved by Hannibal's words, and following that meeting they were reconciled—at least to a degree. But despite what the sources say about their reconciliation, Hannibal apparently never played a major role in the military affairs of the king after that.

Antiochus ignored Hannibal's advice and undertook to invade Greece in the autumn of 191 B.C. He led his infantry, cavalry, and elephants over the body of water known as the Hellespont (The Dardanelles) and once more into Thessaly. The following spring the king moved south to engage the Romans at Thermopylae, the narrow pass that served as the gateway to central Greece.

The two armies faced each other in the same pass where in 480 B.C. three hundred Spartans, immortalized in history, had sacrificed themselves by blocking the massive invading army of the Persian king Xerxes. The Spartans held the Persians at bay long enough for the other Greek city-states to assemble their armies and eventually defeat the threat. But now, instead of Greeks and Persians fighting, it was the Romans under the command of the consul Acilius Glabrio with two military tribunes, Porcius Cato and Valerius Flaccus, facing the Seleucid king and his Greek allies. Hannibal was notably absent. Antiochus held the pass, but in a classic replay of history, a detachment of some two thousand Romans, led by Cato (the pig man) went up and over the mountains at night, just as the Persians had done centuries before. They came down at dawn behind the army of Antiochus in a surprise attack. Caught between two Roman armies, Antiochus, with a small contingent of his advisors and his new teenage wife, extricated himself from the fighting and fled to Asia Minor. Antiochus lost Greece in a single battle. The Roman army under Glabrio remained in Greece, punishing those city-states that had joined Antiochus. Even though Antiochus managed to escape, his troubles with the Romans were far from over.

After the defeat at Thermopylae, the struggle between Antiochus and Rome shifted to Asia Minor and became one for control of the seas off the western and southern coasts of Turkey. The Romans were now allied with the Rhodians, considered to be among the best sailors in the ancient world, and a local king, Eumenes of Pergamum. Eumenes and the Rhodians were anxious to enlist the Romans in countering the steadily encroaching threat of Antiochus, but what they failed to realize at the time was that they were bringing in a Roman tiger to drive out a Seleucid wolf.

A large Roman fleet was dispatched from Ostia, the principal seaport of Rome, to Asia Minor under the command of Livius Salinator, the son of the Salinator who had defeated Hannibal's brother at the Metaurus River. The fleet consisted of some fifty troop transports, which were joined off the coast of Sicily by six ships from Carthage and another twenty-five provided by various Italian allies. At Piraeus, the seaport of Athens, twenty-five more ships under the command of the Roman praetor Atilius Serranus reinforced the fleet, which was joined along the way by an additional fifty ships sent by Eumenes. The opposing Seleucid fleet, equally as formidable as the Roman, was under the command of a Rhodian exile in the service of Antiochus, Polyxenidas. Polyxenidas engaged the Romans near Cape Myonessus, north of Ephesus, near the island of Chios. The Rhodians had the advantage since attached to the prows of their ships were containers of flaming pitch—perhaps an early version of the famed "Greek fire," an incendiary weapon widely used in the eighth century A.D. by the Byzantine Empire. The containers were ignited and then lowered by a system of pulleys onto the decks of the Seleucid ships, setting them on fire. Polyxenidas was defeated and Antiochus lost control of the important sea lanes in the Aegean— another setback for the Seleucid king. Once again, there is no mention in the sources of Hannibal's presence at the battle. The war now shifted to mainland Asia Minor.

Lucius, the younger brother of Scipio Africanus, returned to Rome and won the consular elections for the year 190 B.C. He was assigned Asia Minor by sortition, or lot; then, for some reason, perhaps hostility toward the Scipios, the senate reassigned Asia to his co-consul, Laelius. But Scipio Africanus protested vigorously, and under pressure the senate agreed to return the assignment to his brother—but only if Scipio would accompany him as second-in-command. History was repeating itself, although in a slightly altered scenario. Twenty-five years earlier, the father and uncle of the Scipio brothers died together fighting the

Carthaginians in Spain (217–211 B.C.); then the next generation witnessed the engagement between Scipio and Hannibal in Africa, and
now the possibility loomed that Hannibal might once more come face-
to-face on the field of battle with Scipio and his younger brother. But
circumstances had changed, and this time neither Hannibal nor Africanus was in command—both were serving in second position: Scipio
to his brother Lucius, and Hannibal to Antiochus.

At some point during the year 190 B.C., Antiochus sent Hannibal
to Tyre to raise another fleet. This was a marked change from Hannibal's traditional role as a commander of ground forces to an admiral
although there might not have been such a distinction in the ancient
world. Hannibal assembled the fleet, and as he sailed from Phoenicia
northward with his new ships, the Rhodians, still in alliance with Rome,
sent their navy to intercept him. The two fleets engaged off the coast
of southwestern Turkey, not far from Side, a Greek port on the Gulf of
Pamphylia. While Hannibal had numerical superiority and was able
to take the upper hand initially, the Rhodians, experienced sailors who
manned the best-quality ships of that time, forced him to retreat. Hannibal took refuge in Side, on the east coast of Lycia, where the Rhodian
fleet set up a blockade to confine him. In trying to understand Hannibal's defeat, it may be that, just as at Zama, he was in command of a
hastily assembled force of sailors and soldiers with whom he had never
worked before. Thus, he might have been forced to do the best he could
with what he had. In any event, he remained isolated at Side as the
Rhodian fleet patrolled the coast to keep him contained and the war
went on without him.

Antiochus, having lost control of the seas, had no choice but to ask
for an end to hostilities. He offered to pay the Romans an indemnity
that amounted to half their war costs as well as relinquish his holdings
in northern Greece along with several cities and towns on the west coast
of Asia Minor. Lucius Scipio countered with a demand for payment of

all Rome's war expenses and the relinquishment of all the king's territory up to the western side of the Taurus Mountains; in other words, Antiochus would have to give up practically all his kingdom in Asia Minor. The king circumvented Lucius with a direct appeal to Africanus. He offered to release Scipio's son, who had been captured at the start of the war under circumstances that are unclear in the sources.[14] Instead of demanding a ransom for the young man, Antiochus instead offered Scipio a sizable amount of money and the hint that there would be an important and profitable role for him in the future administration of the Seleucid Empire.[15]

Antiochus and Scipio were men of very different temperament and values. They came from different cultures and clearly they were not cut from the same cloth. While outright bribery and other similar inducements might be commonplace among the despots of the Orient and at Carthage, they were repulsive to a conservative Roman of Scipio's caliber—patriotic and dedicated to the service of his country. Africanus replied that he would be grateful for the return of his son, but that he would neither take nor give anything in exchange that compromised his duty to his country. Scipio pointed out to Antiochus that he had effectively lost the war by failing to secure the crossing points of the Hellespont and thus allowing the Roman forces to cross from Greece into Asia without resistance. The Romans were now in Asia Minor, and with the recent naval defeats, the gates to Antiochus's kingdom were open. Africanus advised the king to accept the terms offered by Lucius Scipio to end the war. Antiochus refused.

More Roman legions moved into northern Asia Minor by way of the Hellespont, the waterway between Europe and Asia which King Eumenes had secured for them. Then they moved southeast, along the coast of Asia Minor, taking cities as they went. Unable to come to terms with the Romans, Antiochus decided to risk everything in a decisive land battle with the Roman army some twenty miles northeast of modern-day Izmir, on the plain of Magnesia ad Sipylum, in December 190 B.C. or January 189 B.C. Before the battle, Antiochus returned Scipio's son unharmed, without a demand for ransom. Apparently, it was done as a simple gesture of kindness—from one father to another. Africanus sent his thanks to the king at his camp, a massive fortification protected by a wide ditch and a high double earthen wall.

When the Roman legions approached the fortification, Antiochus refused to engage them in battle. The king was stalling, waiting for the onset of winter to force the Romans back into their quarters, where they would have to remain until the spring before resuming the war. But Antiochus, pressured by his soldiers, who were anxious to fight, and apprehensive that if he delayed any longer he might lose their support, moved out of his secure position and onto the plains to engage in battle.

Magnesia was a battle for a commander of Hannibal's ability and experience. Yet there are no clear references in the ancient sources to any role he might have played that day or even if he was present. If Hannibal was present, then Antiochus, for reasons of personal insecurity, ego, or mistrust, failed to use him to his best advantage. Among the ancient sources there are only two brief references to Hannibal at Magnesia— the first one surfaced at Rome, sometime after the battle, by a cousin of the Scipio's during his testimony at the trial of Lucius Scipio before the senate on the charge of embezzlement. The cousin commented that during the battle against Antiochus, Hannibal was present on the field along with several other generals. A second brief reference is found in Livy, in a comment that Hannibal was the Seleucid king's director of military operations—whatever that means—but not specifically that he was present on the field that day.

In preparation for the battle, Antiochus had drawn manpower from all parts of his empire, and his army is reputed to have numbered between sixty thousand and eighty thousand. The largest group was the infantry, with an array of scythed chariots, camel riders, regular cavalry,

and Indian elephants to support them. They were arrayed in a traditional deep formation and their flanks extended so far they allegedly
could not be seen from the middle of the battle line, a well-protected
position from which the kings of the ancient eastern world usually commanded. Antiochus appears to have had no strategy that day beyond his
intent to simply overwhelm the numerically inferior Roman army under
the command of Lucius Scipio. The Romans numbered between thirty
thousand and forty thousand. Magnesia was poised to develop into a replay of Cannae, but this time with the Romans in the role of the winner.

In the initial clash, Antiochus was successful. Taking command of the
right wing of his army, he drove back the Roman left and nearly succeeded
in capturing their camp. But on the other side of the battlefield, the king's
left wing was collapsing under pressure from the Roman cavalry. In the
center his elephants became unmanageable and turned on their own soldiers, causing them to break ranks and flee. Antiochus made the tactical
error of using elephants against infantry instead of on the flanks against
cavalry, where, with room to maneuver, they would be more effective.
When driven directly into a clamoring mass of men, the elephants often
would panic and could easily turn back on their own soldiers.

Antiochus lost the battle, and his casualties are reputed to have exceeded fifty thousand men killed—a number that rivaled the Roman
loss to Hannibal at Cannae. If the sources can be believed, the Romans
only lost three hundred foot soldiers and twenty-four cavalry that day—
highly suspicious underestimations. Forced to flee the battlefield, Antiochus initially retreated to the city of Sardis, just a few miles away, but
then quickly moved much farther east into the deeper recesses of his
empire. He settled in Apamea, near the modern Turkish town of Dinar.
Once word of his defeat spread, most of the principal cities throughout
western Asia Minor, like Ephesus, gave themselves over quickly to the
Romans. From Apamea, Antiochus sent emissaries to Africanus with a
request to end the war. Scipio had not participated in the battle because

of illness, and he directed the emissaries to his brother Lucius. Antiochus hoped that Africanus would be inclined to intercede on his behalf with his brother—but there was no negotiation. Lucius demanded unconditional surrender.

The Seleucid defeat at Magnesia decided the outcome of the Roman-Syrian War, and while Antiochus had instructed his envoys to negotiate the best terms they could, ultimately they had to accept what was presented to them. The king was forced to abandon his European territories and cede all of Asia Minor north of the Taurus Mountains to Rome's ally Eumenes. In addition, he was required to pay an indemnity of fifteen thousand talents in annual installments. To guarantee those payments, the Romans took twenty hostages of importance from the royal entourage—including the king's son. Then the Romans demanded Hannibal be turned over to them. This was the first time they had made such a demand. In prior negotiations between the Scipios and Antiochus, before the battle at Magnesia, at the Hellespont for instance, no mention was ever apparently made of Hannibal nor any demand for his surrender. After Magnesia, even though Hannibal's name was prominent among those to be turned over to Rome, he was listed as only one among several Greek exiles who had taken refuge in the court of the king and had been branded as a threat to Roman security.

Antiochus was finished and a power vacuum developed in that part of the ancient world, which the Romans quickly filled, first with proxies such as King Eumenes and later with their own governors. The balance of power in the eastern part of the Mediterranean was recalibrated by Rome, just as it had been in the west at the conclusion of the war with Carthage. The Romans established a presence in Asia Minor and transformed that part of the world while Antiochus came to his end three years later, murdered while looting a local temple near Susa in Iran.

Once the terms of the peace treaty had been agreed to, the king's envoys were instructed to accompany Lucius Scipio back to Rome and

appear before the senate to obtain final ratification. Lucius returned to
Rome in the autumn of 189 B.C. to a triumph more spectacular than
his brother had enjoyed when he returned from Africa in 201 B.C. after
defeating Hannibal at Zama.[16] In recognition of his victory, the senate
and people of Rome bestowed on him the cognomen Asiaticus. Then,
two years later, in a turn of events, the hero of Magnesia was arrested
and put on trial at Rome on charges that he had misappropriated funds
given to him to conduct the war and then held back some of the treasure
taken from Antiochus for his personal use. Publius Scipio Nasica (the
pointed nose), a cousin of the Scipio brothers and consul in 191 B.C.,
appealed to the tribunes and the senate not to put Asiaticus in prison,
citing not only his innocence of the charges, but the sacrifices and service of the entire Scipio family to Rome in the Second Punic War and
in the war against Antiochus. In his testimony, Nasica referred to the
battle at Magnesia, where he said Antiochus had among his many generals on the field that day, Rome's nemesis, Hannibal.[17]

Shortly after the battle, Hannibal fled to the island of Crete.[18] There
has been speculation among historians that Hannibal may have left Antiochus before the battle, although Livy maintains that Hannibal was
rectorum militae, or director of military operations for Antiochus, and
that could imply he would have been present at Magnesia.[19] From the
coast of Pamphylia, the area of southwestern Turkey just to the south
of Apamea, where the king had taken refuge, Hannibal had a limited
number of choices to flee to. The island of Cyprus was nearby, but not
an option because it was allied to Rome. On the coast of Lebanon, Tyre
was still within the Seleucid kingdom and probably subject to the terms
of the Roman peace treaty with Antiochus. The only viable option appears to have been Crete, which, like Cyprus, was only a relatively short
sail away. Hannibal may have chosen Crete as well because of its prox-
imity to North Africa. The island was well placed to serve as a base for

future operations against Carthage and had remained neutral in the conflict between Rome and Antiochus.

But at this point in his life Hannibal was on the run and lacked the resources necessary to mount an invasion of any consequence. He probably went to Crete on a temporary basis, in order, as one ancient source contends, to "deliberate where to seek asylum."[20] The island was a haven for pirates who made a living by kidnapping for ransom anybody they could get their hands on. That Hannibal could find refuge there must have been an indication of the degree of respect and fear in which he was held throughout the ancient world. Following the defeat of Philip and then Antiochus, perhaps the Greeks, even those on Crete, saw him as their last hope of preventing their entire subjugation by Rome. Hannibal settled in Gortyn, the most prosperous city on the island and one with strong ties to Ptolemaic Egypt. Gortyn was known in classical Greek mythology as the place where Zeus, disguised as a bull, took the princess Europa to consummate an illicit affair away from the suspicious eyes of his wife Hera. Europa consequently gave birth to three children, who came to rule the three Minoan palaces on the island, the most famous being Knossos. The city was also famous for its law code, excavated in 1884 and the most complete example of ancient Greek law in existence. The code is currently on display in situ, among the ruins of the city, located some thirty miles south of modern Heraklion.

When Hannibal arrived at Gortyn, he aroused the interest of the local authorities, not only because of his reputation, but because he was reputed to have with him a "large sum of money" in gold and silver coins.[21] He settled into a villa just outside the city and asked the authorities to allow him to deposit his fortune in the temple of Diana for safekeeping. They were only too pleased to accommodate him.

Hannibal had a sizable number of large, narrow-necked jars, probably amphorae, brought to the temple for storage. There was considerable interest among the local people, and a large crowd gathered to watch the proceedings. Unknown to everyone except Hannibal, the jars contained lead, except for the top several inches where the necks narrowed. The necks were filled with gold and silver coins. Believing the jars were filled entirely with precious coins, the priests and officials of the city had them sealed and placed within a secure area of the temple for safekeeping. With the jars stored in their temple, the Gortynians quickly lost interest in Hannibal, who spent his days in the comfort of his villa and the tranquility of its garden. The garden, apparently by design, was in poor condition. It was unkempt, with several very ordinary bronze statues of varying sizes that had been pushed over on their sides and blended into the disheveled surroundings.

Months later, when Hannibal decided to leave, he asked the Gortynians to allow him to leave his jars in the temple until he sent for them. They were only too pleased to oblige and made no attempt to prevent his departure. Among the items that were crated for the move, transported to the seaside, and placed on the departing ship were the statues in the garden, which, unbeknown to the Gortynians, contained the gold and silver.

While Hannibal was at Gortyn, a large contingent of Roman troops landed on the island and began a systematic sweep in search of Roman soldiers and others who had been kidnapped. The consul in charge sent messengers to the Cretan cities and towns, demanding they give up any Romans they held or suffer the consequences. This could account, in part, for Hannibal's sudden decision to leave the island. Hannibal made his way, probably by ship, north to the Hellespont, through the straits, and into the Black Sea. From there he continued by ship along the northern coast of Asia Minor, probably as far east as the Greek port of Trapezus. Then, leaving his ship, he undertook an overland journey south through what is today Georgia and into Armenia, where he sought refuge in the court of a minor king—Artaxias.[22]

Armenia had been a former Persian province or satrapy that Antiochus had brought under his control in 212 B.C. He had placed Artaxias on the throne as his vassal, and that connection between the two could explain how Hannibal found his way there. Armenia was as remote a location in the ancient world as could be found with some degree of civilization—an ideal place to hide from the Romans. With the defeat of Antiochus at Magnesia, Artaxias declared his independence, establishing his capital at Artaxa (modern Artashat) on the river Araxes (Aras). Armenia would not come under Roman domination for nearly another hundred years, after Pompey defeated its king Tigranes, in 66 B.C., and the country became a Roman protectorate. The emperor Trajan visited Artaxa in 114 A.D., and it remained the capital of Armenia until as late as the fifth century A.D., when the site was abandoned.

Artaxias welcomed Hannibal and commissioned him to design and oversee the building of his new capital on a peninsula of land where two rivers came together, the Aras and the smaller Azat. The Aras in ancient times was known as the Araxes, and today it marks the tense and closed border between Turkey and Armenia. The river flows past the biblical Mount Ararat, the legendary resting place of Noah's Ark according to the Book of Genesis. The ruins of the ancient city are twenty miles south and east of the present-day Armenian capital of Yerevan and atop a Urartian citadel that had been abandoned for nearly four hundred years before the king began construction of his new city. Today the site consists of twelve hills, two of which have been excavated, while four were destroyed by marble quarrying operations during the Soviet era, and six, as of the writing of this book, remain relatively untouched.[23]

Artaxa became a prosperous commercial center, something evident from the recent excavations, and came to be known in the ancient world as the "Armenian Carthage." The city came to rival other Hellenistic centers, such as Pergamum, because it was located where the trade routes of Persia and Mesopotamia converged with those from the Caucasus and Asia Minor.

When Hannibal left Armenia, he returned once more to Asia Minor and the kingdom of Bithynia. Bithynia was an area in the northwest corner of Asia Minor, bordering the Sea of Marmara, on the Asian side of the Bosporus. The kingdom was ruled by Prusias, who was at war with Eumenes of Pergamum over an area in Asia Minor known as Mysia. The territory had been given to Eumenes's predecessor, Attalus, by Antiochus, and then seized by Prusias in 196 B.C. Eumenes had been too busy helping the Romans fight Antiochus at the time, so he did not actively contest the loss, but by the time Hannibal arrived in Bithynia, sometime in 187/186 B.C., the dispute between the two kings had escalated into open warfare.

Prusias saw in Hannibal a valuable military advisor in his war against Eumenes. For Hannibal, it was another opportunity to continue his struggle against the Romans and fulfill his oath. While he could have chosen to remain in Armenia, living out his final years in relative comfort and safety, Hannibal returned to the west to wage war against an ally of Rome—something which was sure to bring him to the attention of the Romans. In his war against Eumenes, Prusias was at a disadvantage since his adversary ruled a larger kingdom with greater resources and was allied with Rome. Prusias had limited financial resources and manpower. Hannibal became his director of military operations and immediately launched a diplomatic initiative, cultivating alliances with other smaller kingdoms in the area to increase the king's manpower capabilities. Then he set about to train Prusias's army, ostensibly to fight Eumenes, but probably with the real intent of launching another campaign against the Romans in the future; although unlikely, perhaps he even contemplated another invasion of Italy.

During this same period, Prusias prevailed on Hannibal to oversee the construction of a new city closer to Mysia, the territory which was in dispute between the two kings. Hannibal evidently took on the project, at least the design phase, and today the ancient site lies beneath the modern Turkish city of Bursa. Known as Prusa, the new city eventually prospered, becoming the first capital of the Ottoman Empire in 1326. Prusias intended the new city to eventually supplant his old capital at Nicomedia.

Hostilities between Eumenes and Prusias commenced in 186 B.C., and Hannibal took a prominent role in the conflict. During a naval battle, which took place on the Sea of Marmara in 184 B.C.,[24] the navy of Prusias was considerably outnumbered by the ships of Eumenes. Hannibal had prepared accordingly. His plan was to kill Eumenes at the outset of the battle, reasoning that with their king dead his soldiers would lose their will to continue the fight and the war would end in Prusias's favor. Hannibal's plan was to identify the ship that carried Eumenes at the outset and then concentrate all his forces on isolating that ship and killing the king. As the two navies faced each other, but before they engaged, Hannibal sent a skiff out with a messenger bearing a herald's staff. The staff was known as the *caduceus* and recognized among civilized nations in the ancient Mediterranean world as carried by one who had come to negotiate a truce arrangement under diplomatic protection. The *caduceus* was a short staff entwined by two serpents with wings on them. In modern usage, it is sometimes mistakenly used as a symbol of those in the medical profession, the symbol of Asclepius, the god of healing in the ancient world. That symbol is a rod that has only one snake and no wings. The messenger approached the enemy fleet, holding up his staff and a letter for the king. He was taken immediately to the ship that carried Eumenes, and with that deceptive move Hannibal knew exactly where his target was. What Hannibal had done was to exploit a recognized request to parlay, the modern-day equivalent of a white flag, to gain a tactical advantage over his enemy. It was deceptive, but perhaps to Hannibal's mind, acceptable given his belief that victory, which was always his end, justifies the means used to achieve it.

Hannibal concentrated his forces against the king's ship, and as they closed, the ships in Eumenes's battle line moved to block their advance. Then Hannibal unleashed a second surprise. On board Prusias's ships, hundreds of clay pots were loaded onto catapults and hurled onto the decks of the enemy fleet. The pots broke into pieces on impact and released their lethal contents—venomous snakes of all sizes. The snakes immediately sought cover below decks, where the rowers were, and pandemonium ensued. Ships lost their propulsion and control. Many came to a dead stop in the water. By luck, Eumenes managed to escape from his flagship and reach the nearby shore and the protection of elements of his army that were waiting there. Hannibal won the day, as he had on so many other prior occasions, against a superior force by outthinking his opponents. Following the battle, Prusias hosted a great feast to celebrate the victory, and there was merriment by all except Hannibal. When asked why he remained the only sullen guest on such a festive occasion, Hannibal remarked that Eumenes would return with his Roman allies. The Romans, he warned, would be a much more formidable enemy and not fall for the same trick. Hannibal explained that what he had won for Prusias that day was a temporary respite—not a victory. It was only a matter of time before the final reckoning would come.

Seeking to mitigate his position, Prusias sent envoys to Rome to explain his side of the dispute with Eumenes and if possible negotiate an end to the conflict—with Rome as the broker. During their stay, some of the envoys were invited to dine at the home of the ex-consul Titus Quinctius Flamininus. This was the same Flamininus who had led the Roman armies to victory over Philip of Macedon and considered himself the liberator and protector of Greece. Upon his return to Rome in 189 B.C., Flamininus had been elected censor, the highest office in the Republic and the culmination of a successful political career. Since then, he had ceased to hold public office and was compelled to enter retirement. In an offhand manner during the evening one of the envoys mentioned that Hannibal had taken refuge in Bithynia, and that caught Flamininus's attention. He now saw an opportunity to reenter the political arena and win glory for himself.

The next day Flamininus appeared before the senate and asked to be sent to Bithynia to apprehend Hannibal. There was considerable debate among the senators over whether Hannibal remained a threat to Rome. While many were in favor of his capture and execution, others saw nothing more in Hannibal than a harmless old man who should be left in peace to live out his remaining years in exile—"an old bird, stripped of its tail feathers and unable to fly"' as one senator dismissively referred to him. Flamininus countered that as long as Hannibal lived, he was a threat to Rome. While time may have taken away his youthful vigor, it had not diminished his hatred of Rome or his ability to lead an army. Only his capture and execution would finally free the Romans from their anxiety.

The senate approved the request, and Flamininus sailed for Bithynia with the envoys of Prusias. When he arrived at Nicomedia and confronted Prusias with the demand for Hannibal's surrender, the king pleaded not to be compelled to violate the laws of hospitality— Hannibal was, after all, his guest. But Prusias feared and needed the Romans, so he was reluctant to refuse their demands. The Bithynian king apparently was not among the most principled or strongest of monarchs, and he may well have offered to betray Hannibal in return for an alliance with Rome. In either case, he agreed to allow Hannibal's capture, informing the Romans where he could be found and providing soldiers to accompany them.

Hannibal occupied a small castle on the coast along the Gulf of Izmit, some thirty miles west of Nicomedia. For nearly two decades, he had lived his life with the proverbial sword of Damocles hanging over his head—waiting for the day when the thread would break and the sword would drop. Fate was that thread, and the Romans were the sword—an imminent and ever-present peril faced by a man continually on the run. Hannibal lived with a sense of foreboding engendered by the Roman fear of him and sustained by his loathing of Rome. Never trusting Prusias, and always fearful of the day when the Romans would come for him, Hannibal had multiple secret tunnels dug that radiated out several hundred yards from his castle into the surrounding countryside. When he saw the castle was surrounded and all the exits secured by soldiers, he ended his life rather than be captured.

When news of Hannibal's death reached Rome, there were those who celebrated, while others thought what Flamininus had done was beneath the dignity of a Roman. His critics maintained that Flamininus had not defeated a worthy foe in battle but driven to suicide an old man who was no longer a threat to anyone. They recalled how Scipio Africanus, after the battle of Zama in North Africa, had shown such consideration to Hannibal—even when he remained a formidable threat—by allowing him to remain free and even return to civilian life. The supporters of Flamininus countered that it was precisely Scipio's clemency that was to blame for Hannibal continuing his resistance to Rome in the Hellenistic east for years afterward.

The ruins of what is popularly believed to be Hannibal's castle can be found at Gebze, on the Asian side of the Bosporus some forty miles and an hour's drive east of Istanbul. Known as Eskihisar Kalesi (castle) it is a relatively small, typically medieval-looking structure that sits in a state of disrepair on a windswept and desolate hill just above the tiny picturesque port of the same name. There is no archaeological evidence that links the castle directly to Hannibal—just a long local tradition and the author's perhaps romantic notion that it has the right feel. The word *eskihisar* in Turkish means old fortress and gives the small port its name. The manuscripts place it in the right location, and it certainly fits the mood, which any visitor will readily sense.

Not far from the castle, on another hilltop, equally as barren, is what
is purported to be Hannibal's tomb—known in Turkish as the *Hannibalin Mezari*. The site is difficult to find—isolated, enclosed by barbed
wire, patrolled by guards, and closed to the public. The security there
seems intended to protect the National Metrology Institute, a research
and development institute that shares the grounds with the tomb and
operates under the umbrella of the Scientific and Technological Research Council of Turkey, known as TUBITAK. Ostensibly the aim of
TUBITAK is to ensure the reliability and accuracy of all measurements
used in Turkish commerce and industry and their integration into the
international system, but the wire and guards around the site, the strict
policy of no photographs, and the surrendering of one's passport in return for an identity badge to be displayed during the visit raises suspicions it could be something more than what appears on the surface.

Once past the security and the barbed wire, visitors reach the tomb
by following a dirt road. There is no actual tomb but a large granite rock
placed in a parklike setting. Carved into the middle of the rock is a small
likeness of Hannibal's head. Five walkways radiate out from the rock
to a distance of about a hundred feet, and at the end of each there is a
large marble plaque. The five plaques are each inscribed, one in Turkish,
English, Italian, German, and French. All contain the same inscription:
"This monument was ordered built by Mustafa Kemal Ataturk in 1934
to honor the hundredth anniversary of his [Ataturk's] birth and to commemorate Hannibal, one of history's greatest generals and statesmen.
Hannibal, motivated by his hatred of Rome and the influence of his
father, defeated with the help of his elephants, the Romans at Barletta
[Cannae] in 217 B.C." (There were no elephants used at Cannae.) The
inscription goes on to relate that because of the lack of support from
Antiochus of Syria and Prusias of Bithynia, Hannibal was forced to give
up his struggle against Roman imperialism, and when betrayed to the
Romans by his host, committed suicide in Libyssa (Gebze) in 183 B.C.

The real remains of Hannibal's tomb may lie only a couple of miles to the west of the Ataturk monument, in a rundown industrial site. What is there are some marble pieces, essentially a pile of rubble, from what might be the remnants of a tomb or monument built in 193 A.D. on the order of the Roman emperor Severus, a native of Carthage and Rome's first African emperor.[25] The tomb was built of white marble to honor Hannibal and enclose his grave. Sometime at the turn of the twentieth century, the German archaeologist Theodor Wiegand claimed to have found the site just west of Eskihisar.[26]

Hannibal never believed his life would end in Asia Minor. In his last years, he had relied for comfort on the words of an ancient oracle that "Libyssan soil will cover the body of Hannibal." Libya was the ancient Greek name for North Africa, and it was there Hannibal believed he would die. But what Hannibal apparently did not know was that a small river, called Libyssa by the local people, made its way to the sea just a short distance from his castle. The prophecy was fulfilled. Hannibal died in 183 B.C., and contemporary scholars are generally in agreement that he was sixty-three. Hannibal was more than a general; he was a leader who exceeded his contemporaries in ability. The Roman historian Cornelius Nepos paid him the greatest tribute when he wrote that Hannibal excelled above all other commanders in skill as much as the Roman people are superior to all nations in bravery. For as often as he engaged the Romans in Italy, he was victorious; and if he had not been impaired by the jealousy of his fellow-citizens at home, he would have been able to conquer the Romans. In the end, according to Nepos, it was the disparagement and envy of the multitude that overcame the courage and ability of one great man.[27]

Afterword

HANNIBAL IS AN enigma—a tragic Homeric hero, dedicated to waging war against his sworn enemy, incapable of compromise or accommodation, and doomed in the end to lose his struggle. The sources tell us he was devoted to his father, Hamilcar, and, at his father's urging, took an oath as a young boy on the altar of his gods at Carthage to wage a never-ending struggle against Rome. His relationship with his father, himself a hero from the First Punic War and a figure larger than life, was defined by their pathological hatred of Rome, a hatred that seems to have consumed the entire Barca family. Hamilcar boasted that his three sons were the "lion's brood," and he was raising them to devour Rome. Even his three daughters played their roles as well—not on the battlefields but in the bedrooms. All three were married to advance the family's political and military alliances. When it comes to Hannibal, there are only scant references to his personal relationships, those with his wife and son. And those are rife with conjecture. We have no insight into his family life if, in fact, he had any. His story is one of incessant struggle against his adversary Rome and, as a result, he earned his place in history. He was a commander of extraordinary ability and while he has been called by scholars an "unrivalled success," at the same time, he was, as this book has tried to show, a man of colossal failure. What has never been made clear, even after two thousand years of scholarly effort and endless conjecture, is what motivated Hannibal to leave Africa and undertake his war against Rome in the first place. Was he a dedicated soldier following the orders of his government to wage war in order to retain its commercial domination over the western half of the Mediterranean world, or was he acting alone, *ultra vires* (outside his authority), an independent agent, a rogue, driven by his inner demons and an oath made to his father? Was the Second Punic War, the most destructive in the ancient world at the time and one that changed the course of history, no more than a war caused by a personal vendetta against a hated rival?

What made Hannibal a great leader? The ancient sources, both Greek and Roman, tell us that he possessed an extraordinary ability to inspire those who followed him and instill fear, to the point of paralysis, among any who opposed him. He was innovative in battle, often doing the unexpected and turning the tables on any of his enemies who were stagnant in their thinking and slow to action. What made Hannibal unique was that he was able to think outside the proverbial "box," not remain locked inside it. He is remembered more for the rules of conventional warfare that he broke than for those he followed. His army was unconventional in its makeup, composed of mercenaries, whose common motivation was probably greed. These were men divided by language and culture, who could desert or change allegiance at the slightest shift in fortune and circumstances. They came from Africa, Spain, Gaul, and even Greece—but Hannibal brought them together and then molded them into a unified, coordinated, and effective fighting force that remained fiercely loyal to him for nearly sixteen years. He understood human nature, especially men at war, and realized, as Napoleon wrote, that soldiers are moved by two levers: fear and self-interest. In that regard, Hannibal could be generous in rewarding those who performed well and were loyal to him and brutal in punishing any who opposed him either on the battlefield or in his camps. He was a leader of singular focus; winning was all that mattered and nothing less than victory counted. Leadership for him was about motivating those who followed him to give their best, utilizing them to their greatest capability, and outsmarting his adversaries.

Hannibal's character was as complex as the men he led were diverse. At times, he could be greedy and cruel, or generous, compassionate, and humane, depending on his mood and circumstances. He could be honorable when it came to upholding his word or duplicitous, breaking agreements and treaties that no longer suited him. He could be merciful toward those he defeated one moment and cruel the next. He could be fighting for the cause of freedom—to liberate the Gauls, Italians, and Greeks from the oppression and exploitation of Rome—or for personal gain. According to one Roman source, Juvenal, Hannibal was a man driven by a destructive ego—a man for whom Africa was too small a continent to contain his ambition—even when Spain was added into the mix. Juvenal portrayed Hannibal as a madman, one who wrought havoc on the ancient world; a one-eyed commander riding astride a massive elephant, leading his army over the Alps, splitting the mountains that blocked his path with fire, vinegar, and determination. After he was defeated on the field of battle in North Africa, Hannibal was eventually forced to take refuge in the courts of the Hellenistic kings of Asia Minor. There, without the power and resources he once possessed as supreme commander of the armies of Carthage, he became a shadow of the man he had once been, reduced to a supplicant, sitting patiently, quietly, and obsequiously outside the antechambers of the kings, waiting for them to awaken and give him an audience. According to Juvenal, in the end Hannibal is no more than a figure condemned by history to be little more than a thrill to impressionable schoolboys.[1]

The Second Punic War is often referred to as "Hannibal's War" because he played the principal role in that conflict, just as his father had in the first. Hannibal seized the initiative and turned the power structure of the ancient world upside down by accomplishing what everyone thought impossible at the time. He crossed the Alps with an army at the onset of winter, then he did the unimaginable and brought war to the Romans in their own backyard. Crossing the Alps with an army and elephants earned him his place in the popular imagination and his battlefield victories a place in military history. In Italy, Hannibal defeated Roman armies that outnumbered his forces by two to one, and for years he kept the Romans in a continual state of crisis as his army ravaged the countryside.

Hannibal began the war in Italy with a series of stunning victories that by any measure should have ended the conflict in his favor. His tactics resulted in victories, along the banks of the river Trebbia in northern Italy and Lake Trasimene in central Italy and on the plains of Cannae in southern Italy, that were brilliant by any measure and initially devastating to Rome. The battle of Cannae, Hannibal's greatest victory, became the "archetypical battle of annihilation" and saw the destruction of the Roman army as a cohesive fighting force. It has gone down in the history books as a classic lesson in tactics and is studied in military academies from West Point to Sandhurst. But Hannibal's victory at Cannae was not enough to win the war, as the Romans proved more resilient that he anticipated. When they lost whole armies, the Romans raised new ones to take the field, even filling their ranks with criminals freed from their prisons and slaves from their estates. Like the mythical Greek wrestler Antaeus, every time Hannibal knocked the Romans down, they drew strength from the earth and rose stronger than before. They were a tenacious people and waged a war of attrition against Hannibal, suffering staggering losses in manpower and wealth. But, in the end, it was their tenacity and commitment to see the war to its conclusion that triumphed over Hannibal's tactical genius. It was, as most wars are prone to be, one of resources winning out in the long run over ability.

The Romans won the war and so they wrote the history books. We see Carthage and Hannibal through their eyes—further jaundiced according to some modern academics by a myopic nineteenth- and twentieth-century British and European fascist/racist/orientalizing, imperialistic bias against an inferior Africa in general. These perceptions of ancient Carthage were formulated in part by the influence of Gustave Flaubert's erotic nineteenth-century novel *Salammbo*, which, when it was published, became the rage in Paris. The novel is often cited as a flagrant example of the prejudicial view that portrays Carthage as a society of Philistines, a people obsessed with money, fanatically dedicated to idolatry, and consumed by debauchery. A generation of British and European painters, like Lawrence Alma-Tadema and Jean-Léon Gérôme, put on canvas for the world the distortions about life in the ancient world that Flaubert had put on the page. Movie producers, like the Italian Giovanni Pastrone, in his 1914 film *Cabiria*, amplified that image on a massive public scale. Thus, Carthage, according to this school of academic thinking, has never had a fair shake.

This book, too, admittedly has its biases. It examines Hannibal within the context of Lord Acton's dictum that great men, those who make history and even change its course, are invariably the most evil. Perhaps a capacity for evil is the essential element, the *sine qua non* of effective leadership. Was Hannibal a great hero and patriot of Carthage, a man who devoted his life to the service of his country, or was he driven by his personal demons, ego perhaps coupled with greed, to follow his own agenda? It has always been my belief in writing about great leaders from the ancient world that they invariably turn out to be a complex blend of the worst and a little bit of the best in human nature. The more powerful they become, the more their defects and excesses of ego seem to overpower and subjugate their reason, moderation, and simple empathy. Perhaps Acton is right—power at the highest levels does corrupt and in so doing distorts the best in human nature. Hannibal could be compassionate and merciful, but with more than equal amounts of greed, cruelty, and vindictiveness mixed in. While much of what he accomplished is worthy of admiration and praise, it was attained at tremendous cost in terms of human life and suffering. None more so perhaps than his own. In the end, his brothers died fighting Rome. Hannibal lived the longest of them, but ultimately died, not on a battlefield but by his own hand, far from his native Carthage and without family or friends to ease his passage and mourn him.

In measuring Hannibal as a leader, he stands in time and reputation between two popularly acclaimed giants of successful political leadership and military conquest: Alexander the Great, the Macedonian king who conquered the eastern half of the ancient world in the fourth century B.C., and Julius Caesar, who conquered the western half in the first century B.C. Both men built empires, were admired, worshipped, and hated in their time, and both died violent deaths at the hands of assassins. Alexander and Caesar have wide name recognition and people are generally able to place them in some historical context. We know a great deal about their military and political exploits from the ancient manuscripts and just as much about their personal lives and their philosophies, all of which make them easier for contemporary historians to write about. Hannibal never built an empire, but he waged one of the longest and most devastating wars in Roman history and set the direction for the development of Roman expansion in the ancient world. Even though in the end he lost his struggle, he still stands as one of the great figures in military history—a man driven and consumed by hate and a leader who could never accept defeat or even compromise when it came to fighting his enemies.

ACKNOWLEDGMENTS

SEVERAL PEOPLE CONTRIBUTED in varying degrees to the completion of this book. I am indebted to all of them. In the conceptual stage, my agent Andrew Stuart helped me shape the proposal for presentation and then made it happen. He continues to guide my career with his suggestions for my next book. Steve Forbes and Larry Kirschbaum, both valued friends, gave me encouragement and advice at every stage.

On the logistical side, a longtime friend, Roderick Abbott, former European Union ambassador and deputy director for the World Trade Organization, chauffeured me around Italy in his SUV following the route of Hannibal and visiting every battlefield along the way. I am indebted to Bob Pigeon, my editor, for his suggestions and guidance. Bob and I have worked together off and on for nearly twenty years—first on two of my earlier works, *Xenophon's March* (2001) and *Alexander the Great* (2004) and now on *Hannibal's Oath*. Professor Jonathan Scott Perry of the University of South Florida is a close friend and colleague who took the time to read the manuscript drafts and offer valuable suggestions for improvement.

On the technical side, Sandy Thomas of St. Petersburg, Florida, helped me to develop the maps, which are so crucial to giving the reader the geographical perspective necessary to comprehend the magnitude of Hannibal's odyssey through the ancient Mediterranean world.

Finally, my gratitude to Mavis Gibson, who has been there to support my writing career from the submission of my first manuscript twenty years ago, through the writing and publication of five subsequent books. Over the years, she has travelled with me to Tunisia, and through Spain, France, Italy, Greece, and Turkey to visit and photograph archaeological sites. We have climbed through the Alps more times than either of us can remember, and to her, I owe more than I could ever repay or words could ever adequately express.

NOTES

PREFACE

1. Emmanuel de Las Cases, *Mémorial de Sainte Hélène*, 1823, Volume II, pg. 338.

PROLOGUE: THE ULTIMATE SACRIFICE
TO FULFILL AN OATH

1. In an alternate version by the Roman satirist Juvenal, Hannibal ended his life by consuming poison taken from a ring that he always wore, mixed into a container of wine. Livy, *History of Rome*, Book XXXIX, Chapter 51, and Juvenal, *Satires*, Book IV, Satire X.

CHAPTER I: THE ROAD TO POWER

1. A talent was a brick of approximately 55 pounds of gold or silver.

2. Livy, *History of Rome*, Book XXI, Chapter I.

3. Cornelius Nepos, *On Great Generals. On Historians*, Chapter XXII, "Hamilcar," and Chapter XXIII, "Hannibal," 1.

4. Dexter Hoyos, *Hannibal's Dynasty*, 2005, challenges what he calls Livy's far-fetched tale of Hasdrubal's pedophilic designs on his young brother-in-law Hannibal. However, references to this relationship are multiple and found not only in Livy, Book XXI, Chapter 3, but in Diodorus, *Library of History*, Book XXV, Chapter 12, and Cornelius Nepos, "Hamilcar." While those skeptical of the allegation of pedophilia claim it is little more than

another example of Roman slander, institutionalized pederasty was a characteristically Greek custom and not uncommon at Rome. Richard Stoneman, *Education of Cyrus*, 1992, pg. xviii.

5. *Cambridge Ancient History*, Volume VII, Part II, pg. 515.

6. During the Trojan War, Iphigenia, the daughter of the Greek King Agamemnon, was sacrificed at the port of Aulis in exchange for favorable winds for the Greek fleet to sail to Troy. The Romans sacrificed two couples, from Greece and Gaul, by burying them alive when Hannibal was at the gates of Rome.

7. Diodorus, Book XXV, Chapter 10.

8. Polybius, *The Histories*, Book II, Chapter 1, and Cornelius Nepos, "Hamilcar," Book IV.

9. Cary and Scullard, *A History of Rome*, pg. 125; *Cambridge Ancient History*, Vol. VIII, pg. 30; Leonard Cottrell, *Enemy of Rome*, 1960, pg. 14; Ernle Bradford, *Hannibal*, 1981, pp. 33–34; Serge Lancel, *Carthage*, 1992, pg. 380.

10. Livy, Book XXI, Chapter 3.

11. Livy, Book XXIV, Chapter 41.

12. Polybius, Book III, Chapter 15.

13. Livy, Book XXI, Chapter 10.

14. Livy, Book XXI, Chapter 10, and Silicus Italicus, *Punica*, Volume I, Book II, 300–302.

15. Silicus Italicus, *Punica*, Volume I, Book 11, 395–400.

16. Augustine, *City of God*, Volume III, 20.

17. Livy, Book XXI, Chapter 18.

18. Livy, Book XXI, Chapter 22.

CHAPTER II: ON THE MARCH

1. Livy, Book XXVIII, Chapter 37; Polybius, Book III, Chapter 33. The word *balearic* in ancient Greek means "to throw."

2. The number thirty-seven is given by two ancient sources, Polybius in Book III, Chapter 42, who wrote in the same century that Hannibal died, and Appian, who wrote nearly four hundred years after the events, described in *Roman History*, Volume I, Book VII, "The Hannibalic War."

3. R. Leakey and R. Lewin, *The Sixth Extinction*, 1996, Chapter 2, "Elephant Story."

4. John Wilford, "The Mystery of Hannibal's Elephants," in *New York Times* science section, September 18, 1984.

5. Livy, Book XXI, Chapter 23, and Polybius, Book III, Chapter 35. Both sources are in relative agreement about the numbers in Hannibal's army, his infantry and cavalry. Polybius emphasizes the accuracy of his figures by commenting that he viewed a bronze tablet in the extreme southeast corner of Italy, near the modern Cape Colonna, upon which Hannibal had written these numbers.

6. Polybius, Book. IX, Chapter 24.

7. Livy, Book XXI, Chapter 23.

8. Polybius, Book III, Chapter 35.

9. Polybius, Book III, Chapter 42.

10. Between Fourques and Beaucaire: W. W. Hyde, *Roman Alpine Routes*, 1935; Sir Gavin De Beer, *Alps and Elephants*, 1956; J. F. Lazenby, *Hannibal's War*, 1978; Robert Ellis, *Treatise on Hannibal's Passage of the Alps*, 1853; Cecil Torr, *Hannibal Crosses the Alps*, 1924; S. Lancel, *Hannibal*, 1998, Dexter Hoyos, "Crossing the Durance with Hannibal," 2006. Just below Orange: Napoleon, 1816; Jean-Louis Larouza, *Histoire critique du passage des Alpes par Annibal*, 1826; William J. Law, *Alps of Hannibal*, 1866; Theodore Dodge, *Hannibal*, 1891; R. Hall, *Romans on the Riviera*, 1898; and Douglas Freshfield, *Hannibal Once More*, 1914.

11. A Greek *stade* is calculated at 625 feet or 185 meters.

13. Polybius, Book III, Chapter 46.

14. Livy, Book XXI, Chapter 30.

CHAPTER III: OVER THE ICY PEAKS

1. From the Latin *passu*, which can mean a footpath or track.

2. M. Cary, *The Geographic Background of Greek and Roman History*, 1950, pg. 251.

3. Polybius, Book III, Chapter 49.

4. Livy, Book XXI, Chapter 31.

5. Livy, Book XXI, Chapter 31.

6. Livy, Book XXI, Chapter 35.

7. Livy, Book XXI, Chapter 32.

8. Probably goiter brought on by a lack of iodine in their diet.

9. Diodorus, Book IV, Chapter 39.

10. *Baedeker's Southern France*, 1907, pg. 418.

11. Livy, Book XXI, Chapter 34.

12. Polybius, Book III, Chapters 52 and 53.

13. Livy, Book XXI, Chapters 33–35.

14. Livy, Book XXI, Chapter 35.

15. The author, at the request of a BBC film crew, conducted an experiment to see if in fact a rock on that same mountain could be heated and broken apart in this manner. The experiment was not conducted on a ledge at ten thousand feet, but at a comfortable elevation below the pass on the French side. A sizable rock was selected, and the fire built around it was fed for about four hours. Then several gallons of commercial-grade vinegar, hauled to the site specifically for the experiment, were poured over it, and the rock came apart with the first few blows from a sledgehammer.

16. Polybius, Book III, Chapter 60.

17. The two most reliable historical sources on Hannibal, Polybius and Livy, are slightly at variance on these numbers. Polybius says Hannibal lost half his combined initial force of forty-six thousand crossing the Alps (Polybius, Book III, Chapter 60). This would leave him approximately twenty-six thousand men when he arrived in Italy. Livy says he lost thirty-six thousand and a considerable number of pack animals (Book XXI, Chapter 38).

18. Polybius, Book III, Chapter 60.

19. Livy, Book XXI, Chapter 39.

CHAPTER IV: CRUSHING THE ROMANS

1. Livy, Book XXI, Chapter 40.

2. Livy, Book XXI, Chapter 44.

3. Livy, Book XXI, Chapter 46.

4. Polybius, Book III, Chapter 74, says all but one while Livy, Book XXI, Chapter 58, maintains seven survived only to die the following spring crossing the Apennine Mountains into central Italy.

5. Polybius, Book III, Chapter 78.

6. Silius Italicus, Volume I, Book IV, Lines 763–829.

7. Polybius, Book III, Chapter 83.

8. Livy, Book XXII, Chapter 6.

9. The painting by Joseph-Noel Sylvestre (1847–1926) titled *Ducario Beheads Flaminio* is on display at the Musée des Beaux-Arts in Beziers, France.

10. Livy, Book XXII, Chapter 5.

11. Livy, Book XXII, Chapter 13.

12. Polybius, Book III, Chapter 92 and 93, Livy, Book XXII, Chapters 16–17.

13. Polybius, Book III, Chapter 93, and Livy, Book XXII, Chapters 16–17.

14. Livy, Book XXII, Chapter 23.

15. Some estimates reach as high as 87,200: Lancel, *Hannibal*, pg. 104, based on his interpretation of Livy, Book XXII, Chapter 36, and Polybius, Book III, Chapter 107.

16. Livy, Book XXII, Chapter 39.

17. Polybius, Book III, Chapter 117.

18. Livy, Book XXII, Chapter 49.

19. Livy, Book XXIII, Chapter 12.

20. Silius Italicus, Volume I, Book VII, Lines 675–676.

21. Polybius, Book III, Chapter 117.

22. Livy, Book XXII, Chapter 57.

23. Livy, Book XXII, Chapter 58.

24. Livy, Book XXII, Chapter 51.

25. Livy, Book XXII, Chapter 51, and Book XXVI, Chapter 7.

26. Silius Italicus, Volume II, Books X, Lines 331–332.

27. Livy, Book XXIII, Chapter 24.

CHAPTER V: THE EBBING TIDE

1. Livy, Book XXVI, Chapter 38, and Appian, *Hannibal*, 45.191 and 47.205.

2. Livy, Book XXIII, Chapters 30.

3. Livy, Book XXIII, Chapter 4.

4. Livy, Book XXIII, Chapters 6.

5. Livy, Book XXIII, Chapter 5.

6. Livy, Book XXIII, Chapter 7.

7. This is according to Livy, Book XXIII, Chapter 7, but because he was so pro-Roman and critical of Capua, some scholars like Field Marshall Sir Nigel Bagnall, *The Punic Wars*, 1990, pg. 236, argue the story is an exaggeration designed to portray Hannibal in the worst possible light. Cassius Dio, *Roman History*, relates a similar story when Hannibal captured Nuceria. There, the senators who were pro-Roman were locked into the baths and steamed to

death. These stories might have been invented for propaganda purposes and transferred from one setting to the other by various ancient authors. Conversely, they may well be true.

8. Livy, Book XXIII, Chapter 8.

9. Livy, Book XXIII, Chapter 8.

10. Appian, *Roman History*, Chapter 9, Section 63. Livy, Book XXIII, Chapter 15, mentions no such massacre under a promise of safe conduct but reports the city was looted and burned.

11. Livy, Book XXII, Chapter 14.

12. Livy, Book XXIII, Chapter 13.

13. Livy, Book XXIII, Chapters 17–18.

14. Diodorus, Book XXVI, Chapter 9.11.

15. Livy, Book XXIII, Chapters 18–19; Florus, *Epitome of Roman History*, Book 1, Chapter 22.

16. Silius Italicus, Volume II, Book XI, 385–423.

17. Appian, *Hannibal*, Livy, Book XXVII, Chapter 26, and Plutarch, *Lives Volume V, Marcellus*, 11.

18. Silius Italicus, Volume II, Book XII, Lines 286–287, and Livy, Book XXIII, Chapter 18.

19. Livy, Book XXIII, Chapter 46.

20. Livy, Book XXIII, Chapters 11–12. Livy comments that although four pecks are reported, he suspects the rings filled only one.

21. Justinus, *Epitome of the Philippic History of Pompeius Trogus*, Book XXXII, Section 4.11.

22. Appian, *War Against Hannibal*, Sections 32.35.

23. Livy, Book XXVI, Chapters 12–13.

CHAPTER VI: UNENDING WAR

1. Livy, Book XXVII, Chapter 44.

2. Polybius, Book XI, Chapter 2.

3. Polybius, Book XI, Chapter 3.

4. Hera, the wife of Zeus.

5. Livy, Book XXVIII, Chapter 46, and Cicero, *De Divinatione*, Book I, Section 48.24, who allegedly heard the story from Coelius Antipater who in turn heard it directly from Hannibal's historian, Silenus.

6. Polybius says he saw the bronze plaque when he visited the temple, Book III, Chapter 33.18, and Livy wrote about it in Book XXVIII, Chapter 46.

7. Livy, Book XXX, Chapter 20.

8. Ibid.

9. Livy, Book XXX, Chapter 20; Appian, 59; Diodorus, Book XXVII, Chapter 9.

CHAPTER VII: RETURN TO AFRICA

1. Livy, Book XXX, Chapter 21.

2. Livy, Book XXX, Chapter 22.

3. Livy, Book XXX, Chapter 28.

4. Livy, Book XXX, Chapter 20.

5. Livy, Book XXX, Chapter 20.

6. Polybius, Book XV, Chapter 3.

7. Polybius, Book XV, Chapter 5.3, and Livy, Book XXX, Chapter 29.2.

8. The contemporary Tunisian political activist and author Abdelaziz Belkhodja in his book *Hannibal Barca, l'histoire veritable* and in spirited discussions with this author in Tunis (June 2014), maintains the battle never took place. Zama was, he contends, pure fabrication by the Romans, who wanted to end the story of their long and costly war with a decisive victory over the heretofore undefeatable Hannibal. Belkhodja is the owner and publisher of Apollonia Press.

9. Cassius is cited in a later work by John Zonaras, *Epitome Historiarum*, Volume IX, Book 14, Line 7.

10. Polybius, Book XV, Chapter 5.

11. Polybius, Book XV, Chapter 8, and Livy, Book XXX, Chapter 31.

12. Polybius, Book XV, Chapter 2, and Livy, Book XXX, Chapter 24.

13. Livy, Book XXX, Chapter 35.

14. Polybius, Book XV, Chapter 10.

15. Polybius, Book XV, Chapter 13.

16. Livy, Book XXX, Chapter 36.

17. Livy, Book XXX, Chapter 37.

18. Livy, Book XXX, Chapter 44.

19. The sources are at odds with each other regarding the fate of Syphax. Livy, Book XXX, Chapter 45, contends he died in captivity before Scipio arrived at Rome, while Polybius, Book XVI, Chapter 23, maintains he was dragged in chains behind the triumphal procession that entered Rome and later died in prison.

20. Livy, Book XXX, Chapter 45.

21. Sir Gavin De Beer, *Hannibal,* 1969, pg. 290, and Lancel, *Hannibal,* pg. 180.

22. Livy, Book XXXI, Chapter 10.

23. Livy, Book XXXII, Chapter 30.

24. Livy, Book XXXIII, Chapter 23.

25. Livy, Book XXXIII, Chapter 46.

26. Ibid.

27. Nations that prosper following the destruction of a devastating war: Modern examples are Japan and Germany after World War II, South Korea, and Vietnam.

28. Livy, Book XXXI, Chapter 19.

29. Livy, Book XXXVI, Chapter 4.

30. Livy, Book XLIII, Chapter 6.

31. Livy, Book XXXIII, Chapter 45.

32. Livy, Book XXXIII, Chapter 47.

33. Diodorus, Book XXVIII, Chapter 10, and Livy, Book XXXIII, Chapters 48–49.

CHAPTER VIII: EXILE

1. Polybius, Book XVIII, Chapter 44.4, and 46.5, Livy, Book XXXIII, Chapter 32.5.

2. Lancel, *Hannibal,* pg. 193.

3. Livy Book XXXIV, Chapter 60, 3–6, 61, Justinus, Book XXXI, Sections 3, 7–10.

4. Livy, Book XXXIV, Chapter 61.16.

5. Livy, Book XXXV, Chapter 14.2–3.

6. Polybius, Book III, Chapter 11.2.

7. Livy, Book XXXV, Chapter 14,

8. Lancel, *Hannibal,* pg. 195, maintains Scipio could not have been in Ephesus at that time because he was in Carthage taking part in the senatorial mission to investigate Ariston's mission to North Africa.

9. Livy, Book XXXV, Chapter 18.8.

10. Ibid.

11. *"Odi odioque sum Romanis,"* ibid.

12. Silius Italicus, Volume I, 115–125.

13. Polybius, Book III, Chapter 11.8–9.

14. Livy, Book XXXVII, Chapter 34; the son was in the army, and Livy contends he was either captured at sea or during a reconnoitering mission in Asia Minor.

15. Polybius, Book XXI, Chapter 15.3–4, and Livy, Book XXXVII, Chapter 36.2.

16. Livy, Book XXXVII, Chapter 59.2.

17. Livy, Book XXXVIII, Chapter 58.10.

18. Cornelius Nepos ("Hannibal," 9) and Justinus (Book XXXII, Chapter 4) report Hannibal in Crete, while Livy (Book XXXIX, Chapter 51) and Polybius (Book XXIII, Chapter 13) make no mention of his presence on the island, but report him surfacing in Bithynia.

19. Livy, Book XXXVII, Chapter 51.

20. Cornelius Nepos, "Hannibal," Book XXIII, Chapter 9.

21. Ibid.

22. Plutarch, *Lucullus*, Volume II. Chapter XXXI.

23. Richard Stillwell, ed., *Princeton Encyclopedia of Classical Sites*, 1975; Lori Khatchadourian, "Unforgettable Landscapes," 2007; A. Tonikian, "The Layout of Artashat and Its Historical Development," 1992.

24. Cornelius Nepos, "Hannibal," Book XXIII, Chapters 10 and 11.

25. Tzetzes, Book I, Story 27, Lines 798–805. . Pliny, *Natural Histories*, Volume II, Books 3–7, pps. 332–333, maintains that in his own time, the middle of the first century A.D., Hannibal's tomb was a simple mound close to the castle.

26. Theodore Wiegand, "Zur Lage des Hannibalgrabes," 1902, pp. 322–326.

27. Cornelius Nepos, "Hannibal," Book XXIII. Chapter 1.

AFTERWORD

1. Juvenal, Book IV, Satire 10, 147–167.

BIBLIOGRAPHY

ORIGINAL TEXTS AND THEIR TRANSLATIONS

Appian, 2000, *The Wars of the Romans in Iberia*, translated by J. S. Richardson. Warminster, UK: Aris and Phillips.

———, *Roman History*, 2002, Volume I, translated by Horace White, Loeb Classical Library ed. Cambridge, MA: Harvard University Press.

Appian's Roman History, 4 Volumes, 1913, *History of Rome*, "The Wars with Hannibal," Chapters 1–9, translated by Horace White. London: William Heinemann.

Aristotle, 2001, *Politics*, translated by Benjamin Jowett, edited by Richard McKeon. New York: Modern Library.

Augustine, 2003, *City of God*, translated by Henry Bettenson. New York: Penguin Classics.

Cicero, 1923, *On Old Age, On Friendship, On Divination*, Volume XX, translated by W. A. Falconer, Loeb Classical Library ed. Cambridge, MA: Harvard University Press.

———, 1927, *Tusculan Disputations*, Volume XVIII, translated by J. E. King, Loeb Classical Library ed. Cambridge, MA: Harvard University Press.

———, 1930, *Orations*, translated by J. H. Freese, Loeb Classical Library ed. Cambridge, MA: Harvard University Press.

———, 1933, *Philosophical Treatises, On the Nature of Gods, Academics*, Volume XIX, translated by H. Rackham, Loeb Classical Library ed. Cambridge, MA: Harvard University Press.

———, 1951, *Philippics*, Volumes XV, A and B, translated by W.C.A. Ker, Loeb Classical Library ed. Cambridge, MA: Harvard University Press.

Dio Cassius, 1914, *Roman History*, translated by Ernest Cary and Herbert B. Foster, Loeb Classical Library ed. Cambridge, MA, Harvard University Press, 1914.

Diodorus Siculus, 1933, *Library of History*, Volumes II–III, Books 3–8, translated by C. H. Oldfather, Loeb Classical Library. Cambridge, MA: Harvard University Press.

———, 1954, *Library of History*, Volumes X–XII, Books 20–40, translated by Russel M. Geer, Loeb Classical Library ed. Cambridge, MA: Harvard University Press.

Florus, 1995, *Epitome of Roman History*, translated by Edward Seymour Forster, Loeb Classical Library ed. Cambridge, MA: Harvard University Press.

Frontinus, Sextius Julius, 2003, *Stratagems and Aqueducts of Rome*, translated by Charles E. Bennett, Loeb Classical Library ed. Cambridge, MA: Harvard University Press.

Gellius, Aulus, 1927, *Attic Nights (Noctes Atticae)*, Volumes I, II, and III, translated by J. C. Rolfe, Loeb Classical Library ed. Cambridge, MA: Harvard University Press.

Josephus, 1927, *The Jewish War*, Volumes II and III, translated by H. St. J. Thackeray, Loeb Classical Library ed. Cambridge, MA: Harvard University Press.

Justinus, Marcus Junianus, 1853, *Epitome of the Philippic History of Pompeius Trogus*, translated by the Rev. John Selby Watson. London: Henry G. Bohn.

Juvenal, 1897, *Decimi Iunii Iuvenalis*, translated by E. G. Hardy. London: Macmillan.

———, 2004, *Satires*, translated by Susanna Morton Braund, Loeb Classical Library ed. Cambridge, MA: Harvard University Press.

Livy, 1971, *Ab Urbe Condita*, Books XXI–XXII, Thomas Alan Dorey. Leipzig: Teubner.

———, 1925, *History of Rome*, Volume I, Books 1–2, translated by B. O. Foster, Loeb Classical Library ed. Cambridge, MA: Harvard University Press.

———, 1949, *History of Rome*, Volume V, Books 21–22, translated by B. O. Foster, Loeb Classical Library ed. Cambridge, MA: Harvard University Press.

———, 1951, *History of Rome*, Volume VI, Books 23–25, translated by F. G. Moore, Loeb Classical Library ed. Cambridge, MA: Harvard University Press.

———, 1970, *History of Rome*, Volume VII, Books 26–27, translated by F. G. Moore, Loeb Classical Library ed. Cambridge, MA: Harvard University Press.

———, 1955, *History of Rome*, Volume VIII, Books 28–30, translated by F. G. Moore, Loeb Classical Library ed. Cambridge, MA: Harvard University Press.

———, 1961, *History of Rome*, Volume IX, Books 31–34, translated by Evan T. Sage, Loeb Classical Library ed. Cambridge, MA: Harvard University Press.

———, 1958, *History of Rome*, Volume X, Books 35–37, translated by Evan T. Sage, Loeb Classical Library ed. Cambridge, MA: Harvard University Press.

———, 1938, *History of Rome*, Volume XI, Books 38–39, translated by Evan T. Sage, Loeb Classical Library ed. Cambridge, MA: Harvard University Press.

———, 1938, *History of Rome*, Volume XII, Books 40–42, translated by Evan T. Sage and Alfred C. Schlesinger, Loeb Classical Library ed. Cambridge, MA: Harvard University Press.

———, 1951, *History of Rome*, Volume XIII, Books 43–45, translated by Alfred C. Schlesinger, Loeb Classical Library ed. Cambridge, MA: Harvard University Press.

———, 1972, *War with Hannibal*, translated by A. de Selincourt. London: Penguin.

Lucan, 1957, *De Bello Civili*, translated by J. D. Duff, Loeb Classical Library ed. Cambridge, MA: Harvard University Press.

Lucian, 1961, *Dialogues of the Dead*, Volume VII, translated by M. D. MacLeod, Loeb Classical Library ed. Cambridge, MA: Harvard University Press.

———, 1992, *The Works of Lucian*, Volume III, translated by M. D. Macleod, Loeb Classical Library ed. Cambridge, MA: Harvard University Press.

———, 2009, *Selected Dialogues*, translated and edited by C. D. N. Costa. London: Oxford University Press.

Macrobius, 1969, *Saturnalia*, translated by Percival Vaughan Davies. New York: Columbia University Press.

Manilius, 1977, *Astronomica,* translated by G. P. Goold, Loeb Classical Library ed. Cambridge, MA: Harvard University Press.

Martial, 1993, *Epigrams,* Volumes I, II, and III, translated by D. R. Shackleton Bailey, Loeb Classical Library ed. Cambridge, MA: Harvard University Press.

Nepos, Cornelius, 1886, *On Great Generals, On Historians,* Chapter XXIII, "Hannibal," Section 1, translated by Rev. John Selby Watson, Loeb Classical Library ed. Cambridge, MA: Harvard University Press.

———, 1929, *On Great Generals, On Historians,* Chapter XXII, "Hamilcar," and Chapter XXIII, "Hannibal," translated by J. C. Rolfe, Loeb Classical Library ed. Cambridge, MA: Harvard University Press.

Pliny, 1942, *Natural Histories,* Volume II, Books 3–7, translated by H. Rackham, Loeb Classical Library ed. Cambridge, MA: Harvard University Press.

———, 1945, *Natural Histories,* Volume IV, Books 12–16, translated by H. Rackham, Loeb Classical Library ed. Cambridge, MA: Harvard University Press.

———, 1950, *Natural Histories,* Volume V, Books 17–19, translated by H. Rackham, Loeb Classical Library ed. Cambridge, MA: Harvard University Press.

Plutarch, 1967, *Lives, Volume III, Fabius Maximus,* translated by Bernadotte Perrin, Loeb Classical Library ed. Cambridge, MA: Harvard University Press.

———, 1968, *Lives, Volume V, Marcellus,* translated by Bernadotte Perrin, Loeb Classical Library ed. Cambridge, MA: Harvard University Press.

———, 1970, *Lives, Volume VI, Aemilius Paulus,* translated by Bernadotte Perrin, Loeb Classical Library ed. Cambridge, MA: Harvard University Press.

———, 1921, *Lives, Volume X, Flamininus,* translated by Bernadotte Perrin, Loeb Classical Library ed. Cambridge, MA: Harvard University Press.

Polybius, 2005, *The Histories,* Volume I, Books I–II, translated by W. Paton, Loeb Classical Library ed. Cambridge, MA: Harvard University Press.

———, 2001, *The Histories,* Volume II, Books III–IV, translated by W. Paton, Loeb Classical Library ed. Cambridge, MA: Harvard University Press.

———, 1992, The *Histories,* Volume III, Books V–VIII, translated by W. Paton, Loeb Classical Library ed. Cambridge, MA: Harvard University Press.

————, 2000, *The Histories*, Volume IV, Fragments of Books IX–XV, translated by W. Paton, Loeb Classical Library ed., Cambridge, MA: Harvard University Press.

————, 1979, *The Rise of the Roman Empire*, translated by Ian Scott-Kilvert London: Penguin.

————, 1987, *The Histories of Polybius*, Translated from the Text of F. Hultsch by Evelyn S. Shuckburgh. Lake Bluff, IL: Regnery Gateway.

Seneca, 1971, *Naturales Quaestiones*, Volume VII, Books I–III, translated by T. H. Corcoran, Loeb Classical Library ed. Cambridge, MA: Harvard University Press, 1971.

Sextus, Aurelius Victor, 1993, *Liber de Caesaribus*, edited by F. Pichlmayr. Leipzig: Teubner.

Silius Italicus, 1983, *Punica*, Volume I, Books I–VIII, translated by J. D. Duff, Loeb Classical Library ed. Cambridge, MA: Harvard University Press.

————, 1996, *Punica*, Volume II, Books IX–XVII, translated by J. D. Duff, Loeb Classical Library ed. Cambridge, MA: Harvard University Press.

Strabo, *Geography*, 1923, Volume II, Books 3–5, translated by Horace Leonard Jones, Loeb Classical Library ed. Cambridge, MA: Harvard University Press.

Suetonius, 1927, *Divus Iulius C*, edited with an introduction and commentary by H. E. Butler and M. Cary. Oxford: Clarendon Press.

————, 1979, *The Lives of the Caesars*, translated by J. C. Rolfe, Volumes I and II, Loeb Classical Library ed. Cambridge, MA: Harvard University Press.

Tacitus, 1942, *Annals*, translated by Alfred John Church and William Jackson Brodribb, in *Complete Works of Tacitus*, edited by Moses Hadas. New York: Random House.

Tertullian, 1931, *Apology and De Spectaculis*, *Minucius Felix*, translated by T. R. Glover and Gerald H. Rendall, Loeb Classical Library ed. Cambridge, MA: Harvard University Press.

Tzetzes, John, 1926, *Chiliades or Book of Histories* (Historiarum Variarum Chiliades) by Theophilus Kiesslingius, Book I, Section 27 on Hannibal, reprint 2016. Delhi, India: Gyan Books.

Valerius Maximus, 2000, *Memorable Doings and Sayings*, Volume I, Books I–V, translated by D. R. Shackleton Bailey, Loeb Classical Library ed. Cambridge, MA: Harvard University Press.

Virgil, 2004, *Eclogues, Georgics, Aeneid, 1–6*, Volume I, translated by H. R. Fairclough, Loeb Classical Library ed. Cambridge, MA: Harvard University Press.

Zonaras, John, 1870, *Epitome Historiarum*, edited by L. A. Dindorf. Lipzig: Teubner.

SECONDARY SOURCES

Abbott, Jacob, 1849, *History of Hannibal*. New York: Harper.

Ahl, F. M., M. Davis, and A. Pomeroy, 1986, "Silius Italicus." *ANRW*, II.32.4: 2492–2561.

Amadasi, Guzzo, M. G., 1988, "Did the Phoenicians Land in America?" in *The Phoenicians*, edited by S. Moscati. New York: Abbeville Press.

Anderson, Andrew Runni, 1928, "Heracles and His Successors: A Study of a Heroic Ideal and the Recurrence of a Heroic Type." *HSCP* 39: 7–58.

Armandi, P. D., 1843, *Military History of Elephants: From the Earliest Times Until the Introduction of Firearms*. Paris: Librairie d'Amyot (reprinted 2007 by Adamant Media Corporation).

Astin, A. E., 1967, *Scipio Aemilianus*. Oxford: University Press.

Aubet, M. E., 2001, *Phoenicians and the West*, translated by M. Turton. Cambridge, UK: University Press.

Azan, Paul, 1902, *Annibal dans les Alpes*. Paris: Picard.

Badian, Ernst, 1964, "Rome and Antiochus the Great: A Study in Cold War," in *Studies in Greek and Roman History*, Oxford: Blackwell.

Baedeker's Southern France, 1907. London: Dulau.

Bagnall, Field Marshall Sir Nigel, 1990, *The Punic Wars: Rome, Carthage, and the Struggle for the Mediterranean*. London: Hutchinson.

Baker, George, 1967, *Hannibal*. New York: Barnes and Noble.

Barnes, W. R., 1995, *Silius Italicus*, in *A Companion to the Study of Virgil*, edited by N. Horsfall. New York: Brill.

Barré, M. J., 1983, *The God-List in the Treaty Between Hannibal and Philip V of Macedonia: A Study in Light of the Near East Treaty Tradition*. Baltimore: Johns Hopkins University Press.

Bath, Tony, 1981, *Hannibal's Campaigns*. Cambridge, UK: Stephens.

Beard, Mary, 2007, *The Roman Triumph*. Cambridge, MA: Harvard University Press.

Beard, Mary, and Michael Crawford, 1985, *Rome in the Late Republic*. London: Duckworth.

Belkhodja, Abdelaziz, 2011, *Hannibal Barca, l'histoire veritable*. Tunis: Apollonia.

Belton, John D., 1890, *A Literary Manual of Foreign Quotations, Ancient and Modern*. New York: G. P. Putnam's Sons.

Betlyon, John W., 1999, Review of Serge Lancel, 1998, *Hannibal*, Oxford, in *Classical Journal* 27.4: 183.

Bickerman, Elias, J., 1944, "An Oath of Hannibal." *TAPA* 75: 87–102.

———, 1952, "Hannibal's Covenant." *AJP* 73.1: 1–23.

Billot, F. A., 2005, "*Antonius nove Hannibal*: Cicero's Use of Hannibal in the Philippics and Elsewhere." *Classicum* 31.2: 12–20.

———, 2005, "Hannibal Crosses the Alps: Charting the Changing Perceptions of the Hannibal Figure in Polybius, Livy and Other Ancient Sources," in *Themes in European History: Essays from the 2nd International Conference on European History*, edited by Michael Aradas and Nicholas C. J. Pappas. Athens: Athens Institute for Education and Research.

Bonnet, Corinne, 1988, *Melqart, cultes et mythes de l'Héraklès tyrien en Méditerranée*. Studia-Phoenicia 8. Leuven: Presses Universitaires de Namur.

Bonus, A., 1925, *Where Hannibal Passed*. London: Methuen.

Boser, U., 2007, "Hiking with Hannibal." *Archaeology* 60.1, January/February: 36–41.

Bosworth, Brian, 2003, "Plus ça change . . . Ancient Historians and Their Sources." *Classical Antiquity* 2:167–198.

Bosworth-Smith, R., 1879, *Carthage and the Carthaginians*. London: Longmans.

Bradford, Ernle, 1981, *Hannibal*. New York: Dorset.

Briscoe, John, 1973, *A Commentary on Livy Books 31–33*. Oxford: Oxford University Press.

———, 1980, Review of F. W. Walbank, 1979, *A Historical Commentary on Polybius, Volume III, Commentary on Books XIX–XL*, Oxford, in *The Classical Review* 30.2, 189–191.

Brown, J. E. T., 1963, "Hannibal's Route Across the Alps." *G&R* 10.1: 38–46.

Brown, Shelby, 1990, *Late Carthaginian Child Sacrifice and Sacrificial Monuments in Their Mediterranean Context*, JSOT/ASOR Monograph Series 3, American School of Oriental Research. Sheffield, UK: JSOT Press.

Bruère, Richard T., 1952, "Silius Italicus." *Punica* 3.62–162 and 4.763–822, *CP* 47.4: 219–227.

Brunt, Peter A., 1971, *Italian Manpower*. Oxford: Oxford University Press.

Cambridge Ancient History, 1989, Volume VIII, 2nd ed. Cambridge: Cambridge University Press.

Carcopino, Jerome, 1961, *Profils de Conquerants*. Paris: Flammarion.

Cary, M., 1950, *The Geographic Background of Greek and Roman History*. Oxford: Clarendon Press.

Cary, M., and H. H. Scullard, 1974, *A History of Rome*. New York: Palgrave.

Caven, B., 1980, *The Punic Wars*. London: Weidenfeld and Nicolson.

Centini, Massimo, 1987, *Sulle Ormedi Annibale*. Turin: Piemonte.

Chaabane, Sadok, 2004, *Hannibal Redux: The Revival of Modern Tunisia*, translated by Mounir Khelifa. Tunis: Maison Arabe du Livre.

Charles-Picard, Gilbert, 1967, *Hannibal*. Paris: Hachette.

Charles-Picard, Gilbert, and Colette Charles-Picard, 1961, *Daily Life at Carthage in the Time of Hannibal*. London: Allen and Unwin.

———, 1968, *The Life and Death of Carthage: A Survey of Punic History and Culture from Its Birth to Its Final Tragedy*. London: Sidgwick & Jackson.

Colin, Jean, 1904, *Annibal en Gaule*. Paris: Chapelot.

Coninck, Francis de, 1992, *Hannibal à travers les Alpes*. Montelimar: Ediculture.

Connolly, Peter, 1978, *Hannibal and the Enemies of Rome*. London: MacDonald.

Cope, Anthony, 1590, *The History of Two Most Noble Captains*. London: Hovy.

Cornell, Tim, Boris Rankov, and Philip Sabin, eds., 1996, *The Second Punic War: A Reappraisal*. London: Institute of Classical Studies.

Cottrell, Leonard, 1960, *Enemy of Rome*. London: Evans.

Courtenay, A., 2000, "South of France: In Search of Hannibal the Elephant Man." *Telegraph*, 25 March.

Creasy, Edward, 1851, *Fifteen Decisive Battles of the World*. Ithaca: Cornell University Library.

Daly, G., 2002, *Cannae: The Experience of Battle in the Second Punic War*. London: Routledge.

Davies, Jason P., 1996, Review of P. G. Walsh, ed. and transl.,1996, *Livy Book XL*, Warminster, in *BMCR*, 96.12.13.

Davis, E. W., 1959, "Hannibal's Roman Campaign of 211 BC." *Phoenix* 13.3: 113–120.

Davis, N., 1861, *Carthage and Her Remains: Being an Account of the Excavations and Researches on the Site of the Phoenician Metropolis in Africa, and Other Adjacent Places*. New York: Harper & Brothers.

Davis, Paul K., 1999, *100 Decisive Battles from Ancient Times to the Present: The World's Major Battles and How They Shaped History*. Oxford: Oxford University Press.

De Beer, Gavin, Sir, 1956, *Alps and Elephants: Hannibal's March*. New York: Dutton.

———, 1967, *Hannibal's March*. New York: Viking.

———, 1969, *Hannibal*. New York: Viking.

———, 1969, *Hannibal: The Struggle for Power in the Mediterranean*. London: Thames and Hudson.

De Las Cases, Emmanuel, 1823, *Mémorial de Sainte-Hélène: Journal of the Private Life and Conversations of the Emperor Napoleon at Saint Helena*, Volume II. London: Henry Colburn.

De Witt, N. J., 1941, "Rome and the Road of Hercules." *TAPA* 67: 59–69.

Denina, Carlo, 1805, *Tableau historique, statistique, et morale de la haute Italie*. Paris: Fantin.

Devos, Gabriel, 1966, *D'Espagne en Italie avec Annibal*. Vaison-la-Romaine, Paris: Voconces.

Dodge, Theodore, 1891, *Hannibal*. New York: Houghton.

———, 1968, *Great Captains*. New York: Kennikat.

Eckstein, A. M., 1989, "Hannibal at New Carthage: Polybius 3.15 and the Power of Irrationality," *CP* 84.1: 1–15.

Ellis, Robert, 1853, *Treatise on Hannibal's Passage of the Alps*. Cambridge, UK: Deighton.

Engels, Donald, 1985, "The Length of Eratosthenes' Stade," *AJP* 106.3: 298–311.

Erdkamp, Paul, 1998, *Hunger and the Sword, Warfare and Food Supply in Roman Republican Wars (264–30 B.C.)*. Amsterdam: Gieben.

Erskine, Andrew, 1993, "Hannibal and the Freedom of the Italians," *Hermes* 121: 58–62.

Fantar, M. H., L. E. Stager, and J. A. Greene, 2000, "An Odyssey Debate: Were Living Children Sacrificed to the Gods in Punic Carthage?" *Archaeology Odyssey* 3.6: 28–31.

Flaubert, Gustave, 1977, *Salammbo*, translated by A. J. Krailsheimer. London: Penguin.

Forsythe, Gary, 1999, *Livy and Early Rome: A Study in Historical Method and Judgment*. Frankfurt: Franz Steiner.

Fox, Joseph, 1990, *Hannibal: Enemy of Rome*. Chicago: Adams.

Frederiksen, M., 1959, "Republican Capua." *PBSR* 27: 80–130.

———, 1984, *Campania*, edited by N. Purcell, Rome: BSR.

Freshfield, Douglas, 1886, *Alpine Pass of Hannibal*. London: Arnold.

———, 1914, *Hannibal Once More*. London: Arnold.

Garland, Robert, 2010, *Hannibal: Ancients in Action*. London: Bristol Classical Press.

Garnand, B. K., 2002, "The Use of Phoenician Infant Sacrifice in the Formation of Ethnic Identities: Historical Interpretations of the Classical, Biblical and Archaeological Evidence." Dissertation, University of Chicago.

Garnand, Brien K., undated paper, "From Infant Sacrifice to the ABC's: Ancient Phoenicians and Modern Identities." Chicago: University of Chicago.

Geiger, Joseph, 1985, *Cornelius Nepos and Ancient Political Biography*. Stuttgart: F. Steiner Verlag Wiesbaden.

Gilbert, G., 2008, *Hannibal et Cesar dans les Alpes*. Grenoble: Editions Belladonna.

Glanville, Terrell, 1921, "Hannibal's Pass over the Alps." *Classical Journal* 17: 503–513.

Glover, R., 1944, "The Elephant in Ancient Warfare." *Classical Journal* 39: 257–261.

Glover, R. F., 1948, "The Tactical Handling of the Elephant." *Greece and Rome* 17: 1–11.

Goldsworthy, Adrian, 2001, *Cannae*. London: Cassell.

———, 2001, *The Punic Wars*. London: Cassell.

Gowers, W., 1947, "The African Elephant in Warfare." *African Affairs* 46: 42–49.

Green, A., 1982, *Flaubert and the Historical Novel: Salammbô Reassessed*. Cambridge: Cambridge University Press.

Greene, Joseph, 2005, Punic Project Excavations: *Child Sacrifice in the Context of Carthaginian Religion: Excavations in the Tophet*. American School of Oriental Research, Bulletin 338: 71–92.

Guillaume, Augustin, 1967, *Annibal franchit les Alpes*. Montfleury: Editions des Cahiers des Alpes.

Haight, Elizabeth, 1915, *Carthage and Hannibal*. Boston: Heath.

Hall, R. 1898, *Romans on the Riviera*. Chicago: Ares.

Harden, D. B., 1939, "The Topography of Punic Carthage." *Greece and Rome* 9: 1–12.

Head, D., 1982, *Armies of the Macedonian and Punic Wars (359 BC to 146 BC)*, War-Games Research Group G. Publication, 192.

Henderson, Bernard W., 1898, "The Campaign of the Metaurus." *English Classical Review* 13.52: 625–642.

Hoyos, Dexter, 1998, *Unplanned Wars: The Origins of the First and Second Punic Wars.* New York and Berlin: Walter de Gruyter.

———, 2005, *Hannibal's Dynasty: Power and Politics in the Western Mediterranean, 247–183 BC.* Oxford: Oxford University Press.

———, 2006, "Crossing the Durance with Hannibal and Livy: The Route to the Pass." *KLIO* 88.2: 408–465.

———, 2008, *Hannibal: Rome's Greatest Enemy.* Exeter: Bristol Phoenix Press.

———, ed., 2011, *A Companion to the Punic Wars.* Chichester: Wiley-Blackwell.

Hoyte, J., 1960, *Trunk Road for Hannibal: With an Elephant over the Alps.* London: G. Bles.

Hunt, Patrick, 2006, *Stanford Alpine Archaeology Project, 1994–2006.* Stanford, CA: Stanford University Press.

Hyde, W. W., 1935, *Roman Alpine Routes.* New York: American Philosophical Society.

Jacobs, William, 1973, *Hannibal: An African Hero.* New York: McGraw Hill.

Jaeger, M., 2006, "Livy, Hannibal's Monument and the Temple of Juno at Croton." *TAPA* 136: 389–414.

Johnston, T. C., 1913, *Did the Phoenicians Discover America?* London: Nisbet.

Kaplan, Robert D., 2003, *Warrior Politics: Why Leadership Demands a Pagan Ethos.* New York: Vintage.

Khatchadourian, Lori, 2007, "Unforgettable Landscapes," in *Negotiating the Past in the Past*, edited by Norman Yoffee. Tucson: University of Arizona Press.

Kistler, J. M., 2007, *War Elephants.* Lincoln: University of Nebraska Press.

Lamb, Harold, 1958, *Hannibal.* New York: Doubleday.

Lancel, S., 1995, "Questions sur le tophet de Carthage." *La Tunisie: Carrefour du monde antique. Les Dossiers d'Archéologie* 200: 40–47.

Lancel, Serge, 1992, *Carthage: A History.* Oxford: Blackwell.

———, 1998, *Hannibal*, translated by Antonia Neville. Oxford: Blackwell.

Larouza, Jean-Louis, 1826, *Histoire critique du passage des Alpes par Annibal.* Paris: Dondey-Dupré.

Law, William J., 1866, *Alps of Hannibal.* London: Macmillan.

Lazenby, J. F., 1978, *Hannibal's War: A Military History of the Second Punic War.* Warminster, UK: Aris and Phillips.

———, 1996, *First Punic War: A Military History.* Stanford, CA: Stanford University Press.

———, 2004, "Rome and Carthage," in *The Roman Republic*, edited by H. Flower. Cambridge: Cambridge University Press.

Leakey, R., and R. Lewin, 1996, *The Sixth Extinction.* New York: Doubleday.

Macé de Lépinay, Antonin Pierre Laurent, 1852, *Description du Dauphine.* Paris. C. Vellot.

———, 1861, *Les Chemins de fer du Dauphine; guide-itineraire.* Grenoble: Maisonville et Fils.

Mahaney, W. C., 2008, "Hannibal's Trek Across the Alps: Geo-morphological Analysis of Sites of Geo-archaeological Interest." *Mediterranean Archaeology and Archaeometry* 8.2: 39–54.

Mahaney, W. C., et al., 2016, "Biostratigraphic Evidence Relating to the Age-Old Question of Hannibal's Invasion of Italy, I: History and Geological Reconstruction," *Archaeometry* 10.1111/arcm.12231.

Mahaney, W. C., B. Kapran, and P. Pricart, 2008, *Hannibal and the Alps: Unravelling the Invasion Route.* London: Blackwell Publishing.

Mahaney, W. C., and P. Tricart, 2008, "Hannibal's Debacle in the Combe de Queyras in 218 B.C.: The Unknown Gallic Commander," in *Military Geography and Geology; History and Technology*, edited by C. P. Nathanial, R. J. Abrahart, and R. P. Bradshaw. Nottingham, UK: Land Quality Press.

Maissiat, J. H., 1874, *Annibal en Gaule.* Paris: n.p.

Marks, Raymond, 2005, *From Republic to Empire. Scipio Africanus in the Punica of Silius Italicus.* Frankfurt: Lang.

Mazza, Federico, 1988, "The Phoenicians as Seen by the Ancient World," in *The Phoenicians*, edited by Sabatino Moscati. New York: Abbeville Press.

McCall, Jeremiah B., 2002, *The Cavalry of the Roman Republic.* London: Routledge.

Melvin, M., 1980, *Expedition Alpine Elephant.* Cambridge: Cambridge University Press.

Mills, Frances, 2007, "Hannibal's Childhood." *Punica* 1: 70–139, ASCS XX-VIII Conference Paper, Newcastle.

Mommsen, T., 1959, *History of Rome*, abridged by C. Bryans and F. J. R. Hendy. New York: Philosophical Library.

———, 1982, *Theories of Imperialism*, translated by P. S. Falla. Chicago: University of Chicago Press.

Morris, William, 1897, *Hannibal*. New York: Putnam.

Mosca, Paul, 1975, "Child Sacrifice in Canaanite and Israelite Religion." Dissertation, Harvard University.

———, 1990, "Child Sacrifice at Punic Carthage: Written Evidence and Revisionist History." Paper presented at the Symposium, *Carthage Re-Explored*, University of Cincinnati (30 March–1 April).

Moscati, S., 1968, *The World of the Phoenicians*, translated by A. Hamilton. New York: Praeger.

Moscati, Sabatino, 1988, *The Phoenicians*. New York: Abbeville Press.

Müller, M., R. Debreu, P. Müller, and M. Fontaine, 1952, "Recherches anthropologiques sur les ossements retrouvés dans des urnes puniques." *Bulletins et mémoires de la société d'anthropologie de Paris* sér. 10, 3: 170.

Neumann, J., 1992, "Climatic Changes in the Alps About the Year of Hannibal's Crossing (218 B.C.)." *Climatic Change* 22.2, October: 139–150.

A New Dictionary of Quotations from the Greek, Latin and Modern Languages, 1860. Philadelphia: J. B. Lippincott.

Nicol, John, 1936, *The Historical and Geographical Sources Used by Silius Italicus*. Oxford: Blackwell.

Nossov, K., 2008, *War Elephants*. Oxford: Osprey Publishing.

Palmer, R. E. A., 1997, *Rome and Carthage at Peace*. Stuttgart: F. Steiner.

Peddie, John, 1997, *Hannibal's War*. Stroud, UK: Sutton Publishing.

Pedley J., ed., 1980, *New Light on Ancient Carthage*. Ann Arbor: University of Michigan Press.

Pernoud, Jean, 1962, *Annibal*. Paris: Juilliard.

Perrin, Jean, 1887, *Etude sur Annibal*. Paris: Dubois.

Peyramaure, Michel, 1969, *Les Colosses de Carthage*. Paris: Laffont.

Pézard, M., 1908, "Salammbo et l'archéologie punique." *Mercure de France*, ser. mod. 19.71: 622–638.

Pomeroy, Arthur J., 1989, "Hannibal at Nuceria." *Historia* 38.2: 162–176.

Potter, David, 1998, Review of R. E. A. Palmer, 1997, *Rome and Carthage at Peace*, Stuttgart, in *BMCR*, 1998.08.02.

———, 2004, "The Roman Army and Navy," in *The Cambridge Companion to the* Roman Republic, edited by Harriet I. Flower. Cambridge: Cambridge University Press.

Powers, Alfred, 1944, *Hannibal's Elephants*. New York: Green.

Prevas, J., 1998, *Hannibal Crosses the Alps (the Enigma Re-examined)*. New York: Sarpedon.

Proctor, Dennis, 1971, *Hannibal's March in History*. Oxford: Clarendon.

Radice, B., 1965, "Introduction" in Livy, *The War with Hannibal*, London: Penguin.

Rance, P., 2003, "Elephants in Warfare in Late Antiquity." *Acta Antiqua Academiae Scientiarum Hungaricae* 43.3–4: 355–356.

Renaud, J., 1994, "Reconnaissance de l'itineraire de Hannibal du Rhone au dernier col alpin." *Bulletin de la Société d'Etudes des Hautes-Alpes*.

Ribichini, S., 1988, "Beliefs and Religious Life," in *The Phoenicians*, edited by S. Moscati. New York: Rizzoli.

Rich, J., 1996, "The Origins of the Second Punic War," in *The Second Punic War: A Reappraisal*, edited by P. Sabin, T. Cornell, and B. Rankov. London: Institute of Classical Studies.

Rich, J. W., 1983, "The Supposed Roman Manpower Shortage of the Later Second Century BC." *Historia* 32: 287–331.

Richard, J., 1961, Étude *médico-légale des urnes sacrificielles puniques et de leur contenu*. Lille: Université de Lille.

Rivet, A. L. F., 1988, *Gallia Narbonensis*. London: Mackays.

Rosenstein, Nathan S., 1990, *Imperatores Victi: Military Defeat and Aristocratic Competition in the Middle and Late Republic*. Berkeley: University of California Press.

———, 2004, *Rome at War, Farms, Families and Death in the Middle Republic*. Chapel Hill: University of North Carolina Press.

Rossi, Andreola, 2004, "Parallel Lives: Hannibal and Scipio in Livy's Third Decade." *TAPA* 134.2: 359–381.

Roth, Jonathan P., 1999, *The Logistics of the Roman Army at War (264 B.C.– A.D. 235)*. Leiden: Brill.

Rothschild, J. P., 1995, "Haruspicine, divination, prodiges et invocation des morts dans les Punica de Silius Italicus." *Les écrivains et l'Etrusca disciplina de Claude a Trajan*, Tours.

Sabin, Philip, Tim Cornell, and Boris Rankov, eds., 1996, *The Second Punic War: A Reappraisal*. London: Institute of Classical Studies.

Saint-Simon, Maximilien Henri de, 1770, *Histoire de la Guerre des Alpes*. Amsterdam: Marc Michel Rey.

Salmon, E. T., 1957, "Hannibal's March on Rome." *Phoenix* 11.4: 153–163.

Santini, Carlos, 1991, *Silius Italicus and His View of the Past*. Amsterdam: Gieben.

Schwartz, J. H., 1989, "The Tophet and Sacrifice at Phoenician Carthage." *Terra* 28: 16–25.

Schwartz, J. H., Frank Houghton, Roberto Macchiarelli, and Luca Bondioli, 2010, "Skeletal Remains from Punic Carthage Do Not Support Systematic Sacrifice of Infants." PLOS One 5(2):e9177, February, DOI 10.1371/journal.pone.0009177.

Schwartz, Jeffrey H., 1993, *What the Bones Tell Us*. New York: Holt.

Scullard, H. H., 1930, *Scipio Africanus in the Second Punic War*. Cambridge: Cambridge University Press.

———, 1971, Review of De Beer, 1969, *Hannibal: The Struggle for Power in the Mediterranean*, London, in CR 21.2: 299–300.

———, 1974, *The Elephant in the Greek and Roman World*. London: Thames and Hudson.

———, 2002, *A History of the Roman World, 753 to 146 B.C.* London: Routledge.

Solomon, J., 2001 [1978], *The Ancient World in the Cinema*. New Haven, CT: Yale University Press.

Soren, David, Aicha Ben Abed Khader, and Hedi Slim, 1990, *Carthage*. New York: Simon and Schuster.

Stager, L. E., 1980, "The Rite of Child Sacrifice at Carthage." In *New Light on Ancient Carthage*, edited by J. G. Pedley, Kelsey Museum of Archaeology. Ann Arbor: University of Michigan Press.

Stager, L. E., and S. R. Wolff, 1984, "Child Sacrifice at Carthage: Religious Rite or Population Control?" *Biblical Archaeology Review* 10: 30–51.

Starr, Chester G., 1989, *The Influence of Sea Power on Ancient History*. New York: Oxford University Press.

Stillwell, Richard, ed., 1976, *Princeton Encyclopedia of Classical Sites*. Princeton, NJ: Princeton University Press.

Stocks, Claire, 2014, *The Roman Hannibal: Remembering the Enemy in Silius Italicus' "Punica."* Liverpool: Liverpool University Press.

Stone, Jon R., 2005, *The Routledge Dictionary of Latin Quotations*. London: Routledge.

Stoneman, Richard, 1992, *Education of Cyrus*. London: Everyman's Library.

Tonikian, A., 1992, "The Layout of Artashat and Its Historical Development." *Mesopotamia* 27: 161–187.

Torr, Cecil, 1924, *Hannibal Crosses the Alps*. Cambridge: Cambridge University Press.

Vaccarone, R., 1880, *Bollettino del ClubAlpino Italiano*, Volumes XIV–NN, No. 41. Milan: G. Candeletti.

Vanoyeke, Violaine, 1995, *Hannibal*. Paris: France Empire.

Walbank, F. W., 1965, *Speeches in Greek Historians*, Third Myres Memorial Lecture. Oxford, UK: Blackwell.

———, 1972, *Polybius*. Berkeley: University of California Press.

———, 1985, *Selected Papers: Studies in Greek and Roman History and Historiography*. Cambridge: Cambridge University Press.

———, ed., 2002, *Polybius, Rome and the Hellenistic World: Essays and Reflections*. Cambridge: Cambridge University Press.

Walbank, Frank, 1999, *Historical Commentary on Polybius*. Oxford: Oxford University Press.

Walsh, P. G., 1963, *Livy, His Historical Aims and Methods*. Cambridge: Cambridge University Press.

———, 1982, "Livy and the Aims of *Historia*: An Analysis of the Third Decade," *ANRW*, II.30.2: 1058–1074.

Warmington, B. H., 1969, *Carthage*. New York: Praeger.

Westermann, William L, 1955, *The Slave Systems of Greek and Roman Antiquity*. Philadelphia: American Philosophical Society.

Wiegand, Theodore, 1902, "Zur Lage Des Hannibalgrabes" (On the site of Hannibal's grave), German Archaeological Institute, Athenische Abteiling, October, *Athen. Mitteilungen*, Volume 27, pps 322–326. Berlin: Beck und Barth.

Wilford, John, 1984, "The Mystery of Hannibal's Elephants," *New York Times*, Science section, September 18.

Wilkinson, Spenser, 1911, *Hannibal's March through the Alps*, Oxford: Clarendon.

Wiseman, T. P., and C. Gill, eds., 1993, *Lies and Fiction in the Ancient World*. Exeter: University of Exeter Press.

Xella, Paolo, Josephine Quinn, Valentina Melchiorri, and Peter van Dommelen, "Phoenician Bones of Contention," *Antiquity* 87.338: 1199–1207.

INDEX